Fostering Culturally Diverse Leadership in Organisations

Leveraging academic research and case studies, knowledge as a business leader and diversity practitioner, and personal experience, Karen Loon examines how successful culturally diverse leaders at work resolve the contradictions and tensions of their identities within organisations. What can we learn from those leaders who have thrived and smashed the 'bamboo ceiling'? Moreover, are there other factors holding organisational change back?

The book proposes research-based recommendations for aspiring leaders and corporate practitioners whilst revealing the potential inhibitors to progress. Split into three sections, Loon examines current research on identities in multicultural nations and organisations, delves into the career progression of successful Asian-Australian leaders to explore how they negotiate identity in the workplace, and provides a roadmap of actions for business leaders looking to create more inclusive and diverse cultures in their organisations.

Written for both people new to diversity and those keen on new perspectives, the book is well-suited for aspiring leaders at any stage of their careers looking to accelerate their careers, as well as C-Suite, HR, and Diversity leads.

Karen Loon is a Non-Executive Director and a former senior Big 4 partner. She has worked with the world's leading banks and led diversity initiatives. She has qualifications in system psychodynamics and governance from INSEAD, and research interests in identity work and organisational change.

KAREN LOON

Fostering Culturally Diverse Leadership in Organisations

Lessons from Those Who Smashed the Bamboo Ceiling

Routledge
Taylor & Francis Group

LONDON AND NEW YORK

Cover image: Getty Images

First published 2023
by Routledge
4 Park Square, Milton Park, Abingdon, Oxon OX14 4RN

and by Routledge
605 Third Avenue, New York, NY 10158

Routledge is an imprint of the Taylor & Francis Group, an informa business

© 2023 Karen Loon

British Library Cataloguing-in-Publication Data
A catalogue record for this book is available from the British Library

Library of Congress Cataloging-in-Publication Data
A catalog record has been requested for this book

ISBN: 978-1-032-27079-1 (hbk)
ISBN: 978-1-032-27078-4 (pbk)
ISBN: 978-1-003-29123-7 (ebk)

DOI: 10.4324/9781003291237

Typeset in Joanna
by codeMantra

To my husband, Steven, and parents, Russell and Glenda

Contents

Figures

Tables

If you walk down the street of many of the world's leading business cities, you will hear the voices of people from many different backgrounds. These cities are cosmopolitan, noisy, bustling, and vibrant hubs that attract the world's top talent to them. Their companies are some of the world's leading organisations that are changing, innovating, and disrupting the world. The cities that come to mind – New York, San Francisco, Silicon Valley, and Singapore – are close to leading-edge universities that produce people with state-of-the-art skills.

What is unique about these people and their organisations are that they experiment and learn, take risks, sometimes fail, and then pick themselves up again. They are less likely to be bound by societal traditions and norms. Their leaders are unconventional – frequently breaking stereotypes and smashing boundaries as they progress. Many of them, particularly those in Silicon Valley, are immigrants who overcame significant barriers and succeeded.

Yet, most of the narrative about cultural diversity in leadership talks about why people with culturally diverse backgrounds don't make it – particularly since the release of Jane Hyun's book *Breaking the Bamboo Ceiling*. Despite being the 'model minority' due to their significant mobility attributed to education, many people with Asian backgrounds in multicultural nations – such as the US, the UK, Canada, and Australia – remain seriously under-represented in leadership roles. Why is this the case?

One stereotypical view is that Asians are highly competent, making them appear threatening to some people in the workplace. Another is that Asians lack social skills, which are incompatible with leadership roles. Further, many Asian women in the workplace experience a 'double-bind'. This bias against Asian leaders has been known to deflate their motivation and aggravate and bolster their views that they are unsuitable for leadership.

Nevertheless, culturally diverse leaders *do* make it into leadership positions, albeit in small numbers. Some of their personal stories are in the public domain, although their collective views have not been researched extensively. So, did they face challenges during their careers? If this was the case, how did they overcome the barriers they faced during their careers to make it into leadership roles, particularly in more traditional businesses? And what can we learn from them?

WHY DID I WRITE THIS BOOK?

My own interest in exploring how culturally diverse leaders succeed comes from my own career journey. I'm a fourth-generation Asian-Australian and a former partner of a Big 4 accounting firm,[1] where I worked for twenty-nine years.

When I started work, there were no female partners in the Assurance division in my firm in Australia, let alone any partners of Asian backgrounds. So, like many qualified Chartered Accountants, I decided to do a two-year secondment with my firm overseas but chose the less conventional location of Singapore rather than London. What enlightened me about my firm in Singapore at the time was that it had several female partners – some of whom had three or four children. That, amongst other reasons, was my motivation to build my career in Singapore.

Becoming a partner was one of the most challenging things I've achieved during my career, but also one of the most rewarding. Of course, I had to make some personal sacrifices; however, the longer-term benefits were amazing. I had a huge amount of autonomy, worked with some of the world's leading financial services organisations, and travelled the world.

In 2011, whilst on secondment back to my firm in Australia, I was surprised to discover that it only had a small number of Asian-Australian partners at the time. While I noticed that significant numbers of Asian-Australians[2] join the Big 4 firms as graduates, they seemed to leave their respective firms faster than non-Asian-Australians. When I expressed surprise at the issue, I learnt that this was the case in most Australian companies. This 'a ha' moment was the start of my passion for doing my part to foster culturally diverse leadership in organisations.

Over the decade since, organisations globally, including Australia, have started to implement various cultural diversity initiatives. Yet are there, I wondered, better ways to accelerate the progression of those with culturally diverse backgrounds into leadership positions?

My curiosity led me to investigate this as part of my studies at INSEAD. Using the untold stories of current and former Asian-Australian partners of the Big 4 firms in Australia, I evaluated their experiences of how they resolved the contradictions and tensions between their various identities, and examined how their organisations supported or hindered their journeys. This, together with additional interviews of Asian-Australian leaders in other sectors, my own knowledge as a business leader and diversity practitioner, and experiences as an Asian-Australian, formed the basis for this book.

DRIVING CHANGE, UNDERSTANDING OURSELVES

This book hinges on two ideas. First, we are all shaped by our early experiences at home with our parents in our family system. How we experience growing up at home shapes the roles we take up in later life. The behavioural patterns that we learn at home affect how we deal with the various challenges we face. While some of these behaviours may be influenced by the culture we grew up in, not all of them are, including how we relate to other people. These learned relationship styles affect the types of interactions we seek out and how we act in groups.

Second, change involves a cycle of experimentation and learning, whether as individuals or in groups (including organisations). Yet, we all experience fears and concerns when learning and changing. To overcome the inertia, we need to 'try out' different scenarios to see how they 'fit' and decide whether to adopt the new situation or not. In groups, the challenge is how to encourage people to collectively be open to experiment and learn. Often, conscious and unconscious rules in organisations and broader societal context, well-intentioned and designed to ensure consistency of how we are expected to act, inadvertently hold organisations and individuals back from change. To drive change, such as increasing the cultural diversity of leadership, requires simultaneous ecosystem efforts of individuals, organisations, and society to effect collective behavioural changes. If we adopt piecemeal approaches, such as focusing on individuals or implementing organisational policies, we will make some progress. However, we won't deal with the crux of the issue: the unconscious anxieties that may be holding collective change back.

Whilst much of this intuitively may make sense, in practice, we rarely look at problems such as increasing cultural diversity in leadership using systems thinking. It isn't easy to make progress with multiple interdependencies to resolve. There is no right or wrong way to fix them.

Adopting the more rational approach that we learn at business school to drive change may lead to short-term results. Unfortunately, however, it may lead to other unintended consequences. To illustrate, the push to increase gender diversity in workplaces through extensive use of targets has led to improvements in the number of female leaders in many countries. However, regrettably, it has inadvertently suppressed some people's views on the matter to the subconscious. Unfortunately, issues such as sexual harassment at work still arise.

Some of you may wonder whether and how understanding our individual and collective conscious and unconscious emotions can increase leadership diversity in the workplace. I, too, was sceptical at first, having grown up in a family that taught me that I needed to be tough and resilient to succeed. At work, being able to control our emotions is considered to be a leadership strength.

Understanding how we negotiate our career journeys, including the emotions we experience, provides us with an alternative lens on the blockers to individual and organisational change. Moreover, it allows us to contemplate what we can do to remove them. If you are aware of how your early experiences play out at work, understand how to regulate them, and apply an experimentation and learning mindset, you will be able to support the collective change necessary in today's organisations.

WHAT WILL YOU LEARN FROM THIS BOOK?

This book is written for both people new to diversity, and those who already know about the areas covered but are keen on new perspectives.

In this book, I will show you how these two elements play out in organisations. Through the lens of well-regarded psychological and behavioural theories, the stories of Asian-Australian leaders, and leveraging my experience as a business leader, diversity practitioner, and an Asian-Australian, I explore how our childhood experiences at home in the family system and the influence of organisational systems impact our career journeys. I then outline the steps that aspiring culturally diverse leaders can take to 'smash' the bamboo ceiling, and propose a roadmap on how organisations can foster culturally diverse leadership. Finally, I conclude with my Career Progression Model for Culturally Diverse Leaders, which summarises how people with culturally diverse backgrounds take up leadership roles, considering their relationships with their organisations.

If you are an aspiring leader, whether at the beginning of your career or close to the pinnacle of your organisation, this book will help you to super-charge your career. It will share with you the experiences, learnings, and recommendations of successful culturally diverse leaders who navigated their way through various challenges on their journeys and thrived.

Similarly, if you are a C-Suite leader, an HR leader, or diversity leader looking to increase the diversity of your organisation's leadership as part of your broader talent management initiatives, or a manager looking to build a more inclusive environment in your team, this book will provide you with a valuable roadmap to use. It will also be helpful to you if your company has started implementing various diversity-related initiatives, particularly for gender, and is looking to take them to the next level to cover cultural diversity. Finally, if your company is just starting its diversity journey, you will also find the lessons invaluable.

Finally, this book may be for you if someone close to you – your partner, your respected colleague, your son, or your daughter - is looking to accelerate their career.

Acknowledgements

This book marks the culmination of a three-year self-discovery journey for me as part of my own identity transition. It would not have been possible without many people's encouragement, guidance, and support.

First, I would not have written this book without the support of the Asian-Australian leaders who shared their personal and professional stories as part of my research. Whilst I have shared some of their narratives on an anonymised basis in this book, all of them have been considered in coming up with my findings. I sincerely appreciate the lessons I learned from them and their courage in me. I also wish to thank the people I spoke to who shared their perspectives on fostering culturally diverse leadership with me.

Second, I am also indebted to my INSEAD colleagues. My Executive Master in Change (EMC) programme allowed me to turn my dreams into reality. Special thanks must go to Roger Lehman, Erik van de Loo, Lee White, Michael Jarrett, and Ayin Jambulingam, who stretched my imagination, and taught me the value of using a 'Night Vision' lens. I also thank my EMC colleagues Scott Anthony, Nicky Sparshott, Constantinos Hadjigeorgiou, and Peter Cumming for their thoughts and guidance on my book.

Third, I truly appreciate the encouragement and advice of Sung Lee, a pillar of wisdom, who planted the idea of turning my thesis into this book in my mind. Many thanks must also go to Yongling Lam of Routledge, who gave me, a first-time author, this opportunity, and Kendrick Loo, who patiently guided me through the editorial process. In addition, I must thank Dr Jovina Ang for her invaluable coaching on how to turn a thesis into an academic book.

Finally, much love goes to my husband, Steven, for patiently supporting me through my EMC journey and book-writing process. My research means a lot to both of us personally.

Karen Loon, February 2022

NOTES

1 The Big 4 accounting firms (or Big 4 firms) are global multidisciplinary professional services firms: Deloitte, EY, KPMG and PricewaterhouseCoopers.

2 The term 'Asian-Australians' is generally used to describe Australians of visible Asian ancestry. The Australian Bureau of Statistics and the Australian Census do not collect data on races or ethnicities but do collect information on distinct ancestries. Categories used in Australia include East Asian (for example, Chinese-Australians, Korean-Australians), South East Asian (such as, Vietnamese-Australians or Malaysian-Australians), and Southern and Central Asian (including, Indian-Australians and Sri Lankan-Australians). It does not include people of Middle Eastern ancestries. Estimates of the number of people in Australia with Asian ancestry vary. However, based on the most recent forecast by the Australian National University, Asian-Australians make up 14.7% of Australia's population (Biddle et al., 2019).

REFERENCE

Biddle, N., Gray, M., Herz, D., & Lo, J. Y. (2019). *Research Note: Asian-Australian Experiences of Discrimination*. Australian National University. https://csrm.cass.anu.edu.au/research/publications/research-note-asian-australian-experiences-discrimination-0

One

INTRODUCTION

'No, you can't get a part-time job at McDonalds – you should be spending your time at home studying'.

'Playing the piano won't make you any money'.

These are some of the things I recall my father saying to me when I turned fifteen. Like my school friends, I wanted to get a part-time job to earn some money. Instead, I reluctantly complied with my father's wishes and spent a great deal of the next two years after school studying at home. I am sure that I was not the only one.

Read any of the Higher School Certificate or Victorian Certificate of Education honours rolls each year in Australia, and you'll see that a large proportion of the top candidates have Asian backgrounds. Most studied at the state's top selective schools or private schools. Many of them are super-modest and amazingly talented. Stories abound of how many of them have spent their weekends at 'cramming' schools and have 'Tiger' mums. Moreover, the university lecture halls for degree programmes such as medicine, law, and accounting are crowded with students from Asian backgrounds. Asian-Australians are the 'model minority' – conscientious, self-reliant, compliant, and ambitious. This story is repeated in other migrant-receiving countries like the United States (US), the United Kingdom (UK), and Canada.

Yet, while people of Asian ethnicity are often superstars at school, their success is rarely replicated to the same extent in their nations' most prominent corporations. Well-represented in junior ranks, they remain seriously under-represented in senior levels of leadership.

What is leading to this? Is there a 'bamboo ceiling'[1] that is holding them back? Or are there leadership traits that they don't have? Are leaders in these corporations biased towards those who demonstrate more 'Western' values? Or is there something else at play?

These questions have intrigued me for many years. Ethnically Chinese but a fourth-generation Australian, I am a 'banana' – white on the inside,

1 Introduction

DOI: 10.4324/9781003291237-1

yellow on the outside. I identify as an Asian-Australian of Chinese ethnicity who grew up in Australia's country music capital, Tamworth, five hours by car from Sydney. I'm an anomaly in my own country.

After spending my early years in Australia, at the age of twenty-five, I relocated to Singapore for work and have, for the most part, lived there ever since. Many years later, I realised that one of the main reasons for staying in Singapore was that not only were there no female role model partners[2] in my Big 4 firm in Australia at the time; there were also no Asian-Australian partners.

In 2011, I was seconded back to my firm in Sydney as a partner for nineteen months, where I experienced a mini-culture shock. I was unique – female, Asian, and I even worked full-time! While there were many staff with Asian backgrounds at junior levels, I was one of only two Asian female partners at the time. Aspiring Asian female leaders who had no other role models to look up to or speak to in their business units approached me for coffee and career advice. Yet, when I talked to younger Asian staff, many could not see a career for themselves in the firm and were contemplating leaving. While there were no data to measure this, I knew that our Asian-Australian staff were leaving the firm faster than those of other backgrounds. Further, this issue wasn't just one which my firm faced – it existed in almost all organisations. To me, something felt amiss.

Leadership is a lonely experience at the best of times; however, it can be even more difficult when you don't feel like you belong. And while on paper, I had 'made it', having made partnership at the age of thirty-three, I felt like an 'alien' and alone as an Asian female partner in Australia.

I looked younger than many of my staff. I felt uncomfortable 'selling' my experience to older clients, to have them look uninterestedly at me and tell me that 'you look very young'. I was also not married at the time, so I was rarely invited to work-related dinner parties that revolved around couples.

I specifically recall two discussions that really struck me. The first was in my first week back in Australia. I vividly remember sharing a cab with an experienced businessperson. After telling him that I had come back from Singapore, he responded, 'Your English is very good'.

The second was when I thought there was a pipeline issue, as it seemed that proportionately fewer homegrown graduates were being promoted to partner than those educated in the UK. After mentioning this to a colleague of Asian ethnicity, she told me I was mistaken. In her view, Australia had access to the world's best talent, and I had been in Singapore for too long.

I now knew how those from overseas working in Australia felt – I felt like a second-class citizen in my own country. I sensed I didn't belong and was uncomfortable. This brought up memories of being a child at primary school in Tamworth. Not realising that I was any different from the other kids in my class, I came home crying after being called a 'Ching Chong Chinaman'. In high school, I was told by my English teacher that my written English was like that of a foreign student, even though I only spoke English. To be accepted, I became even more 'Aussie'. I became determined to prove that I was better than the other kids in my class.

I was extremely fortunate that I faced relatively few situations of overt racism in Australia. However, I can't imagine what the experiences of my great-grandparents, grandparents, and parents ahead of me would have been like. Australia is my country – where my ancestors had lived for over 140 years. Yet, something didn't feel right.

I wasn't the only one thinking the same way – some of my fellow Asian-Australian partners had similar thoughts. Their stories were different; most had moved to Australia as young kids or had parents who had migrated to Australia. It was lonely for many of us at the top. Some felt even more alone after making it to partner, which we thought would be the pinnacle of our careers. Other Asian-Australians I spoke to felt that there was nothing they could do to change things and felt misunderstood as they lived between two worlds. A small minority were motivated to act.

Around this time, the Australian government released its White Paper on *Australia in the Asian Century*, which set out a strategic framework to guide Australia's navigation of the Asian Century. My firm was exploring how to best support its clients. I proposed suggestions to the firm on how it could leverage its Asian-Australians' cultural diversity to support its broader Asia business objectives. It was the start of my journey as a diversity leader.

After moving back to Singapore, I've observed the progress made by corporate Australia in increasing the cultural diversity of its leadership. There has been much more discussion of the importance of cultural diversity in mainstream media in the past five years. Companies also began to announce targets to increase the cultural diversity of their leadership. Further, organisations such as the Diversity Council of Australia

(DCA) and the Australian Human Rights Commission (AHRC) have published reports that tackle cultural diversity and inclusive leadership. Finally, in the past few years, Asian-Australians started to take action. One example was the inaugural Asian-Australian Leadership Summit (AALS) held in September 2019, which boosted many Asian-Australians' vision, visibility, and voices.

Unfortunately, there has been an increase in racist incidents involving Asian-Australians since the COVID-19 pandemic. This has led to many Asian-Australians becoming more anxious than the rest of the population (Biddle et al., 2020). Furthermore, some Australian companies have been pivoting their business focus away from China.

While these efforts are encouraging, not all mainstream companies have joined the trend. While some celebrate their cultural diversity, many others still do not focus on how to help aspiring culturally diverse leaders reach their full potential.

One reason is that some corporate leaders believe their organisations are still struggling to increase the proportion of women in leadership positions. While some progress has been made in boardrooms, women still remain underrepresented at leadership and management levels in Australian workplaces.

Like in the US, the UK, and Canada, corporate Australia is becoming increasingly aware of the importance of diversity. Improvements have occurred, and, over time, we have seen advancements in its leadership profile in the right direction. The clubbiness of senior male leaders in leadership slowly is reducing.

However, I sometimes wonder if corporate cultures have really changed, or whether the efforts made to date by some organisations are 'diversity washing?' At times, I've been surprised to see cases where very senior leaders dispute hard facts about gender pay gaps – denying there are issues. Pockets of male chauvinism still exist.

Are we making actual progress? What more can we do? And if it has been so hard to sort our gender issues out, what can we do to move the dial on cultural diversity? Is it appropriate to take what has worked to date for gender and apply it to cultural diversity? Or do we need to do things differently?

WHAT IS CULTURAL DIVERSITY? AND WHY IS IT ESSENTIAL?

Before continuing, it is worth taking a step back. What is diversity, what is cultural diversity, and why are they essential?

What is diversity?

Diversity is what makes each of us unique. It includes our backgrounds, personality, life experiences, and beliefs – all the things that make us who we are. These differences shape our views of the world, our perspectives, and our approaches. In other words, it is who we are as individuals.

When we speak about diversity, our focus tends to be on what we can see and hear – our gender, race, nationality, and languages spoken. However, this is just one lens; there are often other aspects about individuals that are not visible.

What is cultural diversity?

Cultural diversity, a term commonly used in Australia, refers to having diverse ethnic backgrounds and ancestries.

There are no official statistics on Australia's ethnic or cultural population, unlike in other countries such as the UK, which uses the term 'Black, Asian and Minority Ethnic' (BAME).

However, in the context of senior leadership, it usually refers to having an appropriate representation of people with non-Anglo-Celtic backgrounds (in other words, European, non-European, and Indigenous backgrounds). The non-European population includes people of Asian, Middle Eastern and North African, and other non-European backgrounds.

The difficulty of having a more diverse workplace is that the more diverse we all are, the more difficult it can be to work collaboratively. This is where the role of inclusion becomes vital.

What is inclusion?

Inclusion is where the thoughts, ideas, and perspectives of all individuals matter. It is the practice of ensuring that people feel a sense of belonging and support from an organisation.

Often, the words diversity and inclusion are used together.[3] However, some argue that there is also a paradoxical relationship between having a diverse workforce and workplace inclusion. In more recent years, discussions have broadened to include the importance of 'belonging'.

A common way to remember these concepts is: Diversity is being invited to the party. Inclusion is being asked to dance. Belonging is dancing like no one's watching.

What is the difference between meritocracy, equity, and equality?

When we speak about diversity and inclusion, we often use the terms 'meritocracy', 'equity', and 'equality' without fully understanding what they mean.

Many workplaces claim that they are meritocratic and adopt merit-based processes whereby people progress based solely on their capabilities. However, numerous academics believe that such organisations may show more significant bias favouring the majority (such as men over equally performing women).

There is frequently confusion about the difference between equality and equity. While both promote fairness, equality achieves this through treating everyone equally regardless of their needs. In contrast, equity reaches this by treating people differently depending on the circumstances.

In the workplace, having a diverse workplace means having a wide range of diverse individuals.

Today, many organisations are struggling to manage their way through the 'Great Resignation'. Further, talent mobility flows globally have been disrupted. Some countries, such as the UK, have become more open to global talent, as others have shut their borders. Other diaspora groups such as Asian-Australians in Hong Kong are repatriating home. As a result, companies need to work much harder to attract and retain the best available talent so they can thrive.

Numerous studies have shown that having multiple points of view can lead to better business outcomes for organisations and a fair and equal work environment. Further, business leaders increasingly recognise that embracing organisational diversity is critical – one never knows where the next important idea will emerge from. Senior teams that are homogeneous may not come up with the best ideas.

Diversity is not just a 'nice to have' – it is increasingly vital.

INCREASING WORKPLACE LEADERSHIP DIVERSITY – A COMPLEX PROBLEM

Yet, why is moving the dial on workplace diversity and inclusion so tricky?

Even in the US, where diversity initiatives started decades ago, following the #blacklivesmatter campaign, there has been greater societal and workplace debate on improving diversity, equity, and inclusion. In addition, there has been significant commentary on workplace cultural diversity barriers, including discrimination and implicit biases against people with ethnic backgrounds. Regrettably, increasing diversity in the workplace is one of those complex problems we cannot answer quickly; otherwise, we would have resolved it by now.

A helpful way to analyse the challenges of increasing cultural diversity in leadership is to apply the 'Framework for Transforming Experience into Authentic Action through Role' (Long, 2016) (Figure 1.1). This looks at how people take up roles using an 'outside-in' perspective (looking to understand the group or system first, then the context). This will be referred to in subsequent chapters.

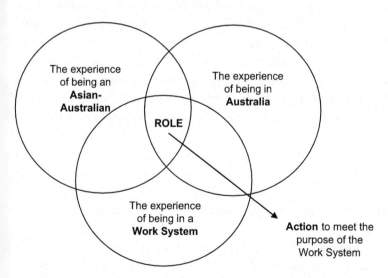

Figure 1.1 The transforming experience framework as applied to an Asian-Australian leader

Source: Adapted from Long (2016, p. 35)

A country's context, the environment in which systems (in this case, companies) operate, is influenced by physical, political, economic, social, historical, international, and emotional factors (Long, 2016). This consequently impacts a country's people, organisations, and social systems.

To illustrate, in Australia, race and ethnicity are topics that people prefer not to talk about, unlike in the US. Historically, Australians have identified themselves by their nationality. Growing up in Australia in the 1970s and 1980s, when there was an expectation that all Australians would assimilate, I defined myself as Australian as I wanted to fit it. Most of my university friends were from varied ethnic backgrounds – Anglo-Celtic, Greek, Italian, Albanian, Singaporean Chinese, and Hong Kong Chinese. Yet, we rarely spoke much about our family backgrounds – we just were who we were. This was due to our nation's history, such as the imposition of the 'White Australia' policy by the 1901 Immigration Restriction Act, which shaped our identities. These policies influenced how many of us with non-Anglo Celtic backgrounds were brought up and identified ourselves, and how our organisations and social systems were founded.

The other challenge is that most organisations are established for a particular purpose, so they have their own culture and rules on how people fit into them and operate. Unfortunately, many older organisations were not initially founded to embrace diversity, making it increasingly difficult for them to pivot to embrace it.

It is not easy to change systems quickly. Doing so may require their people to modify the system's purpose, culture, or rules, which is not easy. This is because there are both rational, conscious, and unconscious dynamics within organisations, the latter of which Russ Vince at the University of Bath describes as 'institutional illogics' (Vince, 2019).

As a business leader and diversity practitioner, my discussions with other C-suite members leading diversity strategies corroborate the challenge of dealing with institutional illogics. Even with the best plans, it takes time for any change initiative to show real and meaningful progress.

Often unspoken or unconscious attitudes can prevent progress and derail change. Common challenges I faced as a diversity leader when seeking to influence change included that initially, people denied that any change was necessary. They then resisted change through rationalisation and scapegoating.

What I found most challenging was getting others to take collective and meaningful action. Some colleagues would tell me, 'Yes – I am supportive of diversity'. Others were silent. Frequently there was inertia among them and a lack of action, individually and collectively. I sensed that their true thoughts on embracing diversity had become repressed and were unsaid. Often, they also had too many other challenges and distractions that they were also trying to manage.

Shifting organisational cultures towards embracing greater diversity and inclusion is a long journey. Many companies can demonstrate that greater diversity in their organisations is beneficial for their clients, people, and organisation. They also have robust accountability frameworks and holistic measures embedded throughout the organisation. Nevertheless, my personal experience, even as a senior business leader and owner, is that increasing leadership diversity in a tangible and meaningful way is extremely challenging. So, I started to wonder if there was a better way.

Many nations have been focusing on improving their gender diversity for some time. For instance, the top Australian- and UK-listed companies now have more than 30% women on their boards. But, on the other hand, our most prominent institutions are rocked by sexual harassment scandals on occasion. So, whilst we may have changed how things appear, have we changed the hearts and minds of our people in our society and organisations?

If we can't make progress in gender, how do we then tackle cultural diversity?

WHERE DO WE START?

There is frequently a view in some countries, such as Australia, that we don't need to act on something unless we have the data to prove the extent of our issues. Sometimes, though, problems stare us in the face without any data.

Case in point – you only need to compare people in the streets of most cities in Australia to the leadership teams of its largest corporations to know that something is amiss. It may surprise many people that over 15% of the Australian population have Asian-Australian ethnicity – a higher proportion than the African-American population in the US. These statistics don't consider people of other ethnic backgrounds, such as those whose ancestors are from the Middle East or Africa. Should this not be a wake-up call?

We intuitively know that many multicultural nations have a problem concerning their cultural diversity – and yet, collectively, action is not taking place to change this. Is this because people unconsciously feel that advancing cultural diversity is a zero-sum game? That if someone else gets the leadership positions, they will lose out?

Furthermore, is it right to take what has worked to increase gender diversity and apply those learnings to cultural diversity to accelerate progress? While specific initiatives in gender, such as targets and disclosure, have moved the dial, have things really changed for good? The accountant in me says yes – we will not make progress unless we can measure change. However, I also know that numbers, if not used sensibly, can lead to inappropriate behaviours that may derail efforts.

While we may desire rapid change, we also need sustainable change, not 'diversity dressing'. Having more inclusive nations, where our business leaders represent our population, requires us to adapt. Society and its organisations must recognise the role they need to take to drive progress. Merely holding feel-good events that celebrate our cultural diversity will not lead to improvements. Improving cultural diversity needs to be part of a broader culture change management initiative and not delegated to the human resources (HR) department. Change initiatives that do not deal with people's (sometimes hidden) concerns and apprehensions will not lead to long-term change.

Unless there is greater recognition, both by our organisations and individuals, of the anxieties that arise unintentionally and unconsciously between us, our progress will remain slow.

We all need to open our minds and look at this differently, possibly unlearning and relearning how to do things. But unfortunately, that is not easy for all of us, individually and collectively.

It is time to look at cultural diversity through a different lens.

TAKING A DIFFERENT ANGLE

Surprisingly, relatively little has been written about workplace cultural diversity in leadership in Australia to date. While there has been a significant focus on gender, research outside of the US on cultural diversity has tended to ignore the treatment and experiences of culturally diverse workers. In addition, the available research has tended to explore the experiences of migrants at work but not in leadership positions.

Significantly more studies from the US have explored race and ethnic diversity from a critical theory perspective. Critical theory focuses on reflective assessment and critique of society and culture to reveal and challenge power structures. Other research on cultural diversity has focused on identity (particularly from a social identity theory (SIT) perspective) and biculturalism.

A great deal of the existing research on cultural diversity in the workplace outside the US offers perspectives on the *barriers* to aspiring culturally diverse leaders reaching leadership roles. However, I could not find concrete answers on what should be done to increase the number of culturally diverse leaders at work.

The research was often focused on either individuals or the system – but did not always deal with both. I felt that I needed to take a step back to find the answers. I pondered – should I ask the culturally diverse leaders who have made it themselves and look at their organisations from within, through their eyes?

I decided to speak to Asian-Australians in leadership roles given their growing presence and unique challenges in reaching leadership positions, and as their voices have seldom been heard.

When looking for potential Asian-Australian business leaders to interview, I found that the pool of leaders was small. Many Asian-Australians in senior positions in their late 40s or 50s that I know, like me, live overseas. Others had chosen to set up their own businesses, like David and Vicki Teoh of TPG and Tim Fung of Airtasker. Of the top twenty companies listed on the Australian Stock Exchange, Shemara Wikramanayake, CEO of Macquarie Group; Sandeep Biswas, CEO of Newcrest; and Mike Henry, CEO of BHP (who has Japanese heritage from his mother) are some of the rare exceptions. Outside of the ASX20, Australian listed company CEOs with Indian backgrounds include Stockland's Tarun Gupta, Orica's Sanjeev Gandhi, Link's Vivek Bhatia, and Pact's Sanjay Dayal. In the past, Ming Long, former CEO of Investa Property Group who has a Malaysian Chinese background and Cleanaway's Vik Bansal, who has Indian ethnicity, have led ASX listed companies (Khadem, 2021). The situation is different in the US, where many more Asian-Americans have led large US companies.

As many Asian-Australians work in the accounting profession where there has been little industry-wide research in Australia to date, I decided to speak to current and former Asian-Australian partners in the Big 4 accounting firms in Australia. In addition, I talked to other senior Asian-Australian leaders across both the public and private sectors. My focus was to understand their experience in the systems where they worked – home, school, and work. After analysing the interviews, some interesting patterns emerged.

DISSIMILAR PATHS, DISSIMILAR EXPERIENCES, SAME DESTINATION

While the career progression of the Asian-Australian leaders overall was in line with what I had expected, what intrigued me were their divergent stories at the age of twelve. This is the age when most kids change schools and are to making new friends in a new environment.

Ben and Michael[4] – same destinations, different paths

Ben was born overseas but moved to Australia at an early age. 'I came here with my family with absolutely no money', he shared with me. 'We weren't poor, we weren't rich. I didn't have the latest Nike shoes, I didn't have the latest t-shirts or anything like that'. Ben moved schools during his childhood, at a time when there was little cultural diversity in his city. He found that his childhood was tough at this age.

Ben recalled being picked on and physically abused by three bigger boys in the playground as he was different. He believes that his experiences in the playground shaped how he operates as an adult.

'It's actually increased my resilience… I think resilience is really important in a professional sense', he told me, noting that it taught him to tolerate people and to problem solve – how could he get out of being teased or physically bashed up? During his work career, I found that he seemed to repeat similar patterns when he faced adversities – to think about how he could resolve problems largely independently.

Michael had a similar ethnic background. He spent his early years growing up in an English-speaking household in Singapore. Just before high school, he moved to Australia.

He recalls a situation at school.

These kids came up to me and they said "Yo – do you speak English?" My immediate response in my head

---

as an 11-year-old was, wow, you know, look at them being discriminatory. [This was] quickly followed by a second thought, which was, well, maybe they just want to know me, right? And then the third thought was, don't they know that everyone in Singapore speaks English? Almost everyone in Singapore speaks English. So, it's kind of three very distinct thoughts, one after the other.

Michael recalls the kids were curious about him; however, he eventually became a good friend with them and had a good school experience overall. He learnt from that incident that we all have pre-conceptions about situations. His leadership style is that he builds long-term trusted relationships with his clients and peers.

Ben and Michael, who both have similar ethnic backgrounds, became successful partners in Big 4 firms. Yet, both approached similar situations in their adolescence in quite different ways. Michael's story wasn't in line with the more typically reported stories of people with culturally diverse backgrounds who are picked on at school and react negatively to the situation.

Pondering further, I realised that there might be a lot more to how Asian-Australian leaders become leaders than working hard and having sponsors within their organisations.

I wondered whether their experiences in early childhood with their parents impacted how they dealt with stressful situations in life and at work. Could their family experiences have also shaped their experiences and relationships with peers? What else aided them in succeeding?

I drilled deeper into their stories further. I concluded that there could be additional influences at play that help us understand how culturally diverse leaders succeeded in the workplace.

OVERVIEW OF THIS BOOK

This book explores how people like Ben and Michael became leaders and seeks to understand their journeys and their experiences of resolving identity conflicts on the way. It also examines their experiences in the organisations in which they work. Finally, incorporating my research findings and leveraging my experience as a business leader and diversity practitioner, the book suggests practical recommendations for aspiring culturally diverse leaders. It also provides a roadmap for fostering culturally diverse leadership in organisations.

Feel free to read the book in its entirety if you are less familiar with the topics covered. Alternatively, deep-dive into different parts of the book if you already have an awareness of specific topics.

The book is divided into three parts.

Part I, Laying the Foundations, introduces some of the concepts I will explore in this book. It examines identities in multicultural nations and efforts by companies to increase their cultural diversity at work to date.

Part II, Lessons from Culturally Diverse Leaders who Smashed the Bamboo Ceiling, delves into the career progression of successful Asian-Australian leaders. It looks at how they manage the various tensions and paradoxes they face in the organisations in which they work. It also explores how their early childhood experiences and adult attachment styles impact their career paths.

I conclude with Part III, which provides a Roadmap for Fostering Culturally Diverse Leadership in Organisations, leveraging my Career Progression Model for Culturally Diverse Leaders. I share what individuals can do to super-charge their careers at work and provide a roadmap for driving organisational change towards greater culturally diverse leadership. Finally, I propose that fostering culturally diverse leadership in organisations will require an ecosystem approach.

Chapter summary

- Culturally diverse leadership is essential for all organisations. Many companies have recognised its importance in supporting their business outcomes and have enhanced their efforts to improve the cultural diversity of their workforces. However, to date, workplace cultural diversity initiatives in many multicultural nations have not gone far enough. Few people with culturally diverse backgrounds have reached their business' highest echelons, particularly those of Asian ethnicity. Further, many of their organisations remain focused on improving gender diversity.
- Often, historical context and institutional illogics in organisations inhibit change. For instance, the unique history of Asian-Australians and race in Australia is frequently an unspoken topic that may hinder real improvement.
- Organisations need to consider using a different lens to understand the potential blockers to change and identify innovative solutions to increase the cultural diversity of their leadership.

Questions to ask yourself and your team members

Yourself

- What does diversity and inclusion mean to me personally?
- To what extent is diversity and inclusion in the workplace important to me? Why?

Your team members

- What is our view on the effort to date by our organisation to increase the diversity of our leadership? What has influenced or inhibited its progress to date?
- What elements of diversity are important in our organisation?
- What are our initial views on what more could be done to foster culturally diverse leadership in our organisation?

NOTES

1 The 'bamboo ceiling' describes the barriers some people of Asian ethnicity believe they face when seeking leadership positions in the workplace in Western organisations.
2 The term 'partner' refers to a senior position within professional services firms (PSFs). 'Partnerships' are the ownership collectives formed by PSFs to carry out work for clients. Historically, PSFs were set up as legal partnerships. The term has remained, even though many have been incorporated as corporations. Most PSFs retain features such as using the title 'partner', their profit-sharing status, and the partnership ethos of 'being there for one another'.
3 In this book, I may use the word 'diversity' without 'inclusion'. However, increasing diversity also requires a simultaneous focus on inclusion.
4 The names and other identifiers of some of the leaders I interviewed for this book have been changed and disguised to protect their anonymity. I am deeply indebted to them for their generosity and courage in telling me their stories.

REFERENCES

Biddle, N., Gray, M., & Lo, J. Y. (2020). *The Experience of Asian-Australians during the COVID-19 Pandemic: Discrimination and Wellbeing*. Australian National University. https://csrm. cass.anu.edu.au/research/publications/experience-asian-australians-during-covid-19-pandemic-discrimination-and

Khadem, N. (2021, December 2). Twitter's New Indian-American CEO Highlights Corporate Australia's Lack of Cultural Diversity. *ABC News*. https://www.abc. net.au/news/2021-12-02/america-indian-ceo-twitter-parag-agrawal-twitter-diversity/100667392

Long, S. (2016). The Transforming Experience Framework and Unconscious Processes: A Brief Journey Through the History of the Unconscious as Applied To Person, System and Context with an Exploratory Hypothesis of Unconscious as Source. In S. Long (Ed.), *Transforming Experience in Organisations: A Framework for Organisational Research and Consultancy* (pp. 29–106). Routledge. https://doi.org/10.4324/9780429484254

Vince, R. (2019). Institutional Illogics: The Unconscious and Institutional Analysis. *Organization Studies*, 40(7), 953–973. https://doi.org/10.1177/0170840618765866

PART I

Laying the Foundations

Two

INTRODUCTION

Who am I?

Well, I'm Karen.

In my case, to the outside world, I'm female, Australian, and ethnically Chinese. To my family: I'm a daughter, a sister, an aunty, and a wife. Then, of course, I also have my religion, my opinions, my attitudes, and my beliefs.

However, when people try to categorise me into different 'boxes', I sometimes get frustrated.

Do I call myself an Australian, an Australian-born Chinese? Or am I an Asian-Australian? Or even a fourth-generation Asian-Australian? In different scenarios, I define myself in various ways, depending on whether I want to be part of the in- or out-group. Sometimes defensively, I 'label' myself to avoid annoying questions, such as 'where are you really from?' and comments like, 'you have a really strong accent'.

Understanding our identity is complex. It often evokes tension within us between our personal motives and social demands.

Some describe it as being like an onion – not just because it has many layers and a virtual centre that disappears when reached – but it also produces tears. Like onions that vary in colour, we may immediately judge other people by external factors when we see them.

Our identity heavily influences our sensemaking and behaviour, even if out of conscious awareness. Therefore, appreciating identity is essential when understanding how to increase leadership diversity at work.

This chapter provides an overview of the concept of identity for people with multiple identities, illustrating this by examining who Australians and 'Asian-Australians' are.

WHAT IS IDENTITY?

When we think about the word 'identity', many concepts often come to mind. If we ask the internet what it means, we will find many definitions, depending on our perspective.

DOI: 10.4324/9781003291237-3

What is identity?

Identity is the meaning attached to the 'self' and 'who one is', based on one's personal and social identities (Figure 2.1).

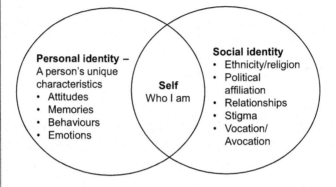

Figure 2.1 Components of identity
Source: Own research

The concept of identity has been examined by both psychologists and sociologists.[1] For psychologists, identity generally refers to our *personal identity* or the distinctive aspects – such as our attitudes, recollections, behaviours, and emotions – that make us distinct from others.

For sociologists, it relates to our *social identity*, the collection of group memberships we develop through our interactions with others that define us. It includes external characteristics we have no control over, such as our ethnicity.

Our own identity is not just a way of distinguishing ourselves from others – it is also a way to see ourselves as similar to a group with which we would like to be associated. Fundamentally a relational and comparative concept formed and sustained by social interaction, the ambiguous nature of identity stems from the fact that we do not fully decide on it, nor is it entirely externally imposed on us.

Some of the more common theories used to explain how individuals incorporate their group memberships into themselves by categorising and comparing their identities highlight that our social identity within a group shapes our norms, attitudes, and behaviours, and it is essential for our self-esteem. Most research on diversity investigates social identity and intergroup behaviour (such as prejudice and discrimination) and centres on people with monocultural, monoracial, heterosexual, and gender-typical backgrounds.

However, in reality, we all have multiple social identities that co-exist and fluctuate based on the person, the context, and their identities. Therefore, at times and in different contexts, we show different combinations of our group memberships. Take me as an example. As a female, an accountant, and an Asian, I could categorise myself with one single compounded identity – a female Asian accountant. However, in another situation, I could also refer to myself as female, *and* an accountant, *and* Asian, which is more complex.

A challenge of managing our multiple identities is that they frequently conflict. For instance, many people with Asian ancestry in Australia feel conflicted between their cultural and national identities. When there are significant cultural differences in groups, some have found that people tend to identify more strongly with their cultural subgroup than the larger group.

To fulfil our need for uncertainty reduction, belonging, and autonomy, we assume, negotiate, or acquiesce our identities. At times, we resist and relinquish restrictive identities and pursue ones that bring us joy. When we become detached from the elements of our identities that we value, we experience social anxiety, such as rejection or status anxiety. Our self-esteem, relationships, and views of identity can protect us from these anxieties (Petriglieri et al., 2018).

Our identity formation starts in childhood and is influenced by our parental upbringing and peers. According to psychologist Erik Erikson, our psychosocial development continues throughout our lifespan. A key influence on how we develop is our sense of self when we interact with others. We are also motivated by our need to achieve competence in certain areas of our lives.

Reconciling our identities during adolescence – Oliver's story

When Oliver was twelve, he was a shy kid. Around that time, he started to get involved in sports. 'One of the things that helped me assimilate and actually click over in confidence was doing a lot more sport', Oliver remembers. 'That teamwork in sport actually helped me quite significantly in terms of growing in confidence', he added, recalling that at that age, he believed that he was a bad public speaker. As he was scared and nervous, he would write down every single word before speaking in public.

(Continued)

However, he also remembered an incident where his mother turned up at a basketball game to watch him play. 'I was so shy because she was there that I didn't call out to my teammates, and I didn't get the ball hardly for the entire first half'.

However, things then changed for him. He recollects:

In the second half, she had to leave because she had to go pick up my sister. And then all of a sudden, I became this bright, bubbly personality again. I was calling for the ball, and getting everywhere, and getting it everywhere, and then having a lot of fun.

And that's one of the key moments I can remember – when I realised that the shyness was somewhat within. But the team was what helped me get over that... What I needed to get over was [that] I was quite shy in front of my parents.

Commenting that he is now pretty outspoken and that his parents are generally quite relaxed, he said that as an Asian, 'there is a certain amount of, you know, you just don't go and scream and shout and yell in front of [your] parents'. Today, Oliver is a very confident public speaker.

During our identity formation, we need to resolve various conflicting ideas. While our identity formation is most acute during adolescence, it continues as we take on new roles or undertake new transitions.

A critical conflict we resolve during adolescence is our 'identity versus role confusion'. This conflict typically arises when we start high school around age twelve and continues until we finish, generally at age eighteen.

One question that we need to resolve at this age is 'Who am I?' Many culturally diverse leaders who grew up in Australia faced this question when they discovered that their schoolyard lunches differed from those of their non-Asian-Australian friends.

Another question is 'What do I want to do with my life?' Again, we face role confusion, as we may not wish to commit to one path.

As we progress, we undergo a period of experimentation before committing, reconciling the pieces of our identity, and emerging into adulthood.

Understanding our childhood experiences is an essential ingredient in our leadership development because these childhood experiences influence our values and behaviours later in life. This is because our leader values and beliefs that motivate our behaviour and decisions tend to be developed in various social contexts through culture, community, and families. The values 'injected' by our caregivers shape our behaviours and attitudes and may vary depending on how we internalise or make meaning of these formative experiences.

THE INFLUENCE OF OUR NATIONAL IDENTITY

Home is where the heart is – how our national identity shapes us

Undoubtedly, our national identity also significantly influences how we identify ourselves.

A national identity is a collective identity – an abstract notion that changes and will continue to change over time and through generations. Nevertheless, it is a shared identity that underpins a sense of belonging among all its members. When we think of a national identity, we usually think about its culture and values.

It is impossible to understand multiple identities without understanding how aspects of identity, such as culture and race, have been managed over time in a country. Historical events and legislation shape people's identities, experiences, and fears in some multicultural countries.

In Australia, the history of Asians in Australia is interconnected with Australia's formation as a nation and the broader Australian identity. The Chinese first came to Australia in the mid-1800s as indentured labourers and for the gold rush. However, Australia's federation was partly motivated by the Australian states' desire to coordinate immigration against non-whites in the 1890s arising from the public's fear of people from Asia taking their jobs. In 1901, the Immigration Restriction Act (commonly known as the 'White Australia' policy), was among the first pieces of Commonwealth legislation enacted, effectively ending non-European immigration to Australia. Edmund Barton, the prime minister at the time, argued in support of the Bill, stating: 'The doctrine of the equality of man was never intended to apply to the equality of the Englishman and the Chinaman... Nothing in this world can put these two races upon an equality' (Barton, 1901, p. 5233).

Rather than naming races or groups for exclusion, the Act required a dictation test in a European language to be administered to prospective immigrants. The result of the Act was that it practically excluded all 'coloured' people from coming to Australia and had a significant influence on views of the Australian people's identity for generations to come. In 1972, in line with changing global attitudes, the government abolished the White Australia policy.

The situation for people with Asian backgrounds in North America has some similarities. Although Chinese labourers had worked in the US since the 1850s, until 1952, the Naturalisation Law of 1790 barred Asian-Americans from gaining US citizenship. Further, the Chinese Exclusion Act of 1882 terminated the immigration of Chinese to the US until 1943. In addition, Japanese-Americans were sent to internment camps during World War II by a government concerned that they would be loyal to Japan. The US immigration laws were changed in 1965 after the rise of the Civil Rights Movement (Thatchenkery & Sugiyama, 2011).

The situation in the UK differs from Australia and the US. Immigration has taken place for education from South Asia to Britain since the early seventeenth century. More significant levels of immigration to the UK took place after World War II and the independence of India and Pakistan. The arrival of people of East Asian ethnicity remained low until the late twentieth century (Thatchenkery & Sugiyama, 2011).

Following policy changes in the 1960s and 1970s, the migration of people of Asian ethnicity to the US, Canada, the UK, and Australia accelerated. As a result, Asian-Americans are now one of the fastest-growing immigrant groups in the US. Likewise, arrivals in Australia from Asian countries have increased markedly, with Asian-born Australians accounting for 5.5% in 1995 and 13.4% in 2016 of the Australian population. While historically, many migrants came to Australia as part of family or refuge migration, more significant numbers came as permanent and temporary skilled migration since 1995 when the focus of the policies changed (McDonald, 2019).

Whilst rules have changed and national identities have evolved, some of the anxieties of the majority over their national identities have remained, and at times, become manifest. In Australia, for instance, not everyone was comfortable with the new policy of multiculturalism. In 2001, Ien Ang of the University of Western Sydney suggested that Australia experiences racial/spatial anxiety with Asia (Ang, 2001). Others feel that 'the fear of "Asians taking our jobs" is still here' (Liaw, 2019, p. 2). Sadly, sporadic incidents such as increased racism against Chinese-Australians since 2020 in the wake of the COVID-19 pandemic still occur.

**The challenges of juggling more than one cultural identity–
Sharon's story**

Sharon moved to Australia to attend university, then spent her formative working years in Australia. Then, in her early 30s, Sharon moved back to her home country to spend time with her parents for personal reasons. She recalls having a huge reverse-culture shock. 'I think I had become more Australian in terms of working very direct and honest'.

As part of her career feedback in Australia, her leaders told her that she needed to express her opinions more. However, she received contradictory feedback when she returned to her home country.

'One of the [pieces of career] feedback I got was, "You are no longer in Australia – you don't have to behave like you are still in Australia"'. Others expected her to keep quiet and not share her own opinions. 'So that was quite an eye-opener to me', she recollects. 'Maybe I've changed, but I'm a very direct person. So, I think if I'm not happy with something, I would say it. I guess that's not [the] culture in Asia'.

A significant challenge for people who migrate to a new country is coping and adapting to the new environment. The experiences of new migrants in multicultural nations have been well documented.

Whenever we join a new culture (with dissimilar people, groups, or social influences), or when another culture is brought to us, we undergo a process which is known as *acculturation*. This is a socialisation process whereby we adopt, acquire, and adjust to a new cultural environment. This leads us to blend our values, customs, norms, cultural attitudes, and behaviours with those of the overarching host culture. Acculturation, which generally covers three domains – *practices*, *identifications*, and *values*, typically occurs over a considerable period (sometimes over a few generations), through social pressure or constant exposure to a more prevalent host culture (Deaux & Verkuyten, 2014).

Historically, there was a view that when we move countries, we acquire the new homelands' values, practices, and beliefs and discard those from our own cultural heritage. However, as more nations have adopted multiculturalism policies, there has been an increasing awareness that when someone embraces a new country's beliefs, values, and practices, they don't simultaneously stop endorsing those of their home country (Schwartz et al., 2010). This has led to a growing recognition that people can have multiple identities and the related concepts of bicultural or dual identities.

Psychologically, when we participate to some degree in two or more intersecting communities that complement or challenge each other, we are confronted with the task of living with diversity and having to integrate different cultural inclinations and group identifications in ourselves. The most used model that explores acculturation, by psychologist John W. Berry examines the independent dimensions of a person's host-culture (receiving) acquisition and home-culture (heritage) retention. These two dimensions intersect to create four acculturation categories. These are:

- Assimilation – Adopts the host culture and discards the home culture
- Separation – Rejects the host culture and retains the home culture
- Integration (or biculturalism) – Adopts host culture and retains the home culture
- Marginalisation – Rejects both the home and host cultures

The acculturation strategies of immigrants are represented diagrammatically in Figure 2.2.

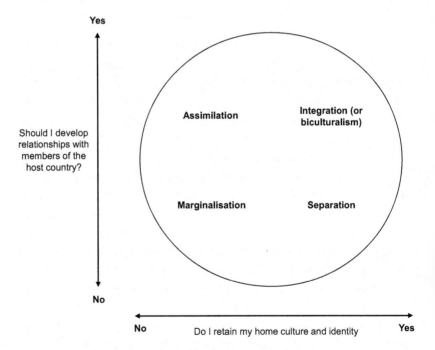

Figure 2.2 Acculturation strategies
Source: Adapted from Berry (1997)

Acculturation in practice

Different acculturation strategies can emerge in any of the three cultural domains of practices, identification, and values. A person may be bicultural in one domain (such as cultural practices) but not in other areas.

Most people with two or more cultural backgrounds who live in multicultural nations adopt a biculturalism acculturation strategy.

A bicultural acculturation approach is most evident in many of the day-to-day *practices* of people in multicultural nations – particularly their food, culture (such as the arts and television), and language. When people speak about embracing cultural diversity, they tend to focus on the practices they can see.

Yet, some choose different strategies privately regarding their cultural identity and values. This may be because some people with bicultural identities have difficulties finding a balance between their two (or more) identities – it can be mentally and emotionally challenging. The more individuals alternate between two identities, the more complexity they may face, as described below.

Cultural identification – the labels we apply

In many Asian families, their ethnic identities are influenced by their family's cultural socialisation practices. These lead to the reconstruction and reproduction of their culture and identity in a way that resonates with future generations. Socialisation takes place through parents teaching their children about their ethnic history, cultural customs, and traditions, either deliberately or implicitly (Hughes et al., 2006; Juang & Syed, 2010). For instance, in Chinese-Australian families, 'gatekeeping' efforts by parents, grandparents, and other extended family members are a frequent reminder of their Chinese heritage among second-, third-, and even fourth-generation Chinese-Australians (Tan, 2001).

Over the years, there has been some sensitivity concerning applying various ethnic labels to people such as those of Asian ancestry. Even using (or not using) the hyphen in some countries has at times been sensitive. Historically, many people of Asian ethnicity defined themselves by their nationality. However, some also referred to their ethnicity, calling themselves 'Chinese-Australian' or 'Australian-born

Chinese' in Australia, which I described myself to minimise questions.

Today, many people self-categorise themselves with a hyphen, such as 'Asian-Australian', forming a distinct 'hybrid' or 'hyphenated' identity that incorporates both 'Asian' and 'Western' elements in their identity. This is in line with the trend that many more people feel they have dual identities, with their feet in two different camps.

Some believe that using hyphenated identities is good for new migrants as they seek to find their place in the world. In addition, researchers have found an individual's affiliation with a hybrid cultural identification plays an integral role in supporting their self-esteem, belonging, and ability to resist adversity, as well as their well-being and happiness.[2]

Cultural values – the less noticeable aspects

Although cultural values may not be as visible, many people with culturally diverse backgrounds in multicultural nations maintain some of their cultural values at home.

People from Asian backgrounds tend to hold more collectivist values, such as consensus, harmony, unity, and community. In particular, the role of the family is significant. However, there is substantial diversity between different backgrounds. For instance, those from East Asian backgrounds may have more group-specific values of filial piety, saving face, humility, conformity, and self-control. On the other hand, parents from South Asian cultures are more likely to encourage their children to be innovative and adaptable.

An example of the influence of cultural values is the continued importance of education to Asian families, as education is a driver of social mobility. According to Christina Ho of the University of Technology Sydney, education is a significant consideration for many migrants, particularly from East Asian societies, who relocate to multicultural countries, as it 'is the cornerstone of families' strategies and dreams for the future' (Ho, 2020, p. 14).

However, maintaining their cultural values in a host country is challenging. Ho stresses that Asian-Australian parents' focus on their children's education reflects the more profound anxiety they face. Deeply aware of their position as newcomers and ethnic minorities, many parents face what they see as racially based exclusion from career opportunities. Fearing that their families will also suffer from racial discrimination, they believe their children's only protection against discrimination is flawless educational qualifications. She argues that these anxieties arise due to Australia's selective migration policies that prioritise skilled migration (Ho, 2020).

Case study – my untold Australian story: a Happy Little Vegemite

My own family story illustrates how historical context influences identities, how families adopt different acculturation strategies across cultural domains, and how ethnic identities evolve through generations.

When people ask me about my family history, most are astounded to learn that one side of my family first moved to Australia 150 years ago, with the other side moving to Australia soon after. The stories of Asian-Australians who have been in Australia for three or more generations are less well known. Understanding my family history and experiences has helped me to understand who I am.

My paternal great-great-grandfather, James Chung-Gon, arrived in Bendigo in 1873 at the age of twenty-one. However, due to racist sentiment in Victoria, he moved to Launceston, Tasmania, in 1878. He worked in tin mines, as a market gardener and as a woodcutter. He learned English in the vestry of the local Baptist church and was naturalised in 1882 (Chung-Gon, n.d.) (Figure 2.3).

(Continued)

Figure 2.3 James and Mary Chung-Gon (my great-great-grandparents) with family in Launceston, in 1899

Source: Chung-Gon family collection

James' eldest daughter, Violet, married my great-grandfather, Dang Loon (Dang Goon Loong). He moved to Australia also aged around twenty-one, sponsored by a relative, and lived in Gundagai and Tumut in New South Wales.

What I have found fascinating is that some of my family members visited China several times after 1901. Yet despite living in Australia for so many years, Dang Loon needed a 'Certificate Exempting from Dictation Test' (CEDT) to leave the country (Figure 2.4). I was fascinated to read about his character reference which accompanied his application for his 1905 CEDT. In the reference, the owner of the Gundagai Times described him as a 'highly respectable man, always quiet and unassuming in manner, and is besides, a worthy townsman in every way' (NAA, 1905). I found this description of him interesting as it was as if my great-grandfather needed to be silent and somewhat invisible for fear of falling afoul of the White Australia policy. It may also explain why my paternal grandfather was relatively laid back.

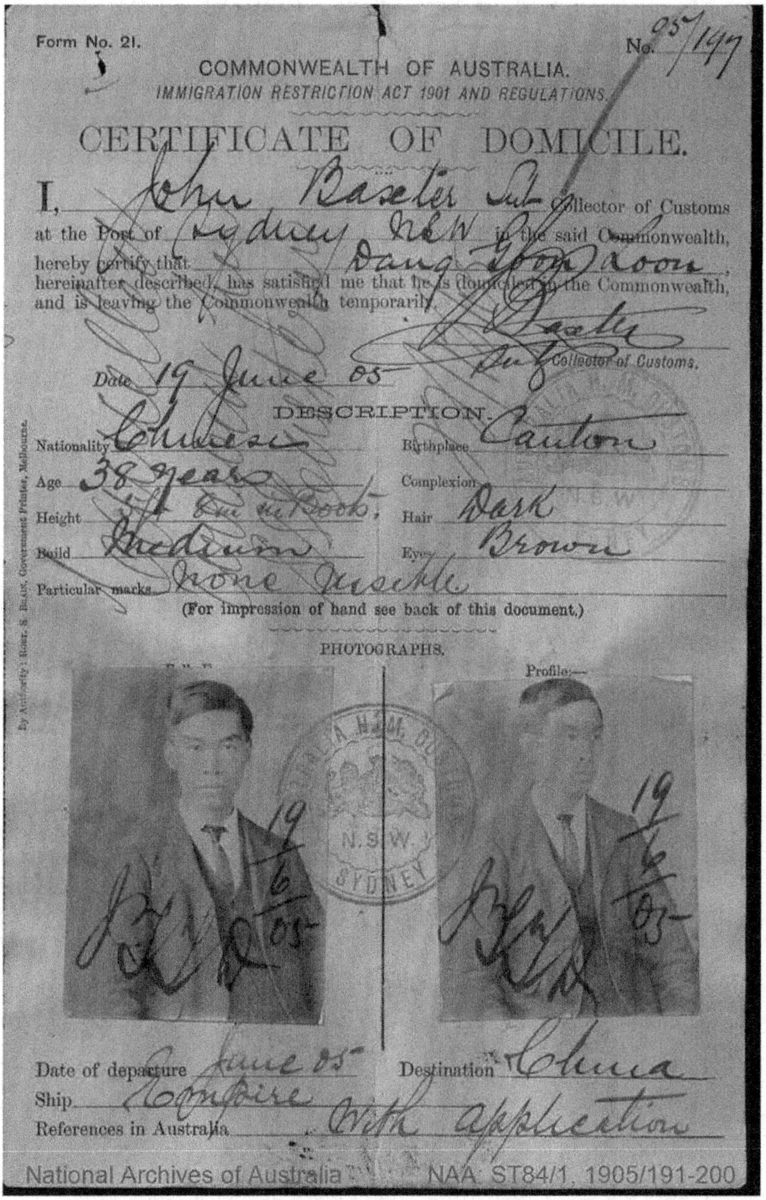

Form No. 21. No. 95/147

COMMONWEALTH OF AUSTRALIA.

IMMIGRATION RESTRICTION ACT 1901 AND REGULATIONS.

CERTIFICATE OF DOMICILE.

I, John Baxter Sub Collector of Customs at the Port of Sydney NSW in the said Commonwealth, hereby certify that Dang Loon, hereinafter described, has satisfied me that he is domiciled in the Commonwealth, and is leaving the Commonwealth temporarily.

J Baxter
Sub Collector of Customs.

Date 19 June 05

DESCRIPTION.

Nationality Chinese Birthplace Canton
Age 38 years Complexion
Height 5ft 6in in Boots. Hair Dark
Build Medium Eyes Brown
Particular marks None visible

(For impression of hand see back of this document.)

PHOTOGRAPHS.

Profile:—

19/6/05

19/6/05

Date of departure June 05 Destination China
Ship Empire
References in Australia With application

By Authority: Robt. S. Brain, Government Printer, Melbourne.

National Archives of Australia NAA: ST84/1, 1905/191-200

Figure 2.4 Dictation test exemption certificate of Dang Loon, my great-grandfather, in 1905

Source: Image courtesy of the National Archives of Australia. NAA: ST84/1, 1905/191–200

(Continued)

My other paternal great-grandfather, (James) Lee Fook, similarly came to Australia from Canton, China, in 1872 at the age of 23, settled in Gladstone in north-east Tasmania and was naturalised in 1883. His wife, Fanny arrived in Australia from Guangdong around 1880 as the maid of Lula Chinn; and together with James had nine children. Living in the remote parts of Tasmania, my family was more assimilated into the community as fewer Chinese were in the area.

My maternal family is from Darwin, where relatively larger numbers of Chinese settled since the late 1800s. The city of Darwin had a relatively racially and ethnically heterogeneous population compared to other Australian cities, and its Chinese residents didn't have any apparent social tension with the majority (Figure 2.5). Additionally, they retained many of their traditional cultural traits, so they were less assimilated (Ngan & Chan, 2012). My grandmother was born in Pine Creek, 225 km from Darwin, and my grandfather was from Palmerston, near Darwin. They married in 1931 in one of the first weddings registered by both the Kuo Min Tang and the Australian government (Unknown, 1931) (Figure 2.6).

Figure 2.5 Dolly Yuen (my grandmother), Selina Hassan, Amy Johnston, Gee Ming Ket, and Arthur Lee in Darwin, in 1930

Source: 'Presenting address' 1930 (Chan Collection), PH0771/0014, in Northern Territory Library Picture NT [online database], https://territorystories.nt.gov.au/10070/3408

Figure 2.6 Clarence Ng and Dorothy Yuen (my grandparents) with wedding party in Darwin, in 1931

Source: Ng family collection

My parents spent their adolescent years growing up in Sydney, at a time when the Chinese population was less than 10,000. My mother's family had a fish-and-chip shop, and my paternal grandmother owned a corner grocery shop. Their circle of friends was primarily of Chinese ethnicity. At the age of twenty-one, my dad started his air conditioning and heating business in Tamworth, 450 km from Sydney, where I grew up. My mother worked in our family business.

While outside our home, my family largely assimilated to the Australian culture, at home, we are primarily bicultural but adopted various practices.

My childhood was typically Australian. We played with the kids in the neighbourhood, and I loved riding my bike around. I played netball and did physical culture. We ate western food most of the time, as it was challenging to buy Asian ingredients in Tamworth. However, we would eat Chinese food once a week – beef with pineapple and lup cheong (Chinese sausage) were favourites. Slightly embarrassingly, my favourite comfort food and staple school lunch

(Continued)

was a vegemite sandwich on white bread. As a baby, my mother also fed me congee (rice porridge) with vegemite and butter – an apt food that describes who I am.

My grandmothers' lifestyles and cooking reflected my upbringing – a mixture of Australian and Chinese elements despite both having been born in Australia. We visited my grandparents in Sydney every holiday. My grandmothers were strong role models to me.

My Por Por (paternal grandmother), Edith Lee Fook grew up in Tasmania. After running her corner grocery shop till she retired, she learnt how to golf at sixty-five and became a regular at her golf club. She played the piano and the organ and spent many hours looking after her garden of beautiful flowers. She cooked both Australian and Chinese food. She was famous for her 1970s favourites – sponge cakes, jelly cakes, pavlova, pasties, and sausage rolls. Por Por kept little bowls of wrapped Cadbury chocolates in her living room, which I would devour. Every Christmas, we would have roast turkey, ham, pork, roast vegetables, and my grandmother's Christmas pudding for lunch, then open presents around the Christmas tree.

My Bor Bor (maternal grandmother), Dorothy (or Dolly) Yuen was from Darwin. A mother to five children, she spoke three Chinese dialects in addition to English. I recall the Buddhas and Chinese ornaments in the house, joss sticks, and red packets for Chinese New Year. In Bor Bor's backyard garden, she grew Chinese vegetables. She had a white Chinese magnolia bush near the front door with a beautiful fragrance and a kumquat tree. On the days when she wasn't spending time out with her Caucasian girlfriends, she watched TV in the lounge room while drinking oodles of Chinese tea out of her Chinese hotpot and nibbling on pumpkin seeds and nuts. I remember walking with her when I was young to the only Chinese grocer in Burwood. We would buy various ingredients that seemed so exotic to me, like wonton skins, dried Chinese mushrooms, and water chestnuts. She was also an excellent Cantonese cook. I loved her wonton soup, deep-fried jian duis (Chinese fried sesame balls) filled with red bean paste and crunchy fried 'beehive' biscuits. She would steam barramundi, which my relatives would bring her from Darwin, and cook soya sauce chicken which we ate with my extended family. On special occasions, I remember visiting Chinatown, where we would eat Chinese food at one of the restaurants on Dixon Street and sit in one of the uncomfortable Formica booths.

Growing up in Tamworth in the 1970s and early 1980s, I was almost always the only Chinese kid in my class, and we were one of a handful of Chinese families. As a result, my cultural upbringing was very Australian. As all of my grandparents, one great-grandmother and my parents went to schools in Australia, I only speak English (although my mother understands a little of some Chinese dialects). Of my grandparents, I can't recall my paternal grandparents speaking anything other than English. However, I am sure they must have understood some Chinese dialects, especially my grandfather, who visited Hong Kong and China as a child to learn Chinese.

While my family is proudly Australian, we were brought up with certain values from our Chinese ancestors. Largely because some of my family did not have a lot of money, we were expected to work hard. As a result, making money and education was crucial – I was the first in my family to go to university well over a hundred years after my great-great-grandfather arrived in Australia. We were also taught to be well-behaved and respect our elders. Consequently, I could never win an argument with our dad as he would (and still does) want to have the last word. Another unspoken expectation was that we would marry someone who was Chinese. However, in my family, we don't live in three-generation households. Further, we don't actively celebrate Chinese New Year, possibly as many of my family are Christians. It was not observed in Australia in the past as much as it is today.

Our historical context, our national culture, and our family cultural background influence our identity. The more complex our identities, the more challenging they can be to manage.

THE EVOLUTION OF BICULTURAL IDENTITIES

Adam Liaw, an Asian-Australian celebrity chef, a television presenter, and an author has described some of the challenges that Asians in Australia face and how this has influenced his identity.

> Asians have been coming to Australia even before Europeans have, but when I was growing up "Asian" and "Australian" were two separate things. You could hardly be both at the same time. Total assimilation was the only game in town.
>
> If you played footy and didn't have an accent you were "just like an Aussie." If your family had been here for three generations you were "basically Australian." And the language here matters, because to be "like an Aussie" or "basically Australian" meant, of course, that you weren't.
>
> In order to be more Australian, you had to be less Asian. But of course, no matter how much beer you could drink, or how little of your parents' language you could speak, you could never change the way people looked at you.
>
> As a kid, the question of identity was a difficult one for me. I'm of mixed race, born in Malaysia to parents of mainly English and Chinese ancestry. As a kid I bought into the idea of exclusivity. I thought that to be more Australian, I had to be less Asian.
>
> As an adult, I know that the more I embrace my heritage, the more Australian I feel. Because that's who I am. That's who we are.
>
> (Liaw, 2019, p. 0)

*****

As the world becomes more global and immigrant populations play a more significant role in multicultural societies, bicultural identities are evolving and maturing. In the last two decades, the narratives of people with multiple identities have been celebrated and popularised in many multicultural nations, particularly in movies such as *Bend It Like Beckham* (UK), and on television screens in TV series such as *Fresh Off The Boat* (US), *Kim's Convenience* (Canada), and *The Family Law* (Australia).

However, the lived experiences of people with bicultural identities vary due to different religious, socioeconomic, gender, and generational circumstances. While a national identity binds people, not all of them may strongly align with it.

Some people with a bicultural identity have difficulties finding a balance between both identities – it can be mentally and emotionally challenging and complex. Even for Australian-born Chinese (ABCs) whose families have been in Australia for many generations, switching identities is not a simple alternation process. While many long-settled ABCs are able to put on different 'masks' and perform 'Chineseness' or 'Australianness' in varied circumstances, many still do not feel they fully belong to either cultural group as they feel suspended in a 'liminal' hybrid zone of in-betweenness – feeling that they are neither Chinese nor Australian (Ngan & Chan, 2012). Liminality is the psychological process of transitioning across boundaries and borders – being between two stages of life or in the middle of changing from one way of existence to another.

Further, the modern-day emergence of transnational communities stemming from the growth of the internet and reduced cost of travel has led to the blurring of the boundaries of place. These factors can lead to situations where the construction of identity by migrants and their children also occurs in a state of liminality (Ngan & Chan, 2012). A growing number of authors and commentators have written about this, with *Growing up Asian in Australia*, edited by Alice Pung being one of the more well-known anthologies of personal accounts, essays and short stories of Asian-Australians.

WHY IS CAREER NAVIGATION SO TRICKY FOR PEOPLE WITH CULTURALLY DIVERSE BACKGROUNDS?

Who we are is shaped by our experiences at home and how and where we are brought up. A key challenge for people with multiple identities is adapting and navigating the different external environments such as at school and work.

The experiences of people with culturally diverse backgrounds are incredibly varied. They are impacted by the number of generations their family has spent in their host countries, where their families migrated from, and the extent of their acculturation. Family values are frequently transmitted across generations through cultural rituals and artifacts such as meals, community events, commemorations, and family narratives. How this is reconstructed and reproduced changes over generations.

Yet, many people with culturally diverse backgrounds such as Asian-Australians feel that their physical appearance inhibits their ability to identify as Australian (Thai et al., 2020) even after many generations in Australia fully. This leads some of them to experience liminality – feeling between cultures.

A practical challenge that everyone faces at work is the expectation that we adopt and embrace the culture of that organisation, which is commonly shaped by the national culture of its founders. This can be challenging and feel uncomfortable and awkward for some, particularly since COVID-19.

Two relevant global research areas which are useful when understanding people's experiences in the workplace, and warrant further research are the integration paradox and the influence of transgenerational collective trauma.

The integration paradox

The concept of the immigrant paradox, where recent immigrants often outperform both more established immigrants and the locally born majority in several areas, is relatively well known. However, one phenomenon that is less well known is the integration paradox. This paradox, explored by Maykel Verkuyten in the Netherlands, describes how more highly educated immigrants are frequently less satisfied and less integrated culturally than less-educated immigrants. Often, highly educated immigrants have high expectations regarding work opportunities; however, they feel disenchanted when they are not provided with equal opportunities. As a result, they emotionally turn away from their host nations rather than embracing them (Verkuyten, 2016).

This paradox also exists in Australia. In general, more highly educated immigrants have had more opportunities to travel overseas and gain broader experiences and networks than those without a university education or professional qualifications (Clark, 2007). As a proportion, more highly qualified Asian-Australians live and work across Asia, particularly in Singapore and Hong Kong, than less-educated Asian-Australians. I suspect that this trend may accelerate with the growing number of aspirational skilled migrants in Australia, which may further exacerbate the anxieties of Asian-Australians. However, this pattern may be offset by changing mobility patterns post-Brexit, and due to COVID-19 and other developments, such as Hong Kong's ongoing transformation.

Transgenerational collective trauma

The notion of transgenerational transmission of collective trauma and how it influences the development of leader values has gained recent interest. Collective trauma (or historical trauma) is emotional and psychological stress which affects a large group and moves across generations. It impacts group members with a strong affiliation with a collective group's identity (Tcholakian et al., 2019). The most well recognised and researched collective trauma is the Jewish Holocaust; however, it includes various other genocides. In each case, there is a process of collective mourning and the development of collective emotions.

In exploring the influence of collective trauma on leadership development, some researchers have concluded that collective trauma shapes leaders' values in second and third-generation descendants. Collective trauma resides in cultural rituals and artifacts, community events and commemorations, and family narratives and is transmitted through social learning, social identity, and psychodynamics (Tcholakian et al., 2019).

While not relevant for all Asian-Australians, some leaders I spoke to (or their parents) may have experienced collective trauma. For example, some Asian migrants (or their parents) escaped the Sri Lankan civil war, the Vietnam war, the 1969 racial riots in Malaysia, and Indonesian anti-Chinese sentiment in 1998 before moving to Australia. These experiences may not have been discussed openly within their families in Australia, as some memories may have been too painful. However, it is likely that their leader values (particularly resilience) and behaviours were influenced by these collective traumas or were transmitted to them.

Reflecting on our early childhood upbringing and experiences navigating our identities allows us to better understand our experiences at work, as we will discuss in Chapter 3.

Chapter summary

- Everyone has multiple identities and labels – including their gender, race, nationalities, and vocations.
- Several factors shape individual identities, including their childhood experiences, interactions with others, and national cultures.
- The identities of people who move countries are influenced by both their receiving and heritage national cultures. As a result, their acculturation generally occurs across three domains – practices, values, and identification.
- People with culturally diverse backgrounds adopt different strategies to manage their identities, which may vary by domain and between their private and public lives.
- Reflecting on the intersection of individual and collective identities and how a person has navigated them allows a person (and others) to better understand their leadership journeys both at work and in private.

Questions to ask yourself and your team members

Yourself

- Who am I, and how do I describe myself?
- How have my ethnic and national backgrounds shaped who I am? Is one of them more dominant? How do I manage my different identities in different situations?

Your team members

- Do you understand the identities of the people in the teams we work with? How do they describe who they are, and why?
- What are our identities within our families? How do they compare to our identities at work?

NOTES

1 Confusion sometimes also arises as to the word 'identity'. It is sometimes also used to replace the term 'role', which generally refers to how one should act in an external situation.
2 It is helpful to remember that there are many cultural identities, such as 'Asian'. Cultural identities also change in different contexts and change over generations. Recognising and understanding people's cultural identifications is crucial in improving cultural diversity in the workplace.

REFERENCES

Ang, I. (2001). *On Not Speaking Chinese: Living between Asia and the West*. Routledge. https://doi.org/10.4324/9780203996492

Barton, E. (1901). Immigration Restriction Bill. *Debates*. House of Representatives. https://parlinfo.aph.gov.au/parlInfo/search/display/display.w3p;db=HANSARD80;id=hansard80%2Fhansardr80%2F1901-09-26%2F0015;query=Id%3A%22hansard80%2Fhansardr80%2F1901-09-26%2F0023%22

Berry, J. W. (1997). Immigration, Acculturation, and Adaptation. *Applied Psychology: An International Review*, 46(1), 5–34.

Chung-Gon. (n.d.). *Welcome to the Site of James Chung-Gon*. https://www.chung-gon.com

Clark, J. (2007). Perceptions of Australian Cultural Identity among Asian Australians. *Australian Journal of Social Issues*, 42(3), 303–320. https://doi.org/10.1002/j.1839-4655.2007.tb00060.x

Deaux, K., & Verkuyten, M. (2014). The Social Psychology of Multiculturalism: Identity and Intergroup Relations. In V. Benet-Martinez & Y. Y. Hong (Eds.), *The Oxford Handbook of Multicultural Identity* (pp. 118–138). Oxford University Press. https://doi.org/10.1093/oxfordhb/9780199796694.013.015

Ho, C. (2020). *Aspiration & Anxiety: Asian Migrants and Australian Schooling.* Melbourne University Press.

Hughes, D., Rodriguez, J., Smith, E., Johnson, D., Stevenson, H., & Spicer, P. (2006). Parents' Ethnic–Racial Socialization Practices: A Review of Research and Directions for Future Study. *Developmental Psychology, 42,* 747–770. https://doi.org/10.1037/0012-1649.42.5.747

Juang, L., & Syed, M. (2010). Family Cultural Socialization Practices and Ethnic Identity in College-Going Emerging Adults. *Journal of Adolescence, 33*(3), 347–354. https://doi.org/10.1016/j.adolescence.2009.11.008

Liaw, A. (2019). *Asian-Australian Leadership Summit - Keynote Address.* Asian-Australian Leadership Summit. https://www.asianaustralianleadership.com.au/speeches

McDonald, P. (2019). Migration to Australia: From Asian Exclusion to Asian Predominance. *Revue Européenne des Migrations Internationales, 35*(1&2), 87–105. https://journals.openedition.org/remi/12695

NAA (National Archives of Australia. (1905). Series SSP244/2, N1950/2/2219, Sydney. https://recordsearch.naa.gov.au/SearchNRetrieve/Interface/DetailsReports/ItemDetail.aspx

Ngan, L. L.-S., & Chan, K.-B. (2012). *The Chinese Face in Australia: Multi-generational Ethnicity among Australian-born Chinese.* Springer. https://doi.org/10.1007/978-1-4614-2131-3

Petriglieri, G., Ashford, S. J., & Wrzesniewski, A. (2018). Agony and Ecstasy in the Gig Economy: Cultivating Holding Environments for Precarious and Personalized Work Identities. *Administrative Science Quarterly, 64*(1), 124–170. https://doi.org/10.1177/0001839218759646

Schwartz, S., Unger, J., Zamboanga, B., & Szapocznik, J. (2010). Rethinking the Concept of Acculturation Implications for Theory and Research. *The American Psychologist, 65,* 237–251. https://doi.org/10.1037/a0019330

Tan, C. (2001). *Chinese Families Down Under: The Role of the Family in the Construction of Identity Amongst Chinese Australians, 1920–1960.* Paper presented at Migrating Identities: Ethnic Minorities in Chinese Diaspora, Centre for the Study of Chinese Southern Diaspora, ANU, 26–28 September 2001, https://eprints.qut.edu.au/916/1/tan_chinese.pdf

Tcholakian, L. A., Khapova, S. N., van de Loo, E., & Lehman, R. (2019). Collective Traumas and the Development of Leader Values: A Currently Omitted, but Increasingly Urgent, Research Area. *Frontiers in Psychology, 10,* 1–13. https://doi.org/10.3389/fpsyg.2019.01009

Thai, M., Szeszeran, N. A., Hornsey, M. J., & Barlow, F. K. (2020). Forever Foreign? Asian Australians Assimilating to Australian Culture Are Still Perceived as Less Australian Than White Australians. *Social Psychological and Personality Science, 11*(6), 812–820. https://doi.org/10.1177/1948550619879907

Thatchenkery, T., & Sugiyama, K. (2011). *Making the Invisible Visible: Understanding Leadership Contributions of Asian Minorities in the Workplace.* Palgrave Macmillan.

Unknown. (1931, April 17). Wedding Bells. *Northern Territory Times*. https://trove.nla.gov.au/newspaper/article/4532617

Verkuyten, M. (2016). The Integration Paradox: Empiric Evidence from the Netherlands. *American Behavioral Scientist*, 60(5–6), 583–596. https://doi.org/10.1177/0002764216632838

The Current State of Culturally Diverse Leadership in Organisations
Three

INTRODUCTION

David, an Asian-Australian who moved to Australia before starting primary school, recalled an incident just after becoming a partner in a Big 4 accounting firm.

> Just soon after I'd [been] made a partner, I actually had one of our managers from another division actually knock on my door. And as soon as he knocked on my door, he blurted out: "Congratulations on making partner. I never thought they made Asians in Australia partners of the firm". That really stuck in my mind. That whole conversation struck me as odd,

he told me.

> And whilst I tried to defend it, I struggled to articulate who else back then was a partner of Asian-Australian background, ignoring Indian and non-East Asian partners, and so that flagged to me, [well] that piqued my interest.

At his next partner conference, David counted how many East and South-East Asian partners were in the room and estimated that it was approximately 2% of the partners at the time.

> And so, it flagged to me that the more general point – a lot of the people in the partnership are very similar in nature – white Anglo-Saxon, Protestant. [The] vast majority, very much male. And there's [a] certain culture about it.
> You have to fit in, you have to look sound and dress like, call it 'them', the 'other' partners.

David's story was not dissimilar to those of many other successful senior Asian-Australian leaders with whom I spoke, who had spent most of

DOI: 10.4324/9781003291237-4

their childhood in Australia. Most were used to being in the minority and were highly culturally adaptable and agile.

After making it into senior leadership roles, many culturally diverse leaders have an 'a-ha' moment when they realise how few people like them reach the pinnacle of their organisations. So, what can we learn from their narratives?

Using illustrations from Australia, this chapter provides an overview of the leadership identity, the experiences of people with culturally diverse backgrounds at work, how cultural diversity has been managed to date, and why fostering culturally diverse leadership in organisations needs to be looked at differently.

WHY IS LEADERSHIP DIVERSITY AT WORK IMPORTANT?

Many organisations now realise that focusing on short-term shareholder value alone is no longer viable. While stakeholder capitalism is critical to unlocking inclusive, sustainable growth, corporate boards and leaders can't overlook the associated risks involved in stakeholder governance. Moreover, the rising importance of environmental, social and governance (ESG) globally means that organisations must create sustainable stakeholder value for economic performance and societal progress.

Further, the growing attention to gender and racial inequity by employees, investors, and activists in the US has fuelled global momentum around increasing diversity on boards and in leadership ranks. Today, most business leaders understand that greater diversity in the workplace is good for stakeholders – particularly shareholders and employees. Further, organisations are expected to embrace inclusiveness, equality, and equity, including cultural diversity in line with the United Nations (UN) Sustainable Development Goals. However, organisations that don't manage their workforce diversity well are likely to face increased external scrutiny and heightened reputational risk from stakeholder groups.

Diversity also makes good business sense. Many studies have shown that effective management of workplace diversity has some links to improvements in organisational performance, effectiveness, profitability, and revenue generation.

There are numerous benefits. First, workplaces that value diversity and are free of discrimination are more productive. This raises employee satisfaction and improves productivity and profitability. Second, they have lower employee turnover, which reduces the cost of replacing skilled and experienced people. This is particularly important given the current talent shortages in many nations and industries since COVID-19. Finally, organisations that harness a diversity of employee skills and perspectives increase creativity and innovation (DCA, n.d.). These are all critical for organisations in today's rapidly changing business environment.

Improving workforce diversity is also the right thing to do for employees. When diversity is combined with an environment that is inclusive and psychologically safe, employee engagement, collaboration and performance increase, and diversity with inclusion become an organisational success factor. In addition, everyone feels they can bring their talents and creativity to the table – an essential accelerant to innovation and productivity.

Why is culturally diverse leadership at work vital?

Cultural diversity in leadership is good for businesses – diverse teams and organisations are superior performers. For example, McKinsey reports that of more than 1,000 large companies in fifteen countries that it analysed, there was a 36% difference in profitability between companies whose leadership teams ranked in the top 25% for cultural diversity compared to those at the bottom (McKinsey, 2020).

In many multicultural nations such as Australia, whose future is extrinsically linked with Asia, there has also been growing recognition that greater cultural diversity in senior leadership is necessary to generate diverse ideas, capabilities, and cultural intelligence (AHRC, 2018; AsiaTaskforce, 2020). This is particularly important as wealth in Asia relative to the rest of the world continues to rise, resulting in greater business opportunities for Australian organisations. To succeed, companies will require leadership skillsets that include Asia-focused capabilities to execute their business strategies successfully. For Australia, Asian-Australians and its Asian diaspora – temporary residents from Asia in Australia for work or study – are well placed to support this (AsiaTaskforce, 2020).

And, of course, ensuring that there is a proportional representation of culturally diverse leadership at work is simply the right thing to do.

Who is a leader, and what is leadership?

Before continuing, it is worth briefly addressing a few critical questions: Who is a leader? And what is leadership?

> **Who is a leader? What is leadership?**
>
> A leader is somebody who people follow. Thus, leadership is a process of social influence with the mutual and reciprocal aid and support of others in the service of accomplishing a collective goal.

A country's historical context plays a critical role in its people's views on a leader. Consider the case of Australia. One recurring theme in Australia's history that influences its leaders' behaviours is egalitarianism (Ashkanasy et al., 2000). Australian leaders are also viewed as ambitious risk-takers – 'mavericks' who manage the tensions 'from the edges', balancing between offering unconventional 'outsider' views and supporting mainstream expectations. These values arose from the earliest days of Australia's colonial history when free settlers and freed convicts set out together to develop the Australian nation. As a result, Australian leaders need to be able to tolerate and contain their emotions enough to allow space for healthy dissent and risk-taking (Long & Chapman, 2018; Western, 2018).

Some academics, particularly in the US, have explored the differences in leadership styles between people of different races or ethnicity (Ospina & Foldy, 2009). Most research concludes that the leadership styles of Asian-Americans are collaborative, empowering, and non-hierarchical, which some view as ineffective leadership characteristics in Western society.

There have been few similar studies in Australia. In 2019, Christine Yeung and Wesa Chau of Cultural Intelligence explored the differences in work styles between Asian-Australian and Australian (other than Asian-Australian) cohorts across roles and levels. They found that Asian-Australian and Australian cohorts had different work styles across all role levels when exploring possibilities, evaluating problems, and establishing rapport. Asian-Australians show higher preferences for solving problems, regardless of role level. In contrast, the Australian cohort shows a higher preference for influencing people and adapting approaches. However, as Asian-Australian and Australian cohorts progress in their careers, differences in work styles decline (Yeung & Chau, 2019).

IS THERE A 'BAMBOO CEILING'? THE CURRENT STATE OF CULTURALLY DIVERSE LEADERSHIP IN ORGANISATIONS

Despite the strong business case for cultural diversity, people with culturally diverse backgrounds, in particular, Asian backgrounds in Western countries, remain under-represented in senior leadership roles, generally defined as Chief Executives and other 'C-Suite' leaders.

In Australia, Asian-Australians occupy a mere 3% of leadership positions (AHRC, 2018), despite making up 14.7% of Australia's population (Biddle et al., 2019). A deep dive into the 2018 data shows only 1.6% of Chief Executives, and 3.3% of senior executive management (non-chief executive 'C-suite') had an Asian background. Similar results were reported by a 2016 *Study of Australian Leadership* by the Centre for Workplace Leadership at the University of Melbourne which found that just over 4% of the senior leaders in the Australian organisations they surveyed were born in Asia (Gahan et al., 2016).

The situation is comparable in the US. According to McKinsey (2021), Asian-American men comprise 20% of entry-level male professionals and 7% of senior male leaders in the US. In contrast, Asian-American women make up 15% of entry-level female professionals and 9% of senior female leaders. Again, East and South-East Asian-Americans experience the steepest drop-off compared to people of other ethnicities.

In the UK, the *Colour of Power* study in 2020 reported that of the 1,059 most senior posts in the UK in business, politics, government, sport, media, and the arts, only 4.7% of the occupants are BAME – compared to 13% of the general British population (Green Park, 2020).

What is the 'bamboo ceiling'?

The term 'bamboo ceiling' was proposed by Jane Hyun in her book, *Breaking the Bamboo Ceiling: Career Strategies for Asians* (Hyun, 2005). It describes the processes and barriers that exclude Asians and Asian-Americans from executive positions based on subjective factors that their job performance or qualifications cannot explain. These include their lack of leadership potential and lack of communication skills.

Many people with Asian cultural backgrounds in multicultural nations believe that they are marginalised and rendered 'invisible' in national dialogues and research due to historical perceptions and stereotypes such as the 'model minority' and the 'perpetual foreigner' (Yip et al., 2021).

In the US, the bamboo ceiling is generally viewed as a subtle and complex form of discrimination. Asian-Americans are frequently labelled as quiet, hardworking, family-oriented, high-achieving in maths and science, passive, non-confrontational, submissive, and antisocial. At work, some of these perceptions are viewed positively at junior ranks but impede their progress in the long term.

Many people also believe that a 'bamboo ceiling' exists in Australia. Various surveys have shown that Asian-Australians are talented, ambitious, motivated, and capable but feel underleveraged and undervalued. In addition, Asian-Australian women experience a 'double jeopardy', lack relationship capital, and think that masculine leadership models work against them.

Is there a bamboo ceiling in Australia? Views of prominent Asian-Australians

High-profile Asian-Australians agree that there is a bamboo ceiling. For instance, Peter Cai noted that

> Asians are typically seen as maths or IT nerds with good quantitative skills. So often they end up as quants at banks or in R&D roles at technology companies. These perceptions can be career limiting for Asians who aspire to leadership positions.
>
> (Cai, 2014)

They also believe that the 'club' or 'tribe behaviour' at the top of organisations creates an invisible barrier to senior leadership (Tan, 2019).

Regarding the expectation in Australia that leaders be extroverted, Ming Long, a Non-Executive Director, has said, 'You have to become that for them to see leadership potential'. But, she added, 'You think about leadership in Australia – it is very white Anglo man. Six foot two, maybe they play rugby. I fit none of those things' (Yun, 2021). She added further that Asian-Australians 'can't be themselves' if they want to succeed, observing that 'I think the perceived nature of the Australian culture – seen as larrikins, jokers, basically loud and obnoxious – is aggressive. It's not intentional, but it makes new groups feel very isolated' (Reynolds, 2016).

While some areas of professional services (Big 4 accounting firms and the legal profession) have made some progress, with some Big 4 firms having announced and reported on progress against targets (Tadros & King, 2016; Sum, 2021), other sectors have lagged behind, including higher education, television new screens, and boardrooms as shown in Table 3.1.

Nevertheless, even without such data, it is apparent that more work needs to be undertaken in this space. As Nicholas Reece said in 2016, 'if you arrived from another planet, you would think there must be a law that mandates the uniform sameness in Australia's leadership ranks, or that white males had more natural talents and skills than everybody else' (Reece, 2016).

While US academics have researched the bamboo ceiling more extensively, less attention has been paid to the issue outside the US. In Australia, academics have focused on understanding the work experiences of skilled migrants. As noted in Chapter 2, an increasing proportion of Australian migrants are skilled migrants from Asia.

Table 3.1 Pale and stale – a report card on Australia's leadership

Sector	Leadership cultural diversity
Legal profession	• A poll in 2019 of almost 5,000 staff of Australia's leading law firms found that while 25% of law graduates and 20% of lawyers have an Asian background, they make up 8% of partnership ranks • In 2015, the Asian-Australian Lawyers Association (AALA) reported that Asian-Australians accounted for 3.1% of partners in law firms, 1.6% of barristers and 0.8% of the judiciary
Higher education	• While Asian-born academics made up 15.4% of teaching and research staff at Australia's universities in 2015, they made up 3.4% of Deputy Vice-Chancellors. No Asian-born academics were Vice-Chancellors • Since then, Peter N Varghese AO was appointed Chancellor of the University of Queensland in 2016, and Xiaoling Liu as Chancellor of QUT in 2020
Television news screens	• 6% of news reporters and presenters have an Indigenous or non-European background, as measured by the frequency of appearance on screen in news and current affairs broadcasts
Board rooms	• 10% of ASX300 board members in 2021 are from a non-Anglo-Celtic background • Analysis of board positions of the ASX 200 boards in 2020 indicates that 5.2% were held by men or women of non-Anglo origin, with 1.8% maintained by non-Anglo women

Source: Compiled from AALA (2015), MDA, (2020), Oishi (2017), Pelly (2019), Watermark (2021), WOB (2020).

Many Asian migrants experience a downward career move upon migration to Australia. They also report biases in recruitment due to a lack of Australian working experience, knowledge of the Australian culture, and 'Australian English' (such as in the accounting profession; see Birrell & Healy, 2008; James & Otsuka, 2009; Rajendran et al., 2019). Studies have also investigated the relationship between an individual's acculturation strategy and job satisfaction for various professional migrants. Skilled migrants from different nations, such as China and India, often have different experiences due to differences in acculturation patterns and English language skills (Lu et al., 2012; Gunasekara et al., 2019). Misunderstandings also arise from differences in communication attitudes and behaviours between Asian and Anglo-Celtic employees, such as speaking in group meetings, self-initiative, self-confidence, and taking or giving feedback (Szkudlarek, 2017).

Yet, some US academics argue that the challenges of smashing the bamboo ceiling differ between various ethnic groups. In a groundbreaking study, Jackson Lu, Richard E. Nisbett, and Michael W. Morris found that East Asians but not South Asians are underrepresented in leadership positions in America as a result of cultural differences in assertiveness (Lu et al., 2020). These differences influence their communication styles. While East Asian cultures value humility, conformity, and interpersonal harmony, South Asian cultures are more likely to encourage assertiveness.

Delving into their evaluation, East Asians were less likely than South Asians and whites to attain leadership positions. In contrast, South Asians were more likely than whites to do so. Further, East Asians faced less prejudice than South Asians and were uniformly motivated by work and leadership as South Asians. However, East Asians were lower in assertiveness, which reliably mediated the leadership attainment gap between East Asians and South Asians. Interestingly, these patterns exist for both international Asians and Asian-Americans. They suggest that this problem is not just driven by language barriers or immigration status. Rather, the issue is 'an issue of cultural fit—a mismatch between East Asian norms of communication and American norms of leadership' (Lu et al., 2020, p. 4599).

In a subsequent study, Lu found that one reason why the bamboo ceiling exists for East Asians but not South Asians was ethnic homophily. This is the tendency to form strong social connections with people who share similar defining characteristics, such as ethnicity (Lu, 2021).

HOW EFFECTIVE ARE THE CURRENT APPROACHES TO DEVELOPING DIVERSE LEADERS?

Current approaches to diversity management

Many diversity management efforts by organisations had their roots in anti-discrimination laws and policies, such as equal employment opportunity (EEO) requirements. They were managed by their HR and legal teams.

In many countries outside of the US, diversity management efforts have traditionally had a narrow focus on gender. In the last decade, this has broadened to areas including LGBTQI+, disability, and in some cases, cultural or ethnic diversity.

What is diversity management?

There are various divergent views on how to manage diversity. Mainstream diversity management literature suggests that managing diversity involves diversity *activities* that employ actions to maximise employee differences' positive effects for business gain. Some of the suggested activities proposed to manage diversity are:

- Activities that increase the identity-consciousness of underrepresented groups.
- Activities that support reducing intergroup conflict and decision-making.
- Employee resource groups (ERGs).
- Flexible work.
- Formal HR policies.
- Fostering an inclusive organisational culture and diversity climate.
- Sponsorship and mentoring schemes.
- Unconscious bias training (O'Leary & Sandberg (2016); own research).

The other stance, advocated in interpretative/critical literature, focuses on people's interpretation of diversity and managing diversity and how it is socially constructed, such as based on power relations.

As managers' understanding of managing diversity varies, practices adopted are wide-ranging (O'Leary & Sandberg, 2016). Further, the methods used vary significantly across ownership types (foreign vs local), organisation types, and sizes.

In practice, many companies strongly focus on the business benefits of leveraging diversity. Most diversity management efforts are part of the talent management initiatives of their organisations, although some also started as part of Corporate Social Responsibility initiatives. Talent management, which aims to improve business performance through practices that make employees more productive, has become a critical business strategy in many organisations over the past two decades, given the increasing focus on people as the key asset by many companies. This has led to what McKinsey has called 'The War for Talent'. A key emphasis of their diversity management efforts is recruiting and retaining talent and being an employer of choice.

One challenge for leaders is an inherent tension between managing talent and diversity, which some call the 'exclusion–inclusion paradox'. Talent management can promote exclusion, as it focuses on identifying and developing a small number of employees, which may be detrimental and undesirable for promoting broader organisational diversity. Some believe this is because organisational leaders and line managers with the power to identify talent are likely to represent the characteristics of dominant groups in their societal context. As a result, they tend to sponsor individuals with similar characteristics.

Over the past decade, many companies globally have also focused on inclusion, recognising that concentrating on diversity does not equate to inclusion. Creating inclusive environments can be challenging. Even where companies are more diverse, some find it difficult to cultivate workplaces that effectively foster inclusive leadership and accountability among leaders and equality and objectivity of opportunities that are free from bias and prejudice (McKinsey, 2020).

In line with a rise in social movements such as #blacklivesmatter, more recently, companies and their CEOs in the US have declared their commitment to diversity and inclusion causes and articulated steps that support greater social justice. Further, many governments and regulators have also put in place various regulations requiring companies to increase the diversity of their boards and disclose diversity-related information. These heightened requirements dovetail with investors' growing interest in ESG factors, including diversity.

However, these changes are challenging for many organisations. For instance, in Australia, 66% of CEOs struggle to keep up with the demands of diversity, equity, and inclusion (Wootton, 2021). Yet, despite greater external disclosure requirements, the establishment of CEO-driven initiatives such as the Champions of Change Coalition, and that 85% of Australian CEOs recognise that millennials want to work for companies that embrace diversity and inclusion (Wootton, 2021), many Australian diversity practitioners believe that senior managers still don't prioritise diversity and inclusion (DCA, 2018). At times, diversity is not generally well understood or appreciated outside HR functions. Further, historically diversity has rarely ranked in their organisation's top business priorities. However, this is starting to change with the more recent push to focus on ESG and increasing numbers of CEOs having their pay based at least partly on ESG issues (Wootton, 2021).

Do diversity programmes deliver financial benefits?

Whilst a number of global studies report a causal link between diversity and financial performance, not all academics are convinced that financial benefits will automatically arise for organisations that apply a level of focus on diversity. Some believe that the methods used in the studies are not robust enough to draw these conclusions. Take one example. In a 2021 paper, applying McKinsey's approach to companies in the S&P 500 index, Jeremiah Green and John Hand did not find a link between racial and ethnic diversity and financial performance (Green & Hand, 2021). Various other studies, such as on the benefits of board diversity, suggest that greater diversity will not lead to benefits unless there is a positive organisational context for diversity.

Leading academics Robin Ely and David Thomas of Harvard Business School remain sceptical and consider that diversity's business case focus is flawed. They believe that if companies are serious about diversity and wish to benefit from increased racial and gender diversity fully, their leaders must reject the notion that maximising short- to medium-term shareholder returns is paramount. Instead, they consider that organisations must adopt a learning orientation and be willing to change their corporate

(Continued)

culture and power structure. This recognises that no research supports the notion that diversifying the workforce automatically improves performance. They also highlight that inequality is bad for both business and society over the long term (Ely & Thomas, 2020).

As Ely and Thomas point out, when diversity programmes suggest financial benefits but fail to deliver, people are likely to retract their support for these programmes (Ely & Thomas, 2020), making it even more important to promote diversity in an effective and supportive manner.

Others remain concerned that increasing business disruption since COVID-19 means businesses will have less bandwidth to support diversity initiatives.

Nevertheless, in a world where the ongoing 'war for talent' has been exacerbated by COVID-19, can businesses afford a higher-than-average turnover of people with diverse backgrounds through failing to support diversity initiatives?

Common strategies to develop cultural diversity leaders

In 2013, Jeff, an Asian-Australian leader was asked to attend a small focus group session of Asian-Australian staff in his company following the release of the *Australia in the Asian Century* white paper. His organisation recognised that having senior staff with Asian cultural and language skills would support its inbound client work from Asia. However, whilst many Asian-Australians joined his company from university, significantly fewer of them were in senior positions to serve these clients. The purpose of the focus group was to understand the challenges that Asian-Australian staff members faced in making it into leadership positions.

Jeff was then struck by the questions raised by an HR representative who attended the session. She asked how many Asian staff were in the company. Further, she wanted to understand what the business cost was of losing Asian-Australians faster than other staff members. At the time, Jeff's organisation did not ask its people to self-disclose their ethnicity, nor was it open to using other ways to estimate the proportion of Asian staff (such as names).

It soon became apparent to Jeff that unless his organisation could quantify the business case for greater cultural diversity in leadership, it would be reluctant to act. This was even though it was evident to most people that staff of Asian ethnicity were leaving the organisation much faster than other staff.

*****

Regrettably, the experiences of culturally and linguistically diverse workers have largely been overlooked by practitioners and researchers in many multicultural countries outside of the US and the UK and their organisations, and consequently, in many workplace-based policies and initiatives (Groutsis et al., 2016).

Anecdotal evidence in Australia is that many business leaders believe that they cannot focus on improving cultural diversity, as they still have much more work to do to improve their gender diversity. This is one of the critical reasons for the lack of progress in enhancing the cultural diversity of leadership in Australia.

Further, most Australian companies do not consistently analyse their workplaces' cultural diversity of their workplaces. This led the DCA and the University of Sydney Business School in 2021 to propose a standardised approach for defining, measuring, and reporting work-force cultural diversity in a respectful, accurate, and inclusive way. This data will allow more significant insight into the cultural diversity of Australia's workforce (DCA, 2021).

Overall, there has been a wide range of organisational responses to managing cultural diversity. A key influence has been whether legal frameworks require organisations to implement procedures that address cultural diversity. As a result, most approaches have not been integrated and vary depending on their organisations' changing culture, climate, and performance.

Over the past decade in Australia, since the release of the government's *Australia in the Asian Century* paper in 2012, some companies have started to focus on increasing the cultural diversity of their leadership to support their business growth in Asia. In addition, some businesses have aligned their cultural diversity initiatives with their business strategies (such as customer segmentation and talent management). Others have started employee resource group (ERG) initiatives.

Leveraging diverse talent – more than celebrations and employee resource groups

One of the first steps many companies take when focusing on diversity and inclusion is to form ERGs. ERGs, affinity groups, or business network groups are voluntary, employee-led groups that come together in their workplace based on shared characteristics or life experiences. Through networking, ERGs provide support, enhance career development, and contribute to personal development at work.

Supporters argue that ERGs foster a diverse, inclusive workplace aligned with the organisational mission, values, goals, business practices, and objectives. Other benefits include developing future leaders, increased employee engagement particularly for first-generation professionals early in their careers (Maldonado & Burwell, 2020), and expanded marketplace reach.

While almost all Fortune 500 companies in the US have ERGs, not all companies support them. For instance, in 2017, Deloitte announced that it was ending its women's network and other affinity groups. Instead, it would offer all managers – including the white males who dominate leadership – the skills to become more inclusive. In addition, it would hold them accountable for building more balanced businesses.

Other studies conclude that ERGs are inconsistent in their effectiveness, as they do not always decrease inequalities. Moreover, while ERGs foster a collective identity, reduce isolation, and increase visibility, they occasionally tame diversity instead of changing the status quo.

Nevertheless, the results of many of these initiatives often have not been measured. If they have been measured, many may not have shown tangible progress. Some of these activities may merely be scratching the surface.

According to Tim Soutphommasane of the University of Sydney, leaders in Australia will need to change some attitudes if their organisations are to foster culturally diverse leadership. First, society and organisations need to stop seeing cultural diversity as just a way for Australia to succeed in Asia. Second, people shouldn't forget the moral and civic reasons behind greater cultural diversity. He emphasises that the reason for more diverse leadership should not be reduced to the business case. Third, leaders must strive to win both hearts and minds of people – they shouldn't just assume that change will come entirely from reason and data alone. And finally, the cause of cultural diversity must be linked with the cause of anti-racism; otherwise, people may lapse into only pursuing celebratory forms of diversity (Soutphommasane, 2019).

DO WE NEED A DIFFERENT LENS?

Could the challenges to increasing cultural diversity in leadership at work reflect broader social issues that include deep-seated beliefs, practices, and assumptions? Have these led to misconceptions about the problems and inadequate responses to tackle them in society and the workplace?

If businesses are serious about sustainable change, they must recognise that they may require a different lens. They need to consider a country's historical context and assess their unique organisational culture and individuals, as they may resist change. Moreover, they should adopt both a top-down viewpoint and a bottom-up perspective through the eyes of their people.

Despite a range of convincing evidence, reasoned arguments, and evolving regulations about diversity, there is frequently a gap between rhetoric and reality. Some organisations and their leaders still have their heads buried in the sand – denying the issue, perhaps due to other unconscious individual or collective fears.

Where cultural diversity initiatives are in place, most focus on changing individuals and not on how to support a change in the conscious or unconscious collective interpersonal and inter-group behaviours and dynamics in organisations. Further, with the increasing focus on diversity and the expectation of 'political correctness' at work, open discussion about diversity could disappear, and concerns buried if organisations are not careful. As a result, many organisations have a collective ambivalence to change.

One only needs to look at the current situation of gender diversity at work. Many countries have had commendable results in increasing the percentage of women on listed boards. Yet, some of them, like Australia, are experiencing a paradox. In Australia, women's educational attainment is high. However, many prominent organisations still face issues like sexual harassment and bullying cases, which its historical context could have been influenced. This could indicate that resistance remains under the surface and demonstrates the power of Australia's masculine 'mateship' cultural core.

To move the dial on cultural diversity will require a broader culture change focus.[1] The initiatives need to consider that ethnicity-related conversations can lead to anxieties in dyads, groups, and organisations, including at work (Foldy & Buckley, 2017). Given this, they need to focus on how constructive dynamics can change potentially destructive diversity dynamics between colleagues and within teams of different ethnic backgrounds.

Understanding how successful culturally diverse leaders take up roles and their experiences in systems using a different lens allows us to identify the barriers to change and potential solutions. I will examine this in Part II, Lessons from Those Who Smashed the Bamboo Ceiling.

Chapter summary

- Having leadership diversity in organisations is the right thing to do and makes good business sense.
- Despite globalisation and increased migration, people with culturally diverse backgrounds remain seriously under-represented in leadership in many countries.
- The 'bamboo ceiling' inhibits aspiring culturally diverse leaders with Asian backgrounds from reaching organisations' top levels of leadership.
- Approaches to managing cultural diversity have been varied and less integrated. Many organisations are focused on increasing the gender diversity of their leadership and are yet to consider cultural diversity in a meaningful way. Managing both diversity and talent can be challenging for organisations.
- Some organisations overfocus on implementing diversity and inclusion programmes for short-term business benefits. However, if interventions are not well thought through, they will be ineffective.
- Increasing the cultural diversity of leadership at work may require a different lens to identify the barriers to change and potential solutions.

Questions to ask yourself and your team members

Yourself

- If I were to describe a typical leader in my organisation, who would they be and their attributes or traits?
- How would I describe my leadership style?
- Have my colleagues or I experienced the 'bamboo ceiling?' If so, what may be the reasons for this?

Your team members

- What are the reasons why is having culturally diverse leadership important in our organisation?
- How has our national identity shaped our views on who a leader is in our organisation?
- To what extent have people of Asian backgrounds hit the bamboo ceiling in our organisation?

NOTE

1 We need to be cautious about balancing individual differences and over-generalisations. People with Asian backgrounds do have diverse backgrounds. Not only are they from different countries of origin but also they have within-group differences, such as immigrant vs. locally born, acculturation levels, and languages spoken. We sometimes categorise people with Asian backgrounds using cultural characterisations – such as collectivist, family-oriented, and face-oriented – which is actually stereotyping. We also need to be careful to frame culture as a general context for understanding individuals within a given culture, as people may vary in acculturation levels. Therefore, context must not be confused with the individual.

REFERENCES

AALA (Asian Australian Lawyers Association). (2015). *The Australian Legal Profession: A Snapshot of Asian Australian Diversity in 2015*. https://www.aala.org.au/publications

AHRC (Australian Human Rights Commission). (2018). *Leading for Change: A Blueprint for Cultural Diversity and Inclusive Leadership Revisited*. https://humanrights.gov.au/sites/default/files/document/publication/Leading%20for%20Change_Blueprint2018_FINAL_Web.pdf

Ashkanasy, N. M., Trevor-Roberts, E., & Kennedy, J. A. (2000). Leadership Attributes and Cultural Values in Australia and New Zealand Compared: An Initial Report Based on GLOBE Data. *International Journal of Organizational Behaviour*, 2(3), 37–44.

Asia Taskforce. (2020). *A Forgotten Advantage: Enabling Australia's Asian-Australian and Diaspora Communities Asia Taskforce Discussion Paper.* Business Council of Australia and Asia Society Australia Asia Taskforce. https://asiasociety.org/sites/default/files/inline-files/Asia_Taskforce_Discussion_Paper_3_Asian-Australian_Diaspora.pdf

Biddle, N., Gray, M., Herz, D., & Lo, J. Y. (2019). *Research Note: Asian-Australian Experiences of Discrimination.* Australian National University. https://csrm.cass.anu.edu.au/sites/default/files/docs/2019/9/Asian-Australian_experiences_of_and_attitudes_towards_discrimination_-_Research_Note_10092019.pdf

Birrell, B., & Healy, E. (2008). Migrant Accountants – High Numbers, Poor Outcomes. *People and Place*, 16(4), 9–22.

Cai, P. (2014, June 14). Is There a Bamboo Ceiling in Australia? *The Australian (Business Spectator).*

DCA (Diversity Council of Australia). (n.d.). *Business Case for Diversity & Inclusion.* https://www.dca.org.au/di-planning/getting-started-di/business-case-diversity-inclusion

DCA (Diversity Council of Australia). (2018). Benchmarking Diversity and Inclusion Practices in Australia. https://www.dca.org.au/research/project/benchmarking-diversity-and-inclusion-practices-australia

DCA (Diversity Council of Australia/University of Sydney Business School (D'Almada-Remedios, R., Groutsis, D., Kaabel, A. & O'Leary, J.). (2021). *Counting Culture: Towards a Standardised Approach to Measuring and Reporting on Workforce Cultural Diversity in Australia.* https://www.dca.org.au/research/project/counting-culture-2021?__cf_chl_jschl_tk__=pmd_36c953c68b76e3308b0129e62f0156b45c362d7b-1627875734-0-gqNtZGzNAjijcnBszQg6

Ely, R. J., & Thomas, D. A. (2020, November). Getting Serious about Diversity: Enough Already with the Business Case. *Harvard Business Review*, 98(6), 114–122. https://hbr.org/2020/11/getting-serious-about-diversity-enough-already-with-the-business-case

Foldy, E. G., & Buckley, T. R. (2017). Reimagining Cultural Competence: Bringing Buried Dynamics Into the Light. *The Journal of Applied Behavioral Science*, 53(2), 264–289. https://doi.org/10.1177/0021886317707830

Gahan, P., Adamovic, M., Bevitt, A., Harley, B., Healy, J., Olsen, J. E., & Theilacker, M. (2016). *Leadership at Work: Do Australian Leaders Have What It Takes?* Centre for Workplace Leadership, University of Melbourne. https://fbe.unimelb.edu.au/cwl/sal#about

Green, J., & Hand, J. R. M. (2021). *Diversity Matters/Delivers/Wins Revisited in S&P 500® Firms.* https://papers.ssrn.com/sol3/papers.cfm?abstract_id=3849562

Green Park. (2020, July 27). The Colour of Power. https://www.green-park.co.uk/insights/the-colour-of-power/s191468/

Groutsis, D., O'Leary, J., & Russell, G. (2016). Capitalizing on the Cultural and Linguistic Diversity of Mobile Talent: Lessons from an Australian Study. *The International Journal of Human Resource Management*, 29(15), 2231–2252. https://doi.org/10.1080/09585192.2016.1239213

Gunasekara, A., Grant, S., & Rajendran, D. (2019). Years Since Migration and Wellbeing among Indian and Sri Lankan Skilled Migrants in Australia: Mediating Effects of Acculturation. *International Journal of Intercultural Relations*, 70, 42–52. https://doi.org/10.1016/j.ijintrel.2019.02.006

Hyun, J. (2005). *Breaking the Bamboo Ceiling: Career Strategies for Asians.* Harper Business.

James, K., & Otsuka, S. (2009). Racial Biases in Recruitment by Accounting Firms: The Case of International Chinese Applicants in Australia. *Critical Perspectives on Accounting,* 20(4), 469–491. https://doi.org/10.1016/j.cpa.2008.02.005

Long, S., & Chapman, J. (2018). Australia: Leadership Identity in the Making. In S. Western & & E.-J. Garcia (Eds.), *Global Leadership Perspectives: Insights and Analysis* (pp. 36–43). SAGE Publications.

Lu, J. G. (2021). A Social Network Perspective on the Bamboo Ceiling: Ethnic Homophily Explains Why East Asians but Not South Asians Are Underrepresented in Leadership in Multiethnic Environments. *Journal of Personality and Social Psychology,* Advance online publication. https://doi.org/10.1037/pspa0000292

Lu, J. G., Nisbett, R. E., & Morris, M. W. (2020). Why East Asians but Not South Asians Are Underrepresented in Leadership Positions in the United States. *Proceedings of the National Academy of Sciences,* 117(9), 4590–4600. https://doi.org/10.1073/pnas.1918896117

Lu, Y., Samaratunge, R., & Härtel, C. E. J. (2012). The Relationship between Acculturation Strategy and Job Satisfaction for Professional Chinese Immigrants in the Australian Workplace. *International Journal of Intercultural Relations,* 36(5), 669–681. https://doi.org/ https://doi.org/10.1016/j.ijintrel.2012.04.003

Maldonado, B., & Burwell, M. (2020). *First Generation Professionals.* https:// firstgentalent.org/

McKinsey. (2020). *Diversity Wins: How Inclusion Matters.* https://www.mckinsey.com/ featured-insights/diversity-and-inclusion/diversity-wins-how-inclusion-matters

McKinsey. (2021). *COVID-19's Impact on Asian American Workers: Six Key Insights.* https:// www.mckinsey.com/featured-insights/diversity-and-inclusion/covid-19s-impact-on-asian-american-workers-six-key-insights

MDA (Media Diversity Australia). (2020). *Australian Television News Is Far More Anglo-Celtic Than the Country It Covers: Lack of Diversity Led from the Top.* Media Diversity Australia and Macquarie University. https://www.mediadiversityaustralia.org/wp-content/ uploads/2020/08/Press-release_final.pdf

O'Leary, J., & Sandberg, J. (2016). Managers' Practice of Managing Diversity Revealed: A Practice-Theoretical Account. *Journal of Organizational Behavior,* 38, 512–536. https://doi. org/10.1002/job.2132

Oishi, N. (2017). *Workforce Diversity in Higher Education: The Experiences of Asian Academics in Australian Universities.* University of Melbourne. https://arts.unimelb.edu.au/__data/assets/ pdf_file/0012/2549496/AA-Report_Final-Copy_Web_5Nov.pdf

Ospina, S., & Foldy, E. (2009). A Critical Review of Race and Ethnicity in the Leadership Literature: Surfacing Context, Power and the Collective Dimensions of Leadership. *The Leadership Quarterly,* 20, 876–896. https://www.sciencedirect.com/science/article/pii/ S1048984309001751

Pelly, M. (2019, April 26). Asian Lawyers Hit 'Bamboo Ceiling'. *Australian Financial Review.* https://www.afr.com/work-and-careers/workplace/asian-lawyers-hit-bamboo-ceiling-20190425-p51h8w

Rajendran, D., Ng, E., Sears, G., & Ayub, N. (2019). Determinants of Migrant Career Success: A Study of Recent Skilled Migrants in Australia. *International Migration,* 58, 1–22. https://doi.org/10.1111/imig.12586

Reece, N. (2016, February 7). The Leadership Whitewash: Our Diversity Problem. *Sydney Morning Herald*. https://www.smh.com.au/opinion/america-not-the-only-country-failing-on-the-diversity-issue-20160206-gmncw7.html

Reynolds, E. (2016, September 2). Asian-Australians 'Can't Be Themselves' If They Want to Succeed. *News.com*. https://www.news.com.au/finance/work/careers/asianaustralians-cant-be-themselves-if-they-want-to-succeed/news-story/265a6aedb58893fe9563d3dc6f3fb69a

Soutphommasane, T. (2019). *Opening Keynote to Inaugural Asian-Australian Leadership Summit.* Asian-Australian Leadership Summit. https://www.asianaustralianleadership.com.au/speeches

Sum, M. (2021, March 19). Does Business Have a Level Playing Field for 'People of Colour'? *KPMG*. https://newsroom.kpmg.com.au/business-level-playing-field-people-colour/

Szkudlarek, B. (2017, March 6). Four Cultural Clashes That Are Holding East Asian Employees Back. *The Conversation*. https://theconversation.com/four-cultural-clashes-that-are-holding-east-asian-employees-back-72661

Tadros, E., & King, A. (2016, March 11). Big Four Accounting Firms Push for More Non-Anglo Partners. *Australian Financial Review*. https://www.afr.com/companies/professional-services/big-four-accounting-firms-push-for-more-nonanglo-partners-20160721-gqag2a

Tan, S.-L. (2019, July 10). The Path to More Diversity at the Top. *Australian Financial Review*. https://www.afr.com/work-and-careers/leaders/the-path-to-more-diversity-at-the-top-20190529-p51suw

Watermark. (2021). *2021 Board Diversity Index*. Watermark Search International. https://www.watermarksearch.com.au/2021-board-diversity-index

Western, S. (2018). Outsider-Leadership: In Search of Lack. In S. Western & E.-J. Garcia (Eds.), *Global Leadership Perspectives: Insights and Analysis* (pp. 218–265). SAGE Publications.

WOB (Women on Boards). (2020). Cultural Diversity Next Frontier in Australia's Boardrooms. *Women on Boards*. https://www.womenonboards.net/en-au/about-us/cultural-diversity-on-boards

Wootton, H. (2021, September 5). CEOs Struggling to Keep Up with ESG, Diversity Demands. *Australian Financial Review*. https://www.afr.com/companies/professional-services/ceos-struggling-to-keep-up-with-esg-diversity-demands-20210903-p58okd

Yeung, C., & Chau, W. (2019). *Asian-Australian Leadership in Australia*. Cultural Intelligence.

Yip, T., Cheah, C. S. L., Kiang, L., & Hall, G. C. N. (2021). Rendered Invisible: Are Asian Americans a Model or a Marginalized Minority? *American Psychologist, 76*(4), 575–581. https://doi.org/10.1037/amp0000857

Yun, J. (2021, March 8). The Bamboo Ceiling 2021: The 'Double Whammy' Asian Women Face in Their Careers. *Yahoo Finance*. https://au.finance.yahoo.com/news/bamboo-ceiling-iwd-2021-023047411.html

PART II

Lessons from Those Who Smashed the Bamboo Ceiling

Four

INTRODUCTION

Macquarie Group CEO Shemara Wikramanayake is one of Australia's most respected business leaders and one of the very few female CEOs of an ASX100. She has Sri Lankan ancestry. In her formative years, Shemara moved countries several times. At three months, she was sent from England to Sri Lanka to live with her grandparents. Aged eight, Shemara moved back to live with her parents in England before moving to Australia at the age of thirteen.

In a keynote address at a 2020 event hosted by Chief Executive Women, Shemara shared how she built her confidence, something she believes goes back to her childhood, where she faced financial hardship and lived in different countries.

In our five years in England, we faced financial hardship, so moved homes a few times. I changed schools three times, changed friends and changed continents. This could have been unsettling for a child, but I looked on it as an opportunity.

Possibly from natural resilience, I was able to accept quickly that I could do nothing about our peripatetic circumstances. But I appreciated that I still had choices and things I could control, including my attitude.

Being curious and social, I resolved to embrace the frequent changes as an opportunity to learn from different cultures and perspectives.

If anyone had told me as a child that I couldn't fulfil my various childhood ambitions to be an astronaut, or pilot or James Bond due to my gender or ethnicity, I would have dismissed their views as irrational. This was my form of resilience.

Shemara's childhood experiences helped prepare her for life in the finance sector, where she's never been part of a majority. In her speech, she shared a story from her early days at Macquarie, where a senior client didn't have confidence in her ability to do her job.

DOI: 10.4324/9781003291237-6

I encountered a senior client who didn't have confidence that a very young-looking, brown-skinned female would be able to get the job done in what was an important moment in the company's journey.

I could have been demotivated or lost confidence from this. I was instead focused on my responsibility to help deliver the necessary outcome for this client.

After the deal concluded successfully, he took me aside and thanked me for teaching him about irrational prejudice and was happy to have me lead further transactions for his company

Source: Hislop (2020) and Patten (2020).

*****

'Tell me about yourself?'

Chances are that when we speak to people that we haven't met before and ask them to tell us about themselves, the first thing they will talk about is their work identity. Similarly, if we were to interview someone for a job, we would usually ask questions about their prior roles, where they studied, and extracurricular activities they did at school or university.

However, we would rarely ask them about their experiences growing up unless we become close friends or speak to them outside of work in a more casual setting. We often prefer to keep strict boundaries between our personal and professional lives. To some extent, it's like we leave parts of ourselves on the office doorstep every morning and don't bring them inside.

Our early family experiences play a big part in shaping who we are, how we behave, and why we act as we do. Our relationships with our parents and other key figures in early life influence how we feel and act in adult life. Yet, many career studies don't consider how our family experiences impact our behaviours in the workplace, particularly for those in subordinate positions (Cardona & Damon, 2019).

The narratives of the culturally diverse leaders that I talked to help bridge this gap. They illustrate how our family dynamics both conscious and often unconsciously, can influence our career journeys and interactions with others at work, and play out in organisational settings.

This chapter explores the link between our family and work, illustrating this link using stories from successful culturally diverse leaders. I also highlight how unearthing hidden family dynamics in individuals can assist them and their leaders in understanding how their teams perceive their work roles.

THE LINK BETWEEN OUR FAMILY AND WORK

When we think about the systems[1] that we are part of, what generally comes to mind are our workplaces or schools. Less frequently, we think about our family.

Like in other systems, each of us occupies several positions in our family system. In my family, I am a daughter to my parents, a wife to my husband, and an aunt to my niece.

Steen Visholm of Roskilde University believes that there are similarities between the dynamics of our roles in family systems and those in management. Furthermore, he considers that there are four solid connections between our family and work life. These are:

1 Our family is the motivation for our work (as our pay goes to provide for our families).
2 Work helps us to determine our value as love objects.
3 Our family serves as an internal and external evaluation team.
4 Our family is the first organisation we have contact with (Visholm, 2021).

The last point is relevant to understanding what we look for in the organisations where we work. Thus, Visholm suggests that our family is our 'organisation in the mind' – a prototype or basic model for our experiences in and of organisations (Visholm, 2021).

These observations are essential to remember as we explore the influences on the career progression of culturally diverse leaders in organisations.

However, before continuing, what is a 'role'?

What is a role?[2]

The term 'role refers to the conscious and unconscious boundary around the way to behave' (Cilliers et al., 2004, p. 74). A role is situated at the intersection between a person and a system. 'Although a role is a structural part of the system, it is filled and shaped by its incumbent, the person' (Long, 2006, p. 127).[3]

Using the 'role biography' framework to guide my discussion, I delved into how people with culturally diverse backgrounds become leaders. 'Role biography' is a term used to describe the biography of a 'person-in-role' expressed through the various work roles they have taken up during their life. This is different from 'role history', which is the history of a specific role shaped by its incumbents over time.

This framework recognises that people are at the intersection of their own role biography and the history of that role, a unique position. It also acknowledges that the influences on a person in their current role come from two sources. The first is the organisation/system, its role history, and how it relates to other roles. The second is the person, their role biography, skills, and attributes (Long, 2006).[4]

From the narratives of the culturally diverse leaders, I found that their family system influenced their leader values, their roles at work, and why they had preferences for taking up certain roles and occupations. Other patterns noted were the concept of transference and the influence of family systems on the expected 'organisation in the mind'.

HOW OUR CULTURAL BACKGROUNDS INFLUENCE OUR LEADER VALUES

Family environments significantly impact how many culturally diverse leaders behave as adults at work. 'I think the background and the environment that one grows up in is super important in terms of how it then forms you', said Fiona.

As we discussed in Chapter 2, our cultural practices, identifications, and values are shaped by the environments we are brought up in. How we learn about life, our early socialisation usually starts at home and continues at school and throughout our working lives. These experiences influence our professional values, orientation, and work ethos.

The impact of family values on relationships at work

Early family experiences influence how culturally diverse leaders build relationships with people, and their preferred leadership style at work. Some culturally diverse leaders leverage lessons from their family experiences at home in the workplace to succeed at work.

Richard, a successful client relationship partner, revealed that his family value of collegiality played a crucial role in shaping him at work. He remarked:

Maybe there's something around people skills – being able to be genuine is a bit of an Asian cultural trait – warmness... I've translated that to clients as well. I bring them into that warm comfy feeling that you're part of my family,

Another, John, spoke passionately about how he learned how to deal with clients and colleagues and be entrepreneurial from his grandfather, who he called his mentor. John's grandfather was a trained doctor that turned into an entrepreneur, operating businesses across several sectors to support his many children. His grandfather taught him many life lessons – not only to be careful how he spent his money but also to always look after his people. On the latter, he recalls his grandfather telling him, 'You need to make sure that they feel valued. But you can't always make sure that they feel like that's good enough. You should always make sure there's always room for… for improvement'.

How John looks at his role in his firm centres on what he learned from his grandfather – with an optimistic mindset and believing that he can make things happen if he can prove the business case for a new idea. 'It's actually that immigrant mentality. What I mean by that is that I see the opportunities more than I see the constraints'.

An additional value of many culturally diverse leaders is respect for elders. As Elizabeth said, 'It's just what I've been drilled into me – respect your elders. It's just fundamental'. As a result, some acknowledged that they were subservient to their parents at home but confident at school. This, however, led to challenges for some of them in the Australian working environment.

Scott, whose family was from South Asia did not like conflict at home. 'At my early age, I probably didn't challenge anybody who was older for a long period because that's what my parents taught me – just respect the people that are ahead of you', he revealed. However, Scott realised that if he were to be heard in the workplace, he had to adjust how he behaved in specific scenarios during his career.

The influence of transgenerational transmission of collective trauma on leader values

Like Shemara Wikramanayake, many culturally diverse leaders also cite resilience as one of their leader values.

As noted in Chapter 2, recent research has found that collective trauma can shape the leaders' values of second- and third-generation descendants. Collective (or historical) trauma refers to the impact of a traumatic experience that affects and involves entire groups of people, communities, or societies. Examples that have been researched extensively include genocides and the Holocaust. It resides in cultural rituals and artifacts, community events and commemorations, and family narratives. Collective trauma can be transmitted to their descendants through psychodynamic means, social learning, and social identity (Tcholakian et al., 2019).

In her research, Lara Tcholakian identified five leader values influenced by collective trauma that shaped leader cognition and behaviour. These values are resilience, forgiveness, empathy, justice, and perseverance (Tcholakian et al., 2019).

Collective trauma may have influenced some Asian-Australian leaders' leader values. Some of them were Vietnamese refugees, whereas others were children of parents who left Sri Lanka due to war, Pakistan due to the 1947 Partition, or Malaysian Chinese whose parents wanted a better life. Some of their parents moved countries more than once before relocating to Australia.

HOW OUR FAMILY INFLUENCES THE ROLES WE TAKE UP AT WORK

Our experiences at home not only shape our leader values but also consciously and unconsciously influence the types of roles that we take up at work and our behaviours.

Take for example Julia, an Asian-Australian leader who recognises that her preference to care for others may have been influenced by her own childhood experience. She was brought up by a single mother who was frequently absent during her childhood. As a result, she didn't get her mother's attention unless she did well in her studies and could bring home an award from school. So, to get her attention, Julia realised that she needed to study hard.

Since her teenage years, she has also been responsible for caring for her significantly younger siblings. As an adult, in addition to looking after her own family, she enjoys mentoring younger staff members and working with teams. However, what really motivates Julia is to help younger leaders.

Why do we take up roles at work?

So, why do certain people have a preference to take on specific roles in groups and organisations, such as becoming a leader? Much of this has to do with their early life experiences.

During our lives, we take up various roles in different systems such as family, society, and work (Long, 2006). Our positive experiences and anxieties at home often influence our adult roles in other systems including our workplaces.

When we take up and participate in work roles, we always do so in the context of a more extensive work system. Conceptualising work systems as systems of role relations is helpful as it emphasises the interactions between roles and their links to the tasks of the organisations. When we look at just a 'person', we always need to consider how the person interacts with others (Long, 2006).

Our valence for roles

Our family dynamics influence the roles we take up and our behaviours later in life.

We often take on roles similar to those we are comfortable with within our families at work. This is because we have a 'valence', a metaphor from chemistry, to take on certain roles and attract certain projections (or feelings) from others. These affirm our self-beliefs and replicate familiar relationship patterns (Petriglieri & Petriglieri, 2020).

When I reflect on the types of roles that I have preferred in my life, I find that I generally enjoy roles where I am the 'organiser' but not always the leader in a group. I only take up roles where it is clear to me and others that I have the authority to take on the role, and that minimise my risk of being criticised or authority challenged. This is a pattern that stems from my relationship with my father. As an example, I prefer to manage activities that I can control from start to finish, from vision to execution, and be respected. As an audit partner, which involved significant collaboration with my clients that had to appoint an audit firm, I would oversee large engagements with up to a hundred people working for me.

According to Jon Stokes, a leadership consultant and Clinical Psychologist, certain personality types are drawn to certain types of work and organisations more than others. Commonly, we choose an occupation and a role because of the defensive function it serves (Czander, 1993). This is because it allows us to express ourselves, manage our concerns and anxieties, and repair 'real or phantasy damage done' (Stokes, 2014, p. 226).[5] Our roles often serve as a defence[6] against anxieties associated with our childhood fantasies and yearnings. Further, we are also more likely to identify with an organisation when it is prestigious and attractive, increasing our self-esteem (Pratt, 1998). Some believe that a social system's broad purpose is to shield its members from their own anxieties and unwanted emotions.

For instance, becoming a professional may offer 'professionalisation' of the role of coping with personal anxieties (Stokes, 2014). A profession 'offers the young person considering a career an opportunity both to express certain needs—for example, to care for others, or to win an argument—but also to contain the anxiety associated with the shadow side of these needs' (Stokes, 2014, p. 229), and 'sort out unresolved issues from the past' (Cardona & Damon, 2019, p. 188). As an example, Stokes suggests that choosing a caring profession can sometimes be a form of defence against the expression of hostility towards others. It offers young professionals a chance to control the anxieties they suffer.

How our parents' expectations influence our formal work roles

Our parents often pass various patterns, themes, and roles (formal and informal – see below) onto us through their anxieties and behaviours. The extent of the influence of these patterns frequently depends on our relationship with our parents.

The backgrounds of many Asian-Australian leaders I spoke to were diverse. Yet most of their parents had high expectations of them. Some were 'parachute-kids'[7] who came to Australia in the 1980s and 1990s from Hong Kong and Taiwan. Others moved to Australia from Vietnam, Korea, Sri Lanka, India, Indonesia, or Malaysia. Their parents wanted them to have a better life. However, in more recent times, many more Asian-Australians came to Australia as skilled migrants, such as Paul and Sharon or the children of skilled migrants.

Working hard was a quality that all the Asian-Australian leaders shared. Many mentioned that their parents and grandparents were strong role models who instilled a strong work ethic, results orientation, and a desire for financial independence in them.

Most leaders from Asian backgrounds generally had strict parents who had strong family values. As a result, many came under pressure from their parents to achieve excellent results at school and have successful careers. Richard recalls the pressure he was under to do well at school. 'The pressure was there in no doubt', he remembered. 'But pressure in a positive way, not negative way. But it was pressure. Let's not underestimate the pressure, but if you came second why didn't you come first. That kind of pressure'. A few others described situations where if they had received a mark of, say ninety-five or ninety-eight out of a hundred, their parents challenged them on what happened to the remaining marks.

As a result, many are competitive at work and are workaholics, such as Paul, who 'chose to work so hard because I want to be the best'.

Some of these behaviours result from their immigrant parents' anxieties about their children's education and work success, as they personally experienced downward social mobility (Ho, 2020). By way of example, the parents of several of the leaders I spoke to were doctors or academics who gave up successful careers overseas to move to Australia and start their careers again. One was Richard, whose parents were medical doctors, and 'sacrifice[d] their lives – to make sure my brother and I had a better upbringing'.

Robert, a highly energetic consultant, also described the substantial measures which his parents took for him and his sister. 'My dad gave up a business. My mother's a qualified chemical engineer', he said.

> And they were working in factories and sewing just to get us through, like not dissimilar to a lot of immigrant families. What... made the biggest difference to where I am right now, and who I am, is my parent's unrelenting, unrelenting quest for my sister and I to get the best education we could ... we moved from suburb to suburb and kept progressing using every single scrapping scrappy cent, to finally get us into a better area and better schools.

Another leader, Ian, who wanted to become a motor mechanic, got the results he needed to study economics at university, so he ended up going to university. His parents had high expectations of him, telling him, "There was no way we came to Australia for you to do a trade. You're going to university. You had better study and get in". This 'intergenerational projection' of anxieties by parents can increase the vulnerabilities of their children.

Family expectations have been frequently found to influence individuals' career goals, interests, and work values. Usually, the career decisions of Asian-Australians leaders are guided by their parents, some of whom are anxious for their future security. As a result, many parents encouraged their children to look for 'safe' career options (Ho, 2020).

Some researchers in the US argue that Asian-Americans often avoid occupations involving ambiguous circumstances, personal contact, and interpersonal communication. Instead, they are driven by extrinsic work values, such as financial gains and occupational repute. Further, those who are less acculturated and have more collective orientations are more likely to base their decisions on family expectations (Tu & Okazaki, 2021).

Many of the leaders I spoke to said they didn't have many choices regarding the degrees they could take at university. Sarah commented, 'when it came to picking a course, from their perspective, you're either going to be a doctor, lawyer or dentist – there really wasn't any other choice', which some described as the 'Asian' thing. Several experienced tensions between complying with their parents' expectations and doing their own thing. Some still appear to be dealing with these tensions later in life, influencing their later career decisions. This can be a double-edged sword in the workplace.

How our family experiences influence the informal roles we take up at work

In organisations (at work and in society), people tend to focus on the 'formal' role defined by the organisation, such as a partner, CEO, or manager. However, individuals (sometimes covertly and often unconsciously) also take on an 'informal' role in line with their emotional and motivational situation (Triest, 1999).

An example of an informal role in a group could be an informal leader, a creative person, a victimised person, a mediator, or an outspoken person. These roles arise from both a person's personality and the group's dynamics. They may resemble familiar roles from childhood that provide them with identity and a sense of security but can limit the freedom they allow themselves and others in groups (Visholm, 2021).

At work, we often take on roles similar to those we are comfortable with within our families or that play a role in helping us cope with personal anxieties. The experiences of some of the leaders I spoke to reflected this.

For many professionals, achieving partnership in a professional services firm (PSF) allows them to be helpful to other people, be respected for their work, and be recognised.

Lisa was one of three PSF leaders I spoke to who described their role as a 'corporate doctor' or surgeon who fixes problems for their clients. These are roles where their clients respect them for the advice they give. 'People come to me because it's like I'm a doctor, I help them to fix problems. I put myself in their shoes... I feel their pain, therefore I'm eager to help them to ease their pain', she said.

In the role biography mini-drawings, I asked the leaders to do at selected ages, the men and women indicated different preferences for what they look for in their work roles. For example, at twenty-two and thirty-two, many men drew corporate logos representing their organisations. These could be viewed as 'phantastic' objects (in other words, an object of fantasy and admiration), indicating that they are looking for recognition from their family and friends. Interestingly, very few women drew logos or other iconic objects – more of them drew themselves with others at work and home.

TRANSFERENCE – CONFUSION IN TIME AND PLACE

Many culturally diverse leaders described their relationships with their sponsors fondly.

Mark, who had two critical sponsors during his career, described one of his sponsors as 'effectively my father figure, because he, like my father, had great discipline'. His sponsor guided him on his way to partnership.

> He's one of the reasons why I remained in the firm because I had options to join investment banks and do other sorts of things, which appeared far more interesting than auditing. But he encouraged me all through, [and] gave me wonderful training. And he also persuaded me to stay. He said, 'Look, you're going to get lots of fantastic experience in the firm. Don't leave too early. Wait until you become a manager or a senior manager. And then you might want to leave if that suits you.' So that was one reason for staying.

Paul also had the opportunity to learn from and be sponsored by a senior leader early in his career, who he described fondly. 'I think that I was a very good senior associate to provide support to the partners. And I learned so much from the partners', he mentioned.

> And he became a bit like a father figure because I learned so much from him, you know, approach to work, approach to life. Yeah, it's difficult to describe it, but imagine working with Steve Jobs for three years. You either really hate it, or you became converted, and you got so much out of it. Because I think I was [a] bit like that.

One of the critical dynamics that supported culturally diverse leaders in achieving leadership roles were their relationships with their sponsors. Some of them may have potentially experienced transference from their parental figures early in life to their sponsors.

Transference and transferential patterns are hidden family dynamics that sometimes repeat themselves later in our lives, including at work. They are aligned to the fourth premise of the Clinical Paradigm, a systems psychodynamic framework used to understand human dynamics in systems explained further in Appendix B. This premise describes the situation where the past is the lens through which we can understand the present and shape the future, which helps us understand our behaviours and relational patterns.

The idea of transference, first explained by Sigmund Freud, is based on how human beings develop and mature. How our parents, family members, teachers, and other authority figures help or hinder us as children in successfully navigating various critical psychological tasks and milestones has a crucial impact on how we behave as adults.

While our identity can change over our lifetime, our early experiences follow us throughout our lives. These can unconsciously play out in later life through transference.

To ensure our memories of early troubling incidents remain unconscious, our minds carry out 'ego defences' that affect our current relationships, and transference occurs. These could include repressing unpleasant thoughts from our minds, taking on characteristics of others, or attributing personal shortcomings to others. Transference patterns from our experiences in family systems can include the following:

- *Parental dynamics* – such as where parents were harsh or forgetful, so we are hypersensitive to criticism or being overlooked.
- *Sibling dynamics* – such as collaborative or protective behaviour, or rivalry, competitiveness, preoccupation with fairness, or a pervasive sense of inferiority.
- *Caretaker dynamics* – where we take on an inappropriate version of a managerial role, try too hard to please others, or ward off reasonable demands.
- *Bullying dynamics* (Cardona & Damon, 2019).

These repressed patterns of relational 'confusion' in time and place can return and be activated by particular cues without our awareness. These lead us to unconsciously repeat the repressed scene in real-life circumstances that are in some way reminiscent of the original incident (Visholm, 2021). Remarkably, it has been detected that these types of transference triggers can sometimes take place multiple times a day (Kets de Vries et al., 2016).

This can happen to all of us. As an example, have you ever been in a situation where you met a supervisor whose tone of voice subconsciously reminded you of your authoritarian father or nagging older sister? Or have had a similar feeling but felt like you had experienced previously it in a completely different context. This may be a result of a transference experience. Occasionally, you may then transfer your repressed memory of your father or sister onto the supervisor. Yet, the supervisor may not comprehend why your actions don't make any sense in the current situation (Visholm, 2021).

Another typical example, mirroring and idealising, has roots in our early interactions with others, starting with our mothers. From there, they become cues on how we behave with others (Kets de Vries & Cheak, 2016).

From my experience working with millennials with Asian backgrounds, transference plays a significant role in how they react in specific settings at work. For instance, those who work for more autocratic leaders are sometimes often reluctant to speak up in front of others and are careful about what they say. But, if their leaders are more collaborative and helpful, like their siblings, millennials open up more and thrive. As a leader, it was vital for me to reduce the hierarchy level between my staff and me to build trust; my team used to call me 'jie jie' or 'big sister'.

Both transference and countertransference, which is essentially the reverse of transference, influence our dyadic relationships at work. These relationships include our sponsors, mentors, and role models – all relationships we leverage for our career advancement.

THE INFLUENCE OF FAMILY SYSTEMS ON THE 'ORGANISATION IN THE MIND'

As mentioned earlier, our family forms our prototype or basic model for our experiences in and of organisations. Sometimes, this is referred to as our 'organisation in the mind'. The family is our primary source of transferences in organisations (Visholm, 2021).

Regardless of its social appeal, people prefer familiar behaviour (Keller, 1999). As such, in groups, individuals unconsciously seek to make them familiar by attempting to assign familial roles from their childhood family (Visholm, 2021).

At times, people feel the need to create idealistic, powerful representations of the organisations in which they work – an idealised 'organisation in the mind'. This organisational ideal could be regarded as a hope, something to be desired, a fantasy of the organisation that a person relishes deep inside themselves. This allows them to feel stronger, more adequate, and more capable, becoming part of their implicit internalised values and social identity. According to Manfred Kets de Vries of INSEAD, like all images in the mind, they can be conscious, pre-conscious, or unconscious (Kets de Vries, 2006).

When I examined the role biographies that I asked the culturally diverse leaders to share with me, I was surprised by some of their drawings. Although I asked interviewees to draw themselves in their work roles at twelve, twenty-two, thirty-two, and so on, I was particularly fascinated by their pictures at forty-two, when almost all were in senior leadership roles.

For those who were partners in Big 4 firms, many men drew themselves with their family at home or on holidays, where they were happy but did not draw themselves at work. In contrast, many women drew themselves at home with their families (who were all happy) and at work with junior staff members. The junior staff members they drew were drawn as small stick figures with no facial expressions and emotions. Intriguingly, many leaders spoke about how they wanted to be role models for the next generation of leaders. Those who did not work in the Big 4 were more likely to describe themselves in their work roles sitting around the boardroom table or leading their teams.

In contrast, at the age of twenty-two, interviewees often drew or described artifacts or icons. Examples frequently included their gradu-ation cap, degree, company logos, office buildings, or them at their desks or in their business attire. A number drew planes, representing travel. These artifacts and icons appeared to indicate they were looking for recognition from others, whether their family or friends and status from their work roles. The women were more likely to draw themselves socialising with work colleagues or with their spouses, indicating that they valued strong friendships with others at work.

At thirty-two, some drew themselves working long hours alone, trav-elling, and stressed. Others drew themselves seeking to balance their family obligations with their spouse and work commitments.

To me, this illustrated the influence of the family system on the 'organisation in the mind' that some of the culturally diverse leaders desired. They were interested in status, recognition, and friendship with their work colleagues. They could work hard; however, many found that certain times in their lives (particularly in their 30s) were emotionally challenging for them.

Interestingly, some of them (more often women) had less of a boundary between their work self and themselves at home as they became more senior. However, fascinatingly, the female leaders were more likely to draw themselves taking up a role as a 'mother' at work – mentoring junior staff members to take on more significant roles (refer to Figure 4.1).

In contrast, others (often the men) put in place stricter boundaries to manage their roles in the various systems as they got older, clearly separating their family and work roles. Often, they did not draw themselves at work once they had families.

In an environment where anxieties and change are the norms, I felt that the 'fantasy' organisation in the mind that some culturally diverse leaders may prefer to work in (particularly those in PSFs) was one that was similar

Figure 4.1 Example of role biography drawing by a female leader who works at a PSF

to their family environment – where there was stability and dependency. In this space, they were part of a stable, happy family, where they were dependent on their senior leaders. However, they were also harmonious and collaborative with their peers, who would always be there to support each other, like brothers and sisters. I also sensed that some female leaders would like to be a 'mother' or 'big sister' to younger staff members, like the types of roles they would be expected to take up at home.

Further, I sensed that some culturally diverse leaders in PSFs might unconsciously be less comfortable working in a (Western) partnership that is managed by a leadership team of elected partners than in an organisation with a more paternalistic leader (where leaders are appointed). But, again, this would be similar to how family roles are often assigned based on seniority.

Finally, if other leaders did not give them the emotional support they needed, they looked for support outside the organisation. This support would often be from their families, who would always be there for them. If they couldn't give them the help they needed, some looked for new opportunities in other organisations.

UNEARTHING THE HIDDEN DYNAMICS THAT SHAPE OUR EXPERIENCES IN THE WORKPLACE

Understanding how our family system influences us and our transference patterns is vital in understanding our roles as leaders and followers. We cannot ignore the influence of patterns such as emotions and transferences in our working life.

Transference explains many of our everyday behaviours in organisations. At its best, it can be viewed as the emotional glue that connects people to a leader (Maccoby, 2004). However, in situations of organisational stress, transference can also be harmful. One action we can all take to minimise this is to acknowledge our transferences.

Understanding our family system also helps us know the organisations and types of behaviours where we may be most comfortable.

Often, when we seek out organisations where we wish to work, we may unconsciously seek a place where we can repeat positive experiences or 'sort out' unresolved issues from the past. If our unconscious desires fit the needs of the system we work in, things can go well. However, often this is not always the case. Over time, even positive dynamics may become dysfunctional as people, roles, tasks, and demands shift (Cardona & Damon, 2019).

For several of the leaders I spoke to, I sensed that their preferred environment at work was one where the dynamics may be similar to their own families.

If, over time, the expectations of an organisation change in a way that is not aligned with the interests of its employees, it may become more difficult to retain them in organisations as talent. As a result, senior leaders have a role in understanding how their teams perceive their work roles.

Undertaking an exercise such as understanding the role biographies of your team members may unearth some interesting patterns about the group's or organisation's hidden dynamics. Further, it can provoke broader yet healthy discussion about some of the barriers to organisational change, and what can be done both by the individuals, groups, and the organisation to remove potential blockers to change.

Chapter summary

- Early experiences in the family have a strong influence on leaders. How the family system operates at home, the first system that people experience, shapes leader values and how they take up subsequent roles.
- For culturally diverse leaders, early roles in the home influence the roles they look for and take up unconsciously at school and work. Often, parental or other caregiver anxieties and expectations impact how they react to situations later in life. This shapes their leader values and behaviours that guide their leadership journeys.
- Transference patterns, where a person projects their feelings about someone encountered in their childhood onto another person, influence their relationships at the workplace.
- Likewise, their family systems influence the types of organisations they are attracted to and how they see themselves in their roles in their organisations. Understanding how a leader's family system guided their career journey is vital for understanding how they take up roles as leaders and followers in the workplace.

Questions to ask yourself and your team members

Yourself

- What are my leader values? What has influenced them?
- What could be the reason(s) for my attraction to certain roles? What do I look for in my work roles?
- To what extent has my family roles impacted the type of roles I take on at work?
- Have I reacted to situations unconsciously to work reminiscent of patterns from my early childhood experiences? If yes, what types of situations were they, and who were you with?
- What type of teams, groups, or organisations do I prefer to work in?

My team members

- What type of roles do you prefer to take on at work, both formally and informally? To what extent have your family dynamics influenced this?
- What situations do you prefer, and which are you less comfortable with at work? What may be the reasons for this?

NOTES

1 A system is a group of components organised to perform a function.
2 However, a 'role' is not our 'identity'. Some academics believe that there is frequent confusion between the two terms. In brief, a role is generally viewed as providing external clues about how one should act. In contrast, identity is the internal meaning attached to the 'self' or 'who one is', based on one's social and personal identities.
3 Republished with permission of Taylor & Francis Informa UK Ltd – Books, from Drawing from Role Biography in Organizational Role Analysis, S. Long, in J. Newton, S. Long & B. Sievers (Eds.), Coaching in Depth: The Organizational Role Analysis Approach, 2006; permission conveyed through Copyright Clearance Center, Inc.
4 Refer to Appendix A for further details on my research background.
5 Copyright © 2015, from Defences against anxiety in the law, by J. Stokes in D. Armstrong & M. Rustin, Social Defences Against Anxiety: Explorations in a Paradigm. Reproduced by permission of Taylor & Francis Group, LLC, a division of Informa plc. This permission does not cover third party copyrighted work which may appear in the material requested. User is responsible for obtaining permission for such material separately from this grant.
6 A defence is an act of defending oneself. I will discuss defences further in Chapter 6.

7 Children sent to a new country to live alone or with a caregiver while their parents remain in their home country.

REFERENCES

Cardona, F., & Damon, S. (2019). Family Patterns at Work: How Casting Light on the Shadows of the Past Can Enhance Leadership in the Present. In A. Obholzer & V. Z. Roberts (Eds.), *The Unconscious at Work: A Tavistock Approach to Making Sense of Organizational Life* (pp. 187–195). Routledge. https://doi.org/10.4324/9781351104166

Cilliers, F., Rothmann, S., & Struwig, W. (2004). Transference and Counter-Transference in Systems Psychodynamic Group Process Consultation: The Consultant's Experience. *South African Journal of Industrial Psychology*, 30(1), 72–81. https://doi.org/10.4102/sajip.v30i1.143

Czander, W. M. (1993). *The Psychodynamics of Work and Organizations.* The Guildford Press.

Hislop, M. (2020, November 27). Dismissing Prejudice as 'Irrational' Has Been Key to CEO Shemara Wikramanayake's Resilience & Leadership. *Women's Agenda.* https://womensagenda.com.au/leadership/macquarie-ceo-shemara-wikramanayake-talks-resilience-leadership/

Ho, C. (2020). *Aspiration & Anxiety: Asian Migrants and Australian Schooling.* Melbourne University Press.

Keller, T. (1999). Images of the Familiar: Individual Differences and Implicit Leadership Theories. *Leadership Quarterly*, 10(4), 589–607. https://doi.org/10.1016/S1048-9843(99)00033-8

Kets de Vries, M. F. R. (2006). *The Leader on the Couch: A Clinical Approach to Changing People and Organizations.* Wiley.

Kets de Vries, M. F. R., & Cheak, A. (2016). Psychodynamic Approach. In P. G. Northouse (Ed.), *Leadership: Theory and Practice* (pp. 295–328). Sage.

Kets de Vries, M. F. R., Korotov, K., Florent-Treacy, E., & Rook, C. (2016). *Coach and Couch: The Psychology of Making Better Leaders* (2nd ed.). Palgrave Macmillan.

Long, S. (2006). Drawing from Role Biography in Organisational Role Analysis. In J. Newton, S. Long, & B. Sievers (Eds.), *Coaching in Depth: The Organisational Role Analysis Approach* (pp. 127–144). Karnac. https://doi.org/10.4324/9780429473029

Maccoby, M. (2004, September). Why People Follow the Leader: The Power of Transference. *Harvard Business Review*, 82(9), 76–85. https://hbr.org/2004/09/why-people-follow-the-leader-the-power-of-transference

Patten, S. (2020, November 26). 'I Had Things I Could Control, Including My Attitude': Macquarie CEO. *Australian Financial Review.* https://www.afr.com/work-and-careers/leaders/i-had-things-i-could-control-including-my-attitude-macquarie-ceo-20201126-p56i84

Petriglieri, G., & Petriglieri, J. L. (2020). The Return of the Oppressed: A Systems Psychodynamic Approach to Organization Studies. *Academy of Management Annals*, 14(1), 411–449. https://doi.org/10.5465/annals.2017.0007

Pratt, M. G. (1998). To Be or Not to Be: Central Questions in Organizational Identification. In D. A. Whetton & P. C. Godfrey (Eds.), *Identity in Organizations: Building Theory through Conversations* (pp. 171–207). Sage Publications, Inc. http://dx.doi.org/10.4135/9781452231495.n6

Stokes, J. (2014). Defences Against Anxiety in the Law. In D. Armstrong (Ed.), *Social Defences Against Anxiety: Explorations in a Paradigm*. Routledge. https://doi.org/10.4324/9780429480300

Tcholakian, L. A., Khapova, S. N., van de Loo, E., & Lehman, R. (2019). Collective Traumas and the Development of Leader Values: A Currently Omitted, but Increasingly Urgent, Research Area. *Frontiers in Psychology*, 10, 1–13. https://doi.org/10.3389/fpsyg.2019.01009

Triest, J. (1999). The Inner Drama of Role Taking in an Organization. In R. French & V. Russ (Eds.), *Group Relations, Management, and Organization* (pp. 209–223). Oxford University Press.

Tu, M.-C., & Okazaki, S. (2021). What Is Career Success? A New Asian American Psychology of Working. *American Psychologist*, 76(4), 673–688. https://doi.org/10.1037/amp0000807

Visholm, S. (2021). *Family Psychodynamics in Organizational Contexts*. Routledge. https://doi.org/10.4324/9781003164913

Five

INTRODUCTION

When I became a partner in Singapore in 2002, I benefited from having a sponsor who supported my promotion to partnership. Although I am ethnically Chinese, I was an outsider in my firm, as I grew up outside Singapore. Further, I was promoted at a time when there were fewer female partners than is the case today. The promotion process at the time was opaque.

I worked hard during those times, serving one of our largest clients in the office and being part of a growing business area. Yet, I would not have made it to partner without my sponsor's support and advice. Further, I may not have won his initial backing were it not for the good words a former partner that I worked for in Sydney said to him and some other Singapore partners about me when I was posted to Singapore on a secondment.

Excellent sponsors, good relationships with colleagues and clients, and strong networks are essential for career success. In addition, we need to continuously experiment, learn, and reinvent ourselves throughout our careers, given the speed of change in businesses and our workplaces.

This chapter explores the actions that culturally diverse leaders with multiple identities take to succeed at work, derived from my interviews with successful Asian-Australian leaders.

HOW DO WE DEVELOP INTO LEADERS AT WORK?

When you think of a leader at work, who do you think of? What makes a great leader?

When I asked some of the Asian-Australian leaders I spoke to how others describe them, expressions they shared included: listens, takes advice, collegiate, collaborative, caring, a person who tries to lead by example, empowering, creative, and visionary. Most of these expressions describe their behaviours – how they relate to others.

DOI: 10.4324/9781003291237-7

The core of leadership – the what, how and why – is about human behaviour, according to Manfred Kets de Vries. It is all about how we behave in organisations (Kets de Vries & Cheak, 2016).

Traditionally, business literature has portrayed world-class organisations as being managed by logical, rational leaders. Yet, being a leader frequently involves dealing with a constantly changing melange of rational behaviours and choices, and frequently irrational forces, which are frequently baffling. Moreover, often organisational incidents remain unanswered and mysterious, particularly as the boundaries between work and home have blurred. As a result, various approaches to leadership development frequently avoid emotions and the psychological spheres of organisational life.

To fully understand ourselves and our behaviours at work requires us to apply both rational and irrational lenses.

What is identity work for leaders?

The concepts of career progression and leadership development have been well-researched from various angles. However, I was curious to understand people's career progression with multiple identities into leadership. This incorporates perspectives from two research areas – identity processes and role transitions. In addition, I wanted to find out more about the intersection of two elements – how we construct our career in organisations, and how the organisations we join shape us.

As discussed in Chapter 2, our own identity is based on our personal and social identities. One aspect of our social identity is our vocation. These elements shape our 'professional identity' – the attributes, beliefs, values, motives, and experiences used to describe people in a professional role.

'Identity work' in organisations generally refers to identity construction processes, where people form, repair, maintain, strengthen, or revise their identities (Sveningsson & Alvesson, 2003). It is a dynamic negotiation process where people negotiate their identities to fulfil their basic needs for uncertainty reduction, belonging, and autonomy. In other words, it is what we do to modify who we are to be accepted, listened to, and engaged with by others.

When we undergo this process, we frequently relinquish restrictive identities and pursue ones that bring us joy. This may include stabilising an existing identity, transitioning into a new one, or negotiating the boundaries between our personal and social identities. Sometimes viewed as a 'living narrative' or described as a socialisation process, identity work can be destabilising, leading to experiences of uncertainty, confusion, and anxiety.

Herminia Ibarra of the London Business School describes this process as experimenting with our 'provisional selves' – being transitory solutions that bridge the gap between our current and future selves. In her seminal 1999 article, Ibarra found that the process of identity transition of junior professionals in consulting and investment banking involved three key components – having role models to identify potential identities, experimenting with provisional selves, and re-evaluating themselves (Ibarra, 1999).

For those in professional services firms (PSFs), on their journeys, professionals need to continue to develop to become successful or remain so (Ibarra, 2004), 'due to professionals' need to continue tailoring their identity to changing opportunities and demands and to their evolving understanding of their roles and in part due to people's desire to move toward a more individuated professional identity that reflects their unique interests and desire' (Petriglieri & Obodaru, 2019, p. 697).

Similarly, identity work for leaders is a social and relational process. According to Ibarra, Sarah Wittman, Gianpiero Petriglieri, and David V. Day, becoming a leader involves three elements. First, leaders acquire a leader identity via experimentation and internalisation of the leadership role. Second, they mould their behaviours in line with group prototypes, embodying what it means to be a leader and becoming part of the leadership group. Finally, they complete the construction of their leadership identity through validation from followers (Ibarra et al., 2014).

Consequently, our work relationships, particularly with sponsors and mentors, role models, peers, managers, and stakeholders, play a crucial role in supporting our identity transitions to become leaders.

Over the past twenty years, our careers have become more global, mobile, and diverse. We work for much longer, the internet/email has created an 'always on' culture, and we no longer work in one company for life. As a result, the traditional psychological contract which bound employers and employees via an exchange of loyalty for job security no longer exists. In addition, many of us embrace flexible working arrangements; however, we spend fewer hours in contact with work colleagues. As a result, our identities have become more malleable and difficult to maintain. As our contemporary careers have become liminal, identity work has become more frequent and necessary.

Many of us increasingly engage in identity 'play' to 'try on' and explore identities. Further, we are also more regularly in a state of being betwixt and between our social roles and/or identities.

I describe it as like trying on new clothes or shoes. Do I like what I see, how do other people react, and can these identities become part of me on a more regular basis? If I do not like these identities, I might then try something else until it feels like something that I can wear daily in due course.

Why career progression is tricky – the paradoxes of working life

One of the challenges of working life is dealing with multiple paradoxes – commonly described as the contradictory and yet interrelated elements (or dualities) that pull us in different directions over time (Smith & Lewis, 2011). Living with tensions is an inevitable part of life, particularly at work.

Most of us would remember a time in the playground when we were at school, when we wanted to be part of a group of friends and feel like we belonged. However, we may also have wished to be ourselves at times and not conform to the group norms. This paradox of belonging continues throughout our life. So, how do we balance belonging and remaining ourselves when we join groups?

Once we start at work, companies generally expect us to behave according to their rules and norms. Yet, we as individuals can also change those rules and norms – this is the paradox of 'embedded agency' at work.

Then, when we reach leadership roles, we often face a tension between our inner world and external reality, between ourselves and others (Jarrett & Vince, 2017). Leaders frequently experience pressure from their followers to act in a certain way. However, deep inside themselves, they may feel insecure. These insecurities may lead them to mismanage their roles and organisations if they cannot manage these tensions. Some of the worst leaders are narcissists – those who act for their own interests and put the needs and interests of others at risk, leading to dysfunctional leadership. This is known as the paradox of authority.

Finally, business leaders who own their businesses, such as partners in PSFs, face another paradox. A partner must simultaneously be a professional and embody the partnership's collective interests. This is generally known as the paradox of belonging/organising (Smith & Lewis, 2011).

Adopting a paradox lens requires that we learn to manage these concurrent and conflicting demands and perspectives. We need to remain aware that, in practice, these conflicts cannot be avoided and will continue over time (Lewis, 2000). Furthermore, managing these paradoxes may also lead to unconscious emotions and behaviours in teams and groups, influencing power relations.

Examining leadership development from another angle

Various leadership literature examines the process of how people take up leadership roles, the challenges they experience, and how individuals construct professional identities.

Less attention has been spent on understanding how individuals with multiple identities negotiate their identity conflicts in the workplace. In other words, how is leadership development complicated by cultural differences and intractable biases in the workplace and society, as is the case for leaders with culturally diverse backgrounds in multicultural nations? And how does leadership development for people with different cultural backgrounds in the workplace differ from those with fewer identities to manage?

As identity is an emotional topic, a systems psychodynamic lens, which focuses on the dynamics of human behaviour in organisations, is appropriate to examine identity and identity work. It helps us understand, analyse, and comprehend some of the hidden undercurrents affecting humans and better understand complexities in organisations (Kets de Vries & Cheak, 2016).

This lens investigates the dynamic tension and interaction between the feelings and goals of members in a system and the collective customs, rituals, and structures of the same system (Petriglieri, 2020a). This is important as identity work cannot be conducted in isolation. It is, by nature, a process between an individual and others (people or organisations), that necessarily has a social validation element (Petriglieri & Petriglieri, 2010) as illustrated in Figure 5.1. Moreover, it recognises that identity work may act as a way to avoid feelings of existential and social insecurities (Petriglieri et al., 2018).

A system psychodynamic lens is beneficial as it allows us to explore how people with multiple identities resolve contradictions and tensions between their identities (Petriglieri, 2020b). It also allows us to understand how unconscious systems-level practices can sustain inequality (Padavic et al., 2020).

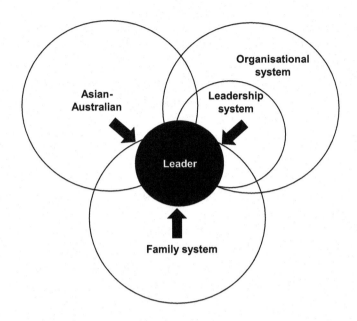

Figure 5.1 Lens adopted for research
Source: Own research

My focus was on Asian-Australians, given their growing presence and unique challenges in reaching senior leadership positions. Outside of the Asian-Australian cohort, the number of people with non-European backgrounds in Australia is small.[1] I initially spoke to thirty current and former Asian-Australian Big 4, and then an additional seven C-suite Asian-Australian leaders in public and private sector organisations to validate my findings.[2]

From their narratives, I identified the steps they took, the tensions and anxieties they experienced, and the actions that supported their career progression. This is what I refer to as *the experimentation and learning career cycle.*

THE EXPERIMENTATION AND LEARNING CAREER CYCLE

When I asked successful culturally diverse leaders for their career advice for aspiring leaders, I was fascinated by Paul's remarks. A partner at a Big 4 firm, he did most of his education overseas before migrating to Australia as an adult.

He started by sharing with me the importance of having a solid business case to make partner, working hard, having good relationships, having a strong brand, having a network, and being a good manager.

He then told me that he had been recently watching Star Wars and described becoming a partner as being like 'learning to be a Jedi' – an evolving process.

'[You] don't become a Jedi overnight. It's just very small things that you'd be building in the last five years', he said. 'You['d] already probably [been] operating as a partner, even before you were admitted as a partner for some time'.

He then said, 'So, it's not like I have one tip that will work for everyone... I think it's really a discipline, a system'.

After speaking to him, I reflected on his comments, my own journey to partnership, and the other stories of the leaders I chatted to. Unfortunately, there is no one silver bullet or one tip on making it into a leadership position. However, progressing into leadership involves efforts by both individuals and the system they work in to help people succeed.

Successful professional adaptation for aspiring culturally diverse leaders involves a continuous and dynamic *experimentation and learning career cycle*. The cycle starts when they join a new group or take up a new role (refer to Figure 5.2).

It includes two elements:

1. *Experiment with possible selves* – Culturally diverse leaders experiment with their provisional and possible selves to assess their potential future work identities. Their trials involved a dynamic cycle where they *experiment with new things; build, enhance and maintain relationships with sponsors; build trusted relationships with others; and enhance their business skills*. By taking risks and creating opportunities that support their growth, they merge and internalise the role and gain competence through having greater

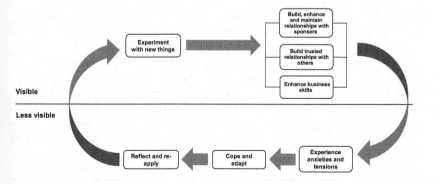

Figure 5.2 The experimentation and learning career cycle
Source: Own research

exposure to different situations over time. These are the *visible* actions that others see.

2. *Negotiate tensions and anxieties, then cope, adapt, reflect, and re-apply.* Throughout their identity transitions, culturally diverse leaders experience various paradoxical tensions and anxieties which arise from their roles and tasks and between themselves and their organisations. Culturally diverse leaders learn to *cope and adapt* to the tensions and anxieties they experience. They make sense of the nature of the systems they enter as part of their self-concept and self-mastery and then *reflect and re-apply* what they have learned. These are the *internal, less visible* steps that aspiring leaders take.

Figure 5.2 illustrates that first; culturally diverse leaders take *visible* steps to progress their careers. This chapter will explore the steps culturally diverse leaders take to make it into leadership roles.

Second, it shows that they take *internal* steps where they learn to *negotiate* their various tensions and anxieties, *cope and adapt, then reflect and re-apply* their learnings. Chapter 6 will explore how they negotiate and manage their journeys.

EXPERIMENTING WITH POSSIBLE SELVES – THE VISIBLE STEPS THAT CULTURALLY DIVERSE LEADERS TAKE TO WIN AT WORK

Culturally diverse leaders take several steps to progress their careers, as illustrated in Table 5.1.

Table 5.1 Visible steps taken by culturally diverse leaders to progress their careers

Experiment with new things	Build, enhance, and maintain relationships with sponsors	Build trusted relationships with others	Enhance business skills
• Open to starting new roles or joining new groups • Try new things and take risks • Build agility skills by working overseas • Learn to manage multiple tasks and stakeholders simultaneously	Find sponsors who are willing to help them with both 'what' and 'who' competencies	• Have mentors • Have supportive networks • Be a team player • Be a people developer	• Excel at what they do beyond technical skills – serving clients, solving problems, being a specialist, growing business • Strong communication skills • Reliable and trustworthy

Source: Own research.

> When starting a new role or joining a new group, culturally diverse leaders are open to experimenting with new things and taking risks. A large proportion of them built agility skills by working overseas. Over time, they learned to manage multiple tasks and stakeholders simultaneously.

Open to starting new roles or joining new groups

Sue, who moved to Australia at the age of twelve, enjoyed her Big 4 firm's environment and community when she started work. Like her, many people in her cohort had migrated to Australia for high school without their families. She appreciated having a group of people around her who supported her and understood what others were going through. 'My first full-time job was kind of exciting in itself… being surrounded by people who were equally determined, quite ambitious, and wanting to achieve something in life', she recalled.

Getting into a role is a complicated process whereby a person 'takes on' the role's expectations. As part of this process, people refrain from acts typically exhibited outside the organisation.

Culturally diverse leaders enjoy starting new roles and joining new groups. For many of them, beginning in any new role or joining a new group involved a period of learning where they moved from being a 'singleton' to becoming a group member. At times, this was a period of flux when aspiring leaders sought to balance their own needs with the team's, yet not lose too much of their own identity.

Work was enjoyable for the culturally diverse leaders who started their careers at a Big 4 firm. They felt a strong sense of belonging and made friends with like-minded people as often they were part of a cohort of colleagues. Few noted anxieties, and some possibly repressed their negative thoughts at the time.

More opportunities came to those enthusiastic about their work, like Robert. He decided that he wanted to work as a consultant in a Big 4 firm after doing work experience as a teenager in the computer support team of one of the Big 4 firms. He thoroughly enjoyed his time as a new graduate as he was keen to learn. 'I'd want to get to work early because I was desperate to learn from the people that were in our team', he remembers. 'I'd sort of volunteer for everything, be involved in everything, be annoyed that I couldn't [as] I wasn't old enough or senior enough to lead proposals just yet, because that was something I always wanted to do'.

Starting work and new roles were more challenging for those not part of a cohort of new joiners, as they had to find their own way and build relationships independently.

A few recalled feeling different. Amanda was one who started work in a Big 4 firm as an audit graduate. 'I was the only Asian person, I think. But also, being at that time, I think people [were] trying to balance out the gender diversity point of view… I don't think that there was even another Asian person', she remembered.

Try new things and take risks

Amanda thoroughly enjoyed her time at work. 'An audit grad at that time did a lot of things that were around… you just have to do everything. So, it was great exposure'. She fondly remembered the training she received, the exposure to different businesses, and meeting a wide variety of people across various industries, which she believes helped her to become a more well-rounded professional. Like other culturally diverse leaders, she was open to trying new things and taking risks.

Those who started their careers in larger organisations were given many opportunities to try new things. This was particularly so for those who worked in PSFs. In line with the apprenticeship model, professionals are frequently given new assignments and roles working with different team members, requiring them to try new things. Peter's advice for young professionals early in their careers in PSFs is to 'just learn as much as you can, take on as many opportunities [as] you can, and don't worry too much about this small stuff at that point.'

Those who started to work in smaller organisations and were not part of a cohort of new joiners tried new opportunities until they found things they enjoyed doing. Their early years were difficult for some, such as Tim who started work in a smaller organisation. 'I hadn't quite figured out what I enjoyed from a career perspective. I knew I liked business. But business is such a broad term.'

Most were self-motivated to work hard, particularly those who embraced the PSF culture. One example was Robert, who said, '[I was] very eager and almost to the point where I always wanted to work overtime. I wanted to stay late, work late and then have dinner with my team because I was enjoying and learning so much'.

Taking risks included working with more complex clients or on higher-profile projects and assignments. Some learned how to be agile and open to taking risks as adolescents, such as Stuart.

From his experience relocating from Mumbai to a much smaller city and school at the age of twelve, Stuart learned 'the ability to walk into the unknown, [to] back yourself and be resilient through change, not overthink and overanalyse', and 'go with the flow.' This helped him when he moved to Australia in his mid-20s, as it gave him the ability to get out of his comfort zone, start over again, and not be afraid of failing.

Another was Mark, who attended several schools when he was young. One of his core strengths was his 'adaptability, versatility, going from one client to another to another to another – it was very easy for me, came very naturally'. Many, like Mark, were open to taking risks and trying new things. Hence, their bosses recognised them for their ability to solve complex problems for clients.

Mark described a situation where he took a risk on a high-profile client, but it paid off.

> We were about to lose a very big client, because they thought the senior manager had done a very bad job. And the partner was an absentee landlord. And so, they put me into the job thinking this is probably lost, but we'll give it a try. I managed to turn it around as a manager, and it [was] very difficult. [The] client wrote to the partner to say I'd done a really fine job, and they're going to retain [the firm] as the auditors. And all of a sudden, my reputation just started to blossom within the firm.

Anne, a tax partner, built her reputation by working with a number of significant clients. One was undergoing a tax audit, and she worked with the managing partner on the engagement. 'There were incredible issues – like issues that were really leading edge at that point in time that no one had really dealt with', she recalled.

With the support of her senior manager, she started to work directly with another iconic partner for a key client. He later became one of her key supporting partners for her promotion to partnership. 'It was technical; it was actually quite interesting...', she recalls.

> I still remember that it was the new part of income tax legislation. And we actually had to lobby for it to be changed because [if] it didn't, the legislation would not work in practice for the client situation the legislation was meant to address.

Anne noted that there were many problems to work through; however, she succeeded in the opportunity. 'So, from that point in time, I worked with him on this client for the rest of my career and assumed the lead partner role when I was admitted to partnership', she said.

Taking risks and speaking up at work can be uncomfortable for some, especially those taught at home in childhood to respect their elders and not challenge authority. Unfortunately, this sometimes means they are not willing to say anything unless they are 100% correct. In addition, in many Asian cultures, it is common for more junior individuals to wait until more senior individuals have finished speaking, which can mean that they are often not heard in time-limited circumstances.

Catherine shared that she learned to change the way she approached matters over time, as clients and internal stakeholders often expect a response on the spot. These expectations increased as her responsibilities expanded across multiple clients and teams. However, over time she recognised that it was impossible to be perfect 100% of the time. For example, if she were 80% certain of her answer, she would present her point of view and reasons but caveat her opinions within the context. Sometimes she needed to forgive herself for expressing her opinion, knowing that she had an opportunity to verify or clarify it later if she needed to.

Build agility skills by working overseas

Many culturally diverse leaders accelerate their careers by working overseas. One such leader I spoke to was Katrina Rathie, Non-Executive Director and former Partner in Charge, King & Wood Mallesons Sydney. She honed her business skills in the US. 'When I went to New York, I really learnt the art of practice development, of client development, [and] of the importance of relationships. [I learnt] how to win business, how to become a rainmaker, how to hustle, how to never take no for an answer, [and] how to knock down doors', she said.

Another leader who benefited from her experience overseas was Rebecca. She worked in a very different role overseas from her technical position in Australia. As a result, she had to learn and adapt to the job.

'I had to throw myself into an area that I didn't know much about and do a lot of self-reading and kind of catch up and try', she remembers of the challenges of having to work out what to do on her own and learn to survive in a much larger office in a new country.

'You had to find your own way. There was no one there to coddle you and go 'Hey, this is what you were expected to do'. It was basically, you get there you go, OK, I think I need to do these things. To achieve that, I'm going to do XY Z, I'm going to meet these partners, [and] I'm going to meet these people', she recalls.

Several of the people I interviewed lived and worked for a few years in countries, including the US and UK, where they immersed themselves in the new culture and environments. They also broadened their perspectives. When they returned to Australia, they performed well and were recognised for their work overseas. Living overseas helps people have greater career decision-making clarity through their reflections (Adam et al., 2018).

Most leaders recognised the importance of being strategic about when to work overseas and when it was essential to re-engage and re-establish ties with their key stakeholders back home.

Learn to manage multiple tasks and stakeholders simultaneously

Tim, a C-suite leader who has worked for organisations in several sectors, credits much of his career growth to the time when he worked in a large organisation in a role where he learned to manage multiple tasks and stakeholders concurrently.

Reflecting on his experience at the age of thirty-two, he recollected that

> I'd gone from a role where it [was] very, very narrow [into] a role that was really, really broad – managing 10 to 15 projects. [In] the role prior, [I was] literally on one project for three months, six months, or even a year. And suddenly, [you] have this wide remit. I think [that] in a large organisation, the way that you do things is very different from in a small place. I think that that experience was quite interesting and quite beneficial.

Culturally diverse leaders learn to manage multiple tasks and stakeholders simultaneously. Taking on new and increasing responsibilities was challenging for some leaders, particularly in their 30s, when some had young families.

Angela found her experience juggling a young child and a part-time middle management role very challenging, especially given she and her husband both had demanding jobs.

'To be honest, I didn't feel like I was doing either thing – work or home – very well and, I was very stretched. However, looking back, I wouldn't have swapped it for anything'. She suggests that women return to the workforce as soon as they feel able to after having a child. When Angela's child started school, she went back to work full time and was immediately promoted into a senior executive role.

Being open to continuous experimentation, learning, adaptation and adjusting to new environments is vital for leaders to survive, particularly in rapidly changing industries and settings.

Still, starting new roles like becoming a new partner in a PSF was, for some like starting again. Ian, an audit partner, described his role as a new partner as feeling like he was in a 'vortex' where you are under pressure, on the go all the time, and you either thrive or die.

'Everything happens so fast', he said.

> You know, like, you're on you're on the go all the time, because you've got client[s], you've got hundreds of things juggling. You just juggle the bits that make sense at the time, and then [the] next day happens. And then a year's gone, and you go arghhh!

He however recognises the skills he gained becoming a partner have subsequently helped him when taking on new roles.

Some leaders put boundaries around different parts of their lives to help them manage all the elements. A few leaders, such as Andrew described being a leader as feeling like they were always 'juggling balls'.

When discussing how he would draw his life on a piece of paper, Andrew replied, 'I'd probably draw that I have just a lot of different balls in the air'.

Recognising that a leader's role involves managing their business, including their people and personal lives, Andrew explained how he manages his various roles.

> So, typically, my life is, I'd have four or five different projects on the go with different teams that I'm not only managing, but I'm also trying to create this cohesive practice as well. So, there's the day-to-day tactical running a project. There's keeping the team together across projects.

There's managing client dynamics as well. But there's also as well the juggling all those balls at work, there's just trying to juggle my family life, juggle my personal sustainability, and also, I do a lot of work with a not-for- profit... so I think there's just lots of things that I'm multitasking all the time.

Build, enhance and maintain relationships with sponsors

> A vital supporting element of the identity work of culturally diverse leaders is sponsors. Sponsors are essential for aspiring leaders because working out what to learn, who to learn from, and how to behave isn't straightforward.

One of the most critical factors that accelerate culturally diverse leaders' careers is having sponsors in their organisations.

Peter's sponsor was one such case. His sponsor 'was keen, supportive and recognised my abilities, and was willing to go into bat for [me] in those discussions that they have, which you're not a party [to]. So, [an] ability to influence', he said.

Sponsors are senior leaders committed to your career success. They invest the time, effort, and resources to prepare you for the top role. They often go out on a limb to advocate and champion for you. As they have power and influence, they have clout at decision-making tables. They can open doors and drive decisions relating to roles, opportunities and even pay rises in your favour. They can also provide 'air cover' that allows you to take risks.

According to pracademic Jovina Ang, sponsors help their sponsees to gain both know 'what' and 'who' competencies in several areas. These cover professional and personal development, not just technical skills (see Table 5.2).

Recognising that you can't mandate a sponsor to spend their personal capital to advocate for someone they don't know well or may not be enthusiastic about, Ibarra explored the concept of sponsorship more broadly. She believes that companies should view sponsorship as an increasingly public spectrum of different behaviours – from strategiser to connector, to opportunity giver to advocate – that allows for various types of commitment (Ibarra, 2019).

Table 5.2 Competencies acquired from sponsorship

'What' competencies	'Who' competencies
• Access to stretch projects	• Access to senior leader networks
• Actionable career guidance	• Battles for promotion
• Confidence	• Ensures candidacy for roles
• Cultivates and teaches	• Opens up external networks
• Image advice	• Provides safety
• Personal advice	• Provides support
• Political acumen	• Provides visibility and exposure

Source: Adapted from Ang (2019).

Sponsors frequently take on talent and train them before nominating them for leadership. Tim's sponsor was a good example. 'I would always have his backing', said Tim. His sponsor would make time to help him resolve issues. 'So that was helpful – to have someone supporting you'.

Many of the successful leaders I spoke to had one to three sponsors who helped them on their career journey. Some leaders in PSFs described their relationships with their sponsors fondly. These relationships were acquired organically through mutual attraction due to similar attitudes, attributes, and traits. Most started working with their sponsors early in their careers.

According to Ang, sponsees typically have a consistent track record and leadership potential. Their characteristics often include passion, enthusiasm, drive, a learning mindset, courage, authenticity, teamwork, and emotional intelligence (Ang, 2019).

Build trusted relationships with others

> Key career success factors of culturally diverse leaders include building trusted relationships with mentors, having support networks with others (role models and other leaders, colleagues, staff or clients), being a team player and collaborator, and being a people developer.

Culturally diverse leaders build strong and trusted relationships with mentors, people across all levels of their organisation, and externally with clients and other stakeholders.

Many recognised the importance of building strong relationships with people at school, on the sports field, or during high school or university.

Others recognised that work relationships were meaningful early in their careers, like Angela. She believes that you have to invest in relationships at work. Her initial view when she started work was, 'I just had to be technically good at my work, and I'd be recognised and promoted. But it soon became clear to me that that's not how a workplace operates and that relationships are so important'. She added, 'all of my mentoring and sponsor relationships with people were informal. There were people who were in my corner and willing to support me and open doors for me'.

In today's dynamic workplaces, where much of our work is undertaken virtually and in teams, collaborating and leveraging internal networks is crucial for successful identity transition. Relationship competencies and interpersonal style are critical contributors to being promoted to leadership roles, such as partners.

It is essential to recognise that whilst having good relationships throughout the organisation is necessary, the composition and quality of their relationships do influence promotion prospects. For instance, not all the culturally diverse leaders I spoke to had sponsors (although they did have mentors and coaches). Some moved to other organisations mid-way during their careers, where they were given leadership roles and got better support.

Have mentors

Kate grew up overseas but did some of her university studies in Australia. She benefited from good advice from a mentor early in her career. She recounts being told by her mentor that her professional work was excellent. However, she learned that she needed to spend more time in the bar on Fridays, as her colleagues didn't know her. 'I still remember one of the counselling conversations or performance review conversations I had with my reviewer at the time', she said.

She recalls that her mentor told her,

> You know, you're really smart – you get on with what you're doing very well. You know how to work professionally. But people don't know you. You need to spend more time mingling. You just spend [need to] more time hanging out with people. Don't just think about going home and go[ing] for a run [by] yourself – spend that social time with people. People in Australia like to hang out in a bar on Fridays.

She remembers the conversation because, at the time, she never expected a career discussion to deal with social aspects, such as how to mingle and blend into the Australian working culture.

Mentors help culturally diverse leaders by providing them with career advice where needed. They can give career and psychological advice to enhance development. In addition, they often act as a sounding board and a listening ear.

Mentors can sit at all levels of the organisational hierarchy. Thus, they can assist aspiring leaders, although they may or may not have as much power and political clout to support career progress as a sponsor.

Mentors provide helpful career advice when needed. For instance, one leader, Fiona, benefited from debating career options with her mentors when deciding whether to stay or leave her firm.

'From a work perspective, I had some fantastic relationships with mentors', she reminiscences.

> I felt like I was the beneficiary of a lot of really good, positive, valuable mentoring. For whatever reason, people took an interest in me and my progress. There are always opportunities to leave the firm. But each serious prospect involved me talking to my mentors… drawing up lists of pros and cons and having long debates. And I just think that they have played an incredible role in my career in helping me navigate [it]. I would sit here and say that none of them have been regretted. So, the importance of having several people who, one can look to is not to be undervalued.

Mentors can also offer sound career advice on the 'rules of the game' – how to progress in the system to the next level. For instance, David's mentor gave him helpful advice, which assisted him to get buy-in from other partners for his promotion to partner. In David's firm, he needed to get written 'sounding' recommendations from other partners to support his promotion. Therefore, it was more beneficial for him to obtain as many positive soundings as possible.

'I remember that one of the final steps is to get sounding recommendations from the other partners. And when I did go to do soundings, because I'd been preparing for it for a year, I was able to actually get 35 soundings, [including] from each of the lines of service. And that, to his credit was because of my mentor, who actually told me you need to actually be thinking about this actively. And I had a clear

objective for the year to build those relationships with those other partners who genuinely want to give me a sounding', he remembers.

After culturally diverse leaders are promoted, mentors continue to
support them, with many of them remaining close personal friends.
Tony benefits from the advice of his mentors even today, even after they
left their firm. 'I was really lucky', he said.

> I had very senior partners who I think took [the] time to coach me from
> day one. Even today, I still keep in touch with them – I mean, they're still
> very good friends, and these are people who are probably 10 years older
> than me, at least. So, when I started as a graduate, they were partners;
> they were already senior partners.

Have supportive networks

Elizabeth benefited from having a supportive network of people who
guided her during her career.

> I've been quite privileged over my time to make good relationships with
> partners as well. And not just, you know, even as a senior con[sultant],
> or even as a con[sultant] or senior con[sultant], you know, I wasn't
> just dealing with managers. So, the importance of having that good
> relationship, and exposure with those, the bonding was really important,
> I guess, for me.

Having strong support networks across all levels of the organisation is
essential for culturally diverse leaders. In addition to sponsors, many culturally diverse leaders benefited from working with iconic leaders and
having role models who inspired them during their careers. However,
networks don't happen by themselves – successful leaders make an effort
to plan, dedicate time, and reach out to others.

Even after making it into leadership roles, in some organisations
building relationships with other leaders and maintaining friendships
was vital to surviving in a more political environment.

As a new partner, John soon learned that he needed 'to very quickly
[work out] who's legit, who is good for me to work with, [and] where
they're going to value me', as not every partner was willing to support
them. Amanda said, 'I think you have to have... senior people who have
your back, and who will support you in whatever environment'.

Be a team player

James, a business unit leader and an enthusiastic team sports player, applied lessons from his experience playing sports as a kid to his work. He started working with his firm at the age of eighteen, so he has known his colleagues for a long time. He feels that there are benefits in people knowing each other well.

As a leader, he values these long-term relationships even more today. 'Knowing a lot about them; they know a lot about you. And having been through a lot of ups and downs together, there's a lot of... inherent value in that', he stated. He collaborates extensively across his organisation, to the extent that work referrals from other parts of the firm to his business unit are his 'best client'.

Being a strong team player and collaborator is an essential skill for aspiring leaders throughout their careers. A number of the male leaders honed their team building and collaboration skills on the sports field during their high school days.

Be a people developer

Being a good people developer is also vital for culturally diverse leaders. Good leaders recognise the importance of having people that follow and support them to do their work well.

Mark recollected, 'I was a group manager. I had a very, very good group. [I] really looked after the people under my care and developed the reputation, I think of being a people person. And that helped enormously'.

Enhance business skills

> Culturally diverse leaders spend significant time developing and enhancing their business skills when adopting their professional and leadership identities.

Whilst early in their careers, technical skills were critical, as they progressed, acquiring business skills became more important to advance their careers.

Providing excellent client service and working with iconic clients was their path to success for some culturally diverse leaders, whilst others excelled at being specialists. Essential skills cited included solving complex problems, having the potential to build and grow a business, and strong communication skills.

Acquiring business skills can be challenging for people of minority backgrounds They often lack the social, economic, and cultural 'capital' required to succeed in leadership roles in specific industries and sectors at the beginning of their careers. For instance, studies have found that many accountants do not start as members of the upper echelons of society (Carter & Spence, 2014). To progress, they need to acquire cultural, social, linguistic, and economic capital to progress (Mueller et al., 2011; Carter & Spence, 2014). Many culturally diverse leaders developed their skills through being open to learning and taking risks.

Being reliable and trustworthy was one of the hallmarks of many leaders. As Angela commented, to be a good leader, you need to do everything well and have a good reputation. 'Do people see you as someone with integrity and somebody they can work with? And are you somebody who delivers?'

Yet beyond client service skills or business skills, senior leaders are often distinguished from managers in many organisations today by their dynamism rather than their technical excellence, client service or efficiency.

For those in PSFs, as they became more senior, leaders needed to refine and articulate their business case for promotion to partner. In addition, they had to prove that they could be a business leader and survive in the partnership system.

As Ian said,

It's all about the business case for you making partner. Can you actually win work, and [have you] got a proven track record for winning work? If you can't win work, they won't make you... If you do make it, you are going to struggle as a partner if you can't win work.

Being able to generate new revenue was even more vital for partners in PSFs, as 'partnership is very revenue-driven', noted Elizabeth. However, the focus moves more towards selling, not execution as a partner, which, as Amanda mentioned, as a partner, 'you're not meant to do the job, you're just meant to win the job'.

As Katrina Rathie added, 'to really succeed as a partner in a professional services firm, it's all about having deep relationships with your clients, and the strength of those'.

Chapter summary

- Successful culturally diverse leaders adopt a dynamic 'experimentation and learning career cycle' of identity work.
- They experiment with new things; build, enhance and maintain relationships with sponsors; build trusted relationships with others; and enhance their business skills. They take risks and create opportunities; merge and internalise the role; gain competence through exposure to different situations over time; and make sense of the system they have entered.
- Having access to sponsors as a 'secure base' is one of the most critical success factors affecting whether someone makes it to a leadership position.

Questions to ask yourself and your team members

Yourself

- What are some of the paradoxes and tensions I experience in my working life?
- How do I normally respond if I am asked to take on something new that I haven't done before? Why?
- Who are the sponsors I can turn to for advice and support? Do they collectively provide me with 'know-how' and 'know-whom' competencies?
- If someone were to describe me as a leader, how would they describe me?

Your team members

- How do we ensure that our aspiring culturally diverse leaders are given equal opportunities for stretch assignments which allow them to experiment and learn?
- How do we ensure that our aspiring leaders are more systematically given access to potential sponsors? How are sponsors

incentivised to sponsor culturally diverse talent through to leadership positions?

- How do we assist our aspiring culturally diverse leaders to have greater access to broader networks and relationships with people, both within and outside our organisation?

NOTES

1 According to the Australian Bureau of Statistics, in 2016 up to 3.55 million or 16.3% of the people resident in Australia who self-nominated their ancestries fell within the definitions of East Asian, South East Asian and Central and Southern Asian. This is the maximum proportion given that some respondents may have nominated two ancestries from the Asian geographical categories; 12.25% of the total population claimed one of the six ancestries of Chinese, India, Filipino, Vietnamese, Korean, and Sri Lankan (Asian Australian, n.d.). Further, of the 7.7 million people resident in Australia who were born overseas where the population resident in Australia is more than 100,000, the only non-European and non-Asian countries on the list were New Zealand, South Africa and the US. The residents of these other countries are likely to have backgrounds similar to those born in Europe (Demography of Australia, n.d.).

2 Refer to Appendix A for further details on my research background.

REFERENCES

Adam, H., Obodaru, O., Lu, J. G., Maddux, W. W., & Galinsky, A. D. (2018). The Shortest Path to Oneself Leads Around the World: Living Abroad Increases Self-Concept Clarity. *Organizational Behavior and Human Decision Processes*, 145, 16–29. https://doi.org/10.1016/j.obhdp.2018.01.002

Ang, J. (2019). *The Game Plan of Successful Career Sponsorship: Harnessing the Talent of Aspiring Managers and Senior Leaders*. Emerald Publishing. https://doi.org/10.1108/9781787562950

Asian Australian. (n.d). Retrieved December 23, 2021 from https://en.wikipedia.org/wiki/Asian_Australians

Carter, C., & Spence, C. (2014). Being a Successful Professional: An Exploration of Who Makes Partner in the Big 4. *Contemporary Accounting Research*, 31(4), 949–981. https://doi.org/10.1111/1911-3846.12059

Demography of Australia. (n.d.). Retrieved December 23, 2021 from https://en.wikipedia.org/wiki/Demography_of_Australia

Ibarra, H. (1999). Provisional Selves: Experimenting with Image and Identity in Professional Adaptation. *Administrative Science Quarterly*, 44(4), 764–791. https://doi.org/10.2307/2667055

Ibarra, H. (2004). *Working Identity: Unconventional Strategies for Reinventing Your Career*. Harvard Business School Press.

Ibarra, H. (2019, August 19). A Lack of Sponsorship Is Keeping Women from Advancing into Leadership. *Harvard Business Review Digital Articles*. https://hbr.org/2019/08/a-lack-of-sponsorship-is-keeping-women-from-advancing-into-leadership

Ibarra, H., Day, D. V., Petriglieri, G., & Wittman, S. (2014). Leadership and Identity: An Examination of Three Theories and New Research Directions. In D. V. Day (Ed.), *The Oxford Handbook of Leadership and Organizations* (pp. 285–301). Oxford University Press. https://doi.org/10.1093/oxfordhb/9780199755615.013.015

Jarrett, M., & Vince, R. (2017). Psychoanalytic Theory, Emotion, and Organizational Paradox. In W. K. Smith, M. W. Lewis, P. Jarzabkowski, & A. Langley (Eds.), *The Oxford Handbook of Organizational Paradox* (pp. 48–65). Oxford University Press. https://doi.org/10.1093/oxfordhb/9780198754428.013.2

Kets de Vries, M. F. R., & Cheak, A. (2016). Psychodynamic Approach. In P. G. Northouse (Ed.), *Leadership: Theory and Practice* (pp. 295–328). Sage.

Lewis, M. W. (2000). Exploring Paradox: Toward a More Comprehensive Guide. *The Academy of Management Review*, 25(4), 760–776.

Mueller, F., Carter, C., & Ross-Smith, A. (2011). Making Sense of Career in a Big Four Accounting Firm. *Current Sociology*, 59, 551–567. https://doi.org/10.1177/0011392111402734

Padavic, I., Ely, R. J., & Reid, E. M. (2020). Explaining the Persistence of Gender Inequality: The Work–Family Narrative as a Social Defense against the 24/7 Work Culture. *Administrative Science Quarterly*, 65(1), 61–111. https://doi.org/10.1177/0001839219832310

Petriglieri, G. (2020a). F**k Science!? An Invitation to Humanize Organization Theory. *Organization Theory*, 1(1), 1–18. https://doi.org/10.1177/2631787719897663

Petriglieri, G. (2020b). A Psychodynamic Perspective on Identity as Fabrication. In A. D. Brown (Ed.), *The Oxford Handbook of Identities in Organizations* (pp. 169–184). Oxford University Press. https://doi.org/10.1093/oxfordhb/9780198827115.013.22

Petriglieri, G., Ashford, S. J., & Wrzesniewski, A. (2018). Agony and Ecstasy in the Gig Economy: Cultivating Holding Environments for Precarious and Personalized Work Identities. *Administrative Science Quarterly*, 64(1), 124–170. https://doi.org/10.1177/0001839218759646

Petriglieri, G., & Petriglieri, J. L. (2010). Identity Workspaces: The Case of Business Schools. *Academy of Management Learning & Education*, 9(1), 44–60. https://doi.org/10.5465/amle.9.1.zqr44

Petriglieri, J. L., & Obodaru, O. (2019). Secure-Base Relationships as Drivers of Professional Identity Development in Dual-career Couples. *Administrative Science Quarterly*, 64(3), 694–736. https://doi.org/10.1177/0001839218783174

Smith, W. K., & Lewis, M. W. (2011). Toward a Theory of Paradox: A Dynamic Equilibrium Model of Organizing. *Academy of Management Review*, 36(2), 381–403. https://doi.org/10.5465/amr.2009.0223

Sveningsson, S. F., & Alvesson, M. (2003). Managing Managerial Identities: Organizational Fragmentation, Discourse and Identity Struggle. *Human Relations*, 56(10), 1163–1193. https://doi.org/10.1177/00187267035610001

Six

INTRODUCTION

Ming Long, a Non-Executive Director, has a formidable CV. She is the chair of AMP Capital Funds Management and a board director of six other organisations, including as the Chair of the Diversity Council Australia. Before that, she was joint managing director of Investa Property Group, CEO of Investa Office Fund and the first Asian-Australian woman to lead an ASX200 company. She has been recognised as a Member of the Order of Australia for her work.

But Long says it wasn't easy. 'Don't assume just because of where I am now that the obstacles don't exist', she said in an interview in 2021. 'They'll continue to exist for the rest of my career' (Yun, 2021).

She says she's never stopped turning cartwheels to fit in. 'It's a tightrope', she said in a 2016 interview.

> I feel like sometimes I'm doing this artistic gymnastic thing on this beam... I'm trying to do these triple spins etc. and stay on that tightrope. Getting into leadership, there is a sense you need to have people who want to work with you. That means you can't be yourself.
>
> (Reynolds, 2016)

This chapter explores how culturally diverse leaders undertake identity work – how they negotiate and construct their identities at work. What actions do they take that are less visible to others to succeed? I also investigate the importance of giving aspiring leaders access to sponsors and holding environments.

HOW DO CULTURALLY DIVERSE LEADERS NEGOTIATE THEIR IDENTITIES AT WORK?

As we discussed in Chapter 5, as identity work for leaders is a social and relational process, it can be destabilising, leading to experiences of uncertainty, confusion, and anxiety.

DOI: 10.4324/9781003291237-8

A key challenge of our modern-day working lives is that we need to learn to manage multiple paradoxes. Aspiring leaders experience numerous tensions and anxieties as their careers progress which arise from their roles/tasks, personal stresses, and pressures from the organisation. Further, as part of their leadership career transitions, they also experience increasing individual and group, system and organisational tensions in the liminal transition period between roles.

As a result, it is common for many leaders to experience a tension between being authentic and feeling like a 'fake' or an imposter (the 'possible-selves' model). Herminia Ibarra calls this the 'paradox of authenticity' (Ibarra, 2015).

For those who seek leadership roles in professional organisations, Ibarra has described their transition into leadership roles such as partner as psychologically challenging.

> At some point in their careers, every management consultant, investment banker, and accountant must attempt the leap from professional to partner. For some, it's an easy jump over the crevasse. They have learned what it takes to woo clients and keep them satisfied; they have learned to lead with confidence. But for most, it's a frustrating and confusing experience in which they arrive at the other side of the crevasse bruised and battered. Still others fail in the attempt and ultimately leave the firm broken.
>
> (Ibarra, 2000, p. 146)

Figure 5.2 illustrates that culturally diverse leaders first take visible steps in the workplace where they experiment (discussed further in Chapter 5), then second, a number of internal, less visible steps.

All identity changes involve periods when leaders experience tensions and anxieties. Aspiring leaders then learn to thrive by:

- Coping and adapting
- Reflecting and re-applying their learnings

This chapter explores the steps that aspiring leaders take to negotiate and manage their journeys. However, before doing so, it is worth taking a moment to understand how we think and behave when we experience anxieties.

HOW WE BEHAVE WHEN WE EXPERIENCE ANXIETIES

It is normal for all of us to experience some anxiety and stress when we face personal or organisational challenges such as taking on new roles. We may also experience survival or performance anxiety. Anxiety is interwoven with our human condition.

Amy Edmundson of Harvard Business School has described interpersonal anxiety as something that keeps us in a little cage of our own (Edmundson, 2021). It makes us feel that we cannot express ourselves or get the help we need. As a result, we may feel vulnerable, experience tension, worrying thoughts, and physical changes. We may then exhibit individual and group defence mechanisms and ambivalence as we seek to defend ourselves against these anxieties and gain control.

The concept of anxiety is fundamental to system psychodynamic theory and understanding organisational role dynamics.

Individual defence mechanisms

I once had a colleague, Tom, who by nature was a pleasant and friendly colleague outside of work. He was a technical specialist who prided himself on his work. However, as Tom got more senior and took on more significant management roles, he became even more entrenched in his ways. For example, staff would tell me how Tom would raise numerous review queries on their work on areas they felt were not relevant, which would take a long time to clear with him. He also developed a reputation for making insensitive and sometimes inappropriate comments to peers and favouring staff with certain types of backgrounds. At other times, he would be passive-aggressive. Finally, Tom would approach very senior leaders directly to raise matters without briefing his boss or other colleagues beforehand.

Does this story resonate with you? Do you have colleagues like Tom, who behave in similar ways under stress?

As adults, we all have unconscious, self-protecting defences that have their roots in our infancy. When we experience stresses and anxieties later in our lives, we sometimes unconsciously have regressive acts. These can alter our experiences of the absolute truth, providing us with a way of dealing with the situation, even if the actions may be inappropriate for the actual circumstance.

Defence mechanisms are sometimes described as 'psychological painkillers' – ways to protect ourselves when under attack. Like all painkillers, we need to take precautions when using them, such as not driving a car if a drug could make us tired. We also need to ensure that we don't become too overdependent on our medication (Kets de Vries et al., 2016).

Melanie Klein, a leading psychoanalyst, identified three different 'ego defensive mechanisms'. These are splitting, projection, and projective identification.

Splitting is sometimes called all-or-nothing thinking. When people *split*, they cannot cohesively hold opposing thoughts, feelings, and beliefs about themselves and others. To tolerate shameful, negative, or shadow emotional aspects of themselves, they categorise other people in black and white terms – either good or bad, idealised, or devalued. This makes it easier for them to manage the emotions that they are feeling. People with narcissistic personalities commonly use splitting.

Splitting often occurs together with *projection*, where people project their feelings onto someone or something else. Take the case of Matthew, a leader who feels inferior and has low self-esteem. He may project his feelings of not being good enough onto his junior staff member, Pamela.

Projective identification is where an individual receiving the projection identifies with it rather than rejecting it. Hence, both are unconsciously connected by the emotion or characteristics they share. An example of projective identification could be where Pamela resonated or identified with Matthew's projection. As a result, she feels inferior – and acts or feels in a way that combines both Matthew's projection and her feelings.

Other common defences include denial, repression, rationalisation, and intellectualisation (Table 6.1).

Table 6.1 Definitions of selected unconscious defence mechanisms

Defence mechanism	Definition and example
Denial	Refusing to acknowledge an unpleasant reality, such as feedback from a negative performance review
Intellectualisation	Avoidance and suppression of the emotional component of an event, using reason and logic to avoid uncomfortable or anxiety-proving emotions. For instance, if Bob was rude to Sally, Sally may rationalise that Bob was having a stressful day
Rationalisation	Distortion of 'the facts' to make an event or an impulse feel less threatening. As an example, if Daniel was passed over for a promotion, he might rationalise his disappointment by claiming that he didn't want as much responsibility in the first place
Repression	Blocking unpleasant encounters from recollection, such as painful memories

Source: Own research.

Defence mechanisms can also be exhibited in groups. One defence mechanism often shown by a group of individuals is scapegoating – denial by a group of individuals through projecting responsibility and blame on others. This allows the perpetrators to reduce negative feelings about themselves and provides them with a sense of satisfaction. In this case, the person blamed for the wrongdoings often ends up being removed from the group, as is frequently the case in politics.

Group behaviours/defence mechanisms

Imagine a situation where we have seen or felt suboptimal behaviours between group members, such as people building alliances, fighting, backstabbing, and mistrust. Or where the organisation feels lacklustre, has an atmosphere of fear or confusion, or never-ending gossip and drama. Sounds familiar?

We all have experienced groups or organisations with positive vibes and those that feel dysfunctional or even toxic.

In analysing human dynamics in groups, the psychoanalyst Wilfred Bion theorised that groups have two parallel modes of functioning. These are work and *basic assumptions*.

- *Work group mode* – In work group mode, members organise themselves and operate in line with the task that the group was set up to undertake. For most companies, this is to maximise productivity and, therefore, the company's shareholder value.
- *Basic assumptions group mode* – In basic assumptions mode, a group is driven by internal environmental anxieties about its psychological survival. Therefore, its members' behaviours are directed towards meeting the unconscious needs of its group members.

When a group is operating in basic assumptions mode, Bion suggests that group members mobilise three types of behaviours – *dependency, fight/ flight,* and *pairing*.

The most common of these group behaviours is *dependency*, where group members depend on a leader. In this case, the group's members unconsciously assume that the leader or an organisation can and should protect and guide them as their parents did in their childhood. These groups are goal-focused and cohesive – generally united by feelings of helplessness, inadequacy, neediness, and fear of the outside world. The individuals within them give up their independence, so they may not have their own points of view or take the initiative (Kets de Vries & Cheak, 2016).

Another typical group behaviour is the *fight/flight* assumption, where members fight or flee from a hypothetical enemy. These groups desire protection from and conquest of 'the enemy'. These groups are often competitive and split into camps of friends or foes (or even in-groups and out-group divisions). Its members exhibit aggression against peers, authority, avoidance, absenteeism, and resignation (Kets de Vries & Cheak, 2016).

According to Jon Stokes, professions can be viewed as 'social institutions' authorised to manage 'basic assumptions'. They allow professionals to retain a 'professional' unconscious connection with a feared emotion in a 'vicarious' way with their clients who are grappling with the same problem, but knowingly (Stokes, 2014).[1]

Ambivalence

Ambivalence has sometimes been described as being 'torn' – experiencing two opposing forces towards something. It can occur in individuals that face individual triggers, such as role conflict or membership dualities. It can also be prompted in organisations when there are contradictory goals and role conflicts. When people experience ambivalence, they sometimes exhibit denial and split. In organisations when people experience ambivalence, they use defence or coping mechanisms, including avoidance, domination, or compromise (Ashforth et al., 2014).

There isn't a great deal of specific research that applies these perspectives to diversity in organisations. However, a general view is that individuals tend to attach themselves to sameness, forming identity groups to reduce the anxiety arising from diversity and uncertainty, with 'racism and ethnocentrism being communal- or societal-level splitting and projection' (Foldy & Buckley, 2017, p. 271). Scapegoating is also a familiar dynamic in multi-racial groups. In teams and groups, individuals generally split and project in situations of anxiety stemming from diversity.

As such, the work of valuing (and managing) diversity relates to how constructive dynamics can replace inter-group diversity dynamics that can ostracise and minimise those with diverse backgrounds.

In summary, defence mechanisms influence several areas at work. These include leadership, culture, and identity dynamics (such as identification, identity work, and organisational identity), as well as a wide range of organisational behaviour issues such as resistance to change, power and politics, stress, organisational learning, and human resource management (Pratt & Crosina, 2016). It is essential to understand this as we examine how culturally diverse leaders manage their journeys to leadership.

EXPERIENCING TENSIONS AND ANXIETIES DURING CAREER TRANSITIONS

Work transitions are not easy. All leaders experience different challenges and pressures as their careers progress (Figure 6.1).

Aspiring leaders learn to manage their role and task anxiety, individual tensions, and individual vs collective tensions.

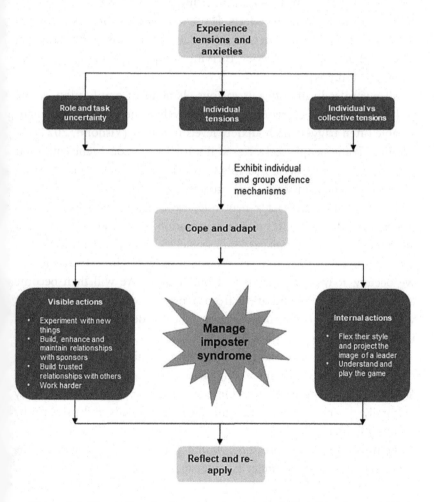

Figure 6.1 How culturally diverse leaders navigate their identity transitions
Source: Own research

Role and task uncertainty

In today's knowledge economy, many people face increasing tension and anxieties arising from their roles. This is particularly the case for people in knowledge industries as their work is inherently ambiguous. Frequently, it takes time to determine whether the output of their work is successful and to evaluate the quality of their work. As a result, they experience pressure to justify the value of their work (Empson, 2017).

This uncertainty can arise early in their careers. Ian, who started work in a Big 4 firm, relished life as a new graduate, especially the camaraderie. 'The socialising aspect was good because you earn a good income. You work hard and you party hard at night, so that was really good. I really enjoyed that', he recollects. However, he didn't always enjoy the work, admitting that at times, 'I had no idea what I was doing – ticking, making photocopies, deliveries, carrying computers – all of that wasn't enjoyable' [laughs].

All our roles in life offer us various elements of gratification, stress, and risk. However, everyone is different. What one person finds manageable often triggers high anxiety levels in others (Visholm, 2021). In addition, some people feel stressed if a role is not consistent with their fantasy of what they wish that role to be. This leads them to use various 'defence' mechanisms to manage anxiety.

To reduce the stress of a new role, we can join the organisation's informal social system to provide gratification or incorporate aspects of an authority figure (manager) into ourselves through identification. If there is a fit between us and the role, and we internalise part of the role we occupy, it will become part of our identity. We will then become a member of the organisation from a psychological sense. However, when a fit doesn't occur, and we cannot use our defences, our role stress increases over time (Czander, 1993).

As culturally diverse leaders became more senior and took on more challenging work, their increasing demands created further anxieties. Determined and motivated to achieve success through promotion, many culturally diverse leaders cope with heavy workloads and pressure by working harder.

At times, the work pressures would get to them. Kate recalls the pressure she put herself under as a manager to get promoted.

> He had a performance discussion with me, or counselling discussion
> [as] people call it... I still recall that day I burst into tears; that's how hard

I work. And burst[ing] into tears is not tears of joy that I feel I deserve it. Rather, I knew I would get it as I had never had a doubt on that. But I guess it's the emotion... the pressure I put on myself.

Individual tensions

Aspiring culturally diverse leaders also experience stress adapting to the expected professional or leadership identity.

Several leaders spoke about feeling tensions between their personal and organisation's values. While some coped by building up relationships with others, others worked hard. A few appeared to hide or repress their emotions.

At thirty-two, a time when many are seeking to accelerate their careers and simultaneously manage their family commitments, when I asked the leaders to draw themselves in their work roles, several drew pictures of themselves stressed at work or in situations where they were reflecting on what was important to them. Some appeared a bit more stressed and emotionally distant during our discussions. Several male leaders also mentioned that becoming a father was a life-changing experience for them as 'parenting is probably one of the most difficult jobs in the world and yet, there is no manual for it' (Stewart). Others expressed heightened tension between fitting in and being authentic, such as Julie, who felt 'brain-scream' and that she was 'selling her soul'.

Another example was shared by Kim, a partner in a Big 4 firm. She personally felt that partners were expected to show entrepreneurial drive as a personal value rather than growing the collective, an expectation that made her feel somewhat uncomfortable.

There is this idealistic view of what a professional is. Here the words that come to mind [are] 'hungry' in the market, 'entrepreneurial' and all these attributes, which are, I think, you know, good attributes. But it describes a certain type of person who I don't think that I am. I might be in a different way... So, seeing those kinds of attributes get put on a pedestal above other attributes, which I think are just as valuable but maybe not as visible like that.

One of the growing and popular areas of academic research in more recent years is authentic leadership. Authentic leaders are generally leaders who are profoundly aware of how they think and behave. At the same time, others perceive them as being mindful of their own and others' values/moral outlooks, knowledge, and strengths. They are also positive, resilient, and of high moral character.

Herminia Ibarra however, argues that authenticity is a paradox and that feeling like a fake can signify growth. Further, she believes that we often latch onto authenticity as an excuse for sticking with what is comfortable, which few jobs allow, limiting leaders' growth and impact (Ibarra, 2015). She has written about how this impacts the psychological journey of professionals to partnership:

> Unfortunately, aspiring partners are in a Catch 22: They are expected to act like partners before they have the competencies and client relationships-in short, the credibility-to actually do so. They are also in the difficult position of having to change their view of themselves-where they fit in with the firm and how they can contribute. They must speak and act with confidence as representatives of their firms and as peer advisers to more senior, experienced managers. In short, they must assume a new and different professional identity, a change that can be a wrenching, self-questioning experience.
>
> It is an experience made worse by the fact that most junior professionals take the leap to senior roles without much formal guidance from their organization. They fly solo. They improvise. For most, therefore, the transition process feels random and erratic, and the criteria by which they are judged, amorphous. Unguided, some take wild stabs at what they think acting like a partner entails. Others take an inordinately long time to discover what it takes to become truly effective. Frustrated, they may eventually assume they are just not right for the job and seek other employment opportunities. Many firms have lost precious talent in just this way.
>
> Of course, some professionals stick with it, and most of them ultimately develop a new but genuine identity as a partner. But even for those individuals, the journey is still trying, for in the midst of it, most individuals question their authenticity. They struggle with the "fake it till you make it" approach they feel obliged to adopt as a stopgap measure. They struggle with issues of integrity. Indeed, there are few professional transformations quite as psychologically complex as the transformation to partner.
>
> (Ibarra, 2000, p. 147)

Individual vs collective tensions

Many culturally diverse leaders also feel tensions between their individual and collective selves. This is common for partners in professional services firms (PSFs) who seek to balance their own identity, meet their revenue targets, and be part of the collective. As a result, a few pondered whether they should change themselves to adapt to the expected organisational identity.

On this tension, David explained the challenge of being a member of a Big 4 partnership and contributing individually as a partner simultaneously. He remarked,

> There is a lesson around that collegiate nature... the firm takes it as given [that] if you haven't achieved the client metrics, you will never make it. But then there's a secondary dimension, that's probably the other learning – you can't just be good at your work, you have to be good at being part of the firm.

Several leaders who are partners also experienced survival anxiety due to the high-performance culture of their firms. As Ben, a partner in a Big 4 firm, mentioned, it's the 'client pressure, and its internal pressure... financial pressure meeting your KPIs'. Chris added,

> You've got certain privileges as a partner. And that comes with earning that partnership. But you know, if you don't continue to demonstrate value to the firm, [do] not bring in the right amount of work, [do] not [look] after your people, or stuff something up, you're gone.

Ben stated,

> I think a lot of the pressure comes from myself. I've got high expectations of myself. So, a lot of the pressure does come from myself. But a lot of the pressure comes from clients. You know, 'I sent you an email six hours ago, why haven't you replied to me' sort of stuff.

Others, such as Sarah, indicated that becoming a partner was not what they expected. Some of the other partners she worked with experienced survival anxiety and projected their fears onto her. She said,

> I just think that everyone's just too busy trying to look after themselves. And when I actually turned to the other partner that I've supported as a director for ten years, and asked him for help, he pretty much (this is exactly what he) said to me – "I've got my own problems".

Once they became more senior leaders, they had to deal with increased politics. Elizabeth described how she felt like as a partner.

> I'm a partner now... you've got a lot to learn, you go again, and you start from the bottom, and actually, it's way more political than you could ever think of, because the incomes are directly related to the escalation of the scale.

Individual and group defence mechanisms exhibited

As a result of their work tensions and anxieties, culturally diverse leaders exhibit various individual and group defence mechanisms – these increase as they progress towards leadership.

Professionals in PSFs who advise their clients frequently experience role and task anxiety. This is because they are expected to be 'containers' for their clients' fears and solve their complex problems (Shongwe & Cilliers, 2020). Containment is defined as creating a safe, reliable environment that enables the expression of strong emotions and impulses (Kahn, 2001). Unfortunately, some believe this often leads professionals psychologically to develop professional detachment and repress or deny certain feelings (Hirschhorn, 1989; Stokes, 2014).

As aspiring leaders progressed and constructed their leadership identities, they showed more individual social anxieties, such as status anxiety (Gill, 2013) or a fear of rejection. As Amanda noted, 'It's a big crowd... you have to somehow stand out in some shape or form'. A typical individual defence was that many of them unconsciously projected an image as a partner, with others mirroring and reinforcing it as legitimate.

Finally, the leaders exhibited group defences arising from the system pressures on them, which we will discuss further in Chapter 7. Partners in PSFs described experiencing increased competition, politics and fighting with peers for client business and revenues. The period before they became senior leaders was not easy for some as they were now competing against their friends, as was the case for Rebecca. 'So, there was an element of for me, you know... these are my peers, these are my friends'.

LEARNING TO THRIVE

What can we learn from culturally diverse leaders who took the leap, made it across the crevasse and survived? Here are the actions that culturally diverse leaders take to navigate their career journeys.

Culturally diverse leaders find ways to cope and adapt to the individual and group tensions and anxieties they face at work. This involves enhancing relationships with others, working harder, and pushing themselves. They also cope and adapt by flexing their style, projecting the image of a leader, and understanding and playing 'the game'. However, sometimes they experience imposter syndrome.

Culturally diverse leaders adopt various strategies to cope with and adapt to anxieties and tensions during their career transition. The most common was enhancing relationships with others, such as through networking (as discussed in Chapter 5), working harder, and pushing themselves.

A particular challenge for many culturally diverse leaders when they started work was how to build relationships in the workplace. Angela highlighted that a challenge for her was that Australians are very enthusiastic about their sport. 'In the workplace, there's a lot of talk about rugby league and cricket, which aren't sports that I'm into. So, I [had] to find other ways to connect with people', she said.

After starting work, Peter quickly learned important conversations were taking place at the pub after work. If he didn't make an effort to go, he would miss out on the discussions. So, he made an effort to join them and seek to fit in.

Becoming a leader requires a social and relational process of experimentation and internalisation, moulding behaviours in line with group prototypes, and getting validation from followers. In addition, career progression requires people to learn how to cope and adapt to their various identity changes as they become more senior and take on leadership roles.

For some such as Tony, a Big 4 partner on making it to partnership, 'it was very much what I expected. I was working with the same people, so overnight, nothing changed'.

For others, it was the start of another new and unknown journey for others, such as Ian, which was not what they expected it to be. 'It's like you are starting out again, you're at the bottom of the rank, and you go, 'Well, now what do I do? How do I get to the next level of partnership?'', he said.

Others recognised that they changed after taking senior leadership positions. One example was Paul's wife, who told him, "You totally changed into a different person".

Flexing their style and projecting the image of a leader

A common way for culturally diverse leaders to cope and adapt was to learn to flex their style and project themselves as a leader.

Peter found that 'listening, understanding an organisation and then trying to work from within [how] to change it and move yourself forward' worked well in his career.

As they got closer to becoming senior leaders, some culturally diverse leaders experimented with their appearance and self-promoted themselves, to ensure that others recognised them as leaders. For those working in PSFs, the 'tournament model' requires professionals to have a positive outlook, differentiate themselves from others, and self-promote themselves. At times, they adopted a more a masculine model of success.

David, who was one of these leaders, shared one of the ways he learned how to cope and adapt. As he said,

'You have to fit in, you have to look, sound and dress like... call it 'them' – the other partners. And that is something that I learned in my partnership journey... I would actually wear a suit. Especially if you look physically different from others, then you have to use all the tricks in the world to make yourself look like them'.

However, for some, this made them feel uncomfortable.

Others were able to cope by adapting – like a 'chameleon' – like Greg, a skill he learned as a young adult in Australia. He shared how he managed this.

I'm very comfortable just walking through a room, and I don't know anyone, and I'll just go and introduce myself to someone and talk to them. [I'm] very comfortable engaging with them. I do find it tiring because I'm not naturally an extrovert. So, if I do it for a prolonged period of time, I do have to come home and kind of, you know, cocoon and recuperate. But I do have absolutely the ability to do it.

Katrina Rathie, Non-Executive Director and former Partner in Charge, King & Wood Mallesons, Sydney agrees that leaders need to project themselves as leaders. They need to be confident to be their authentic selves but understand that the Western leadership style requires visibility, presence and gravitas in the market.

> So, I've never been great at managing up, but I've always felt that you've got to get in the game, you've got to engage in politics, and you've got to do a bit of self-promoting. If you're not promoting yourself, someone else will be promoting themself. In the Western world, as they say, the squeakiest wheel gets the grease, so you will find that people will promote themselves to others... It's really awful if they're promoting themselves at your expense. I'd say, don't sit there quietly and be a bystander,
>
> (Rathie, 2020)

Understanding and playing the game

As they become more senior, leaders learn to handle various institutional power relations and politics at work. They recognise that informal promotion factors and politics could inhibit career progression. The strength of and extent of influence of these power relations varies depending on the size and complexity of the organisation. Leaders in PSFs were more likely to mention that the path to leadership was subjective and impacted by bias, politics, and power plays than leaders working in other sectors.

Some academics suggest that aspiring partners in PSFs need to know how the hierarchy operates, how to impress stakeholders (including those outside the firm) when building their personal brand, and to respect the rules and engage with the game if they are to be awarded the freedom and individual autonomy to operate as a partner (Coffey, 1994; Anderson-Gough et al., 2001; Cohen, 2015). Those who adopt professional 'habitus' (or the feel for the game) are most successful at 'playing the game' and are more likely to be absorbed and live by it (Lupu & Empson, 2015).

Katrina Rathie agrees that leaders need to be 'in the game' and part of the action to succeed in leadership roles. In an interview with Professional Development Forum, she shared,

> I always used to be of the view that if you did your best work, that people would figure that out and that you'd be rewarded. But I found that sadly, that is not always the case, and that life is full of politics and people that do play the game... You've got to be in the game to be part of the action.
>
> (Rathie, 2020)

Managing imposter syndrome

Having a flexible style didn't always alleviate the anxieties of culturally diverse leaders, particularly if they felt that they had been over-promoted and were out of their league. Sometimes this led them to experience fear, as they felt like an imposter, as was the case for Michael. He shared about his experience as a partner:

> It's weird because I still feel a great sense of an imposter syndrome, which many of us do, but I also feel a responsibility too – and I wrestle with this, right? Am I the token Asian? Or am I someone who is successful and has a responsibility to be a role model to others who might be looking up, like I did many years ago saying, "I don't see myself in the partnership."

The term 'imposter syndrome' generally describes an internal feeling of fraudulence in areas of success and development. Although traditionally identified in women, it also can be exhibited by men. Often people who suffer from it think that they don't deserve` their success, it was not achieved through genuine ability but was accidental, or they worked harder than others. People who suffer from imposter syndrome are frequently anxious about being exposed for their 'phoniness' and are critical of their work and performance.

For some leaders, family is one of the biggest influences on whether they feel imposter syndrome. This is particularly the case for those from dysfunctional families whose parents are overinvested in achievement and lack human warmth, who often produce children prone to neurotic imposture. As a result, they often become insecure overachievers over time (Kets de Vries, 2005).

While many believe that imposter syndrome is a curse, author Naomi Shragai suggests that a fear of success also underlies the syndrome. For instance, some people may unconsciously feel guilty about having a better life than their parents or people who look after them. This survival guilt can often hold people back (Shragai, 2021).

Reflect and re-apply

Culturally diverse leaders reflect on what they have learned from their experiences and re-apply their learnings to their work.

Culturally diverse leaders take the time to reflect on their experiences, then learn and apply these learnings to their future endeavours.

When he experienced setbacks, or things didn't go to plan, Vivek Bhatia, CEO and Managing Director of Link Group used the opportunity to understand and learn what he could have done better. 'I always go to the decision-maker and say, "could I have done something differently", and have an open mind'.

One thing he learned was to be positive about the experience.

> The one thing that I make sure that I don't do is to go into victim mentality mode. Because it is really easy to point the finger at someone else and say, "Oh, just because of that person or it's because of this circumstance, that I didn't get the opportunity." Because then, what you're doing is you're going into prisoner mode where you are putting yourself as a prisoner of circumstance.

He added, 'I strongly believe that individuals need to take ownership of their own situation, which means [that they should] learn from mistakes… [do] not worry about the uncontrollable but focus on what you can do differently' (Layton, 2021).

On the need to continue experimenting and learning, Kate added,

> If you don't have the mindset of continuous learning growth and be willing to put your heart and soul into what you do and feel that meaning and fulfilment, I think probably the pressure, and all would overtake you'.

Peter added, 'my key is always to take all opportunities and learn as much as you can'.

Attributes they learned included being resilient, having mindset control, and having a positive attitude. In addition, these experiences taught them new perspectives, made them more self-aware, and reinforced their values. Examples included being aware of their strengths and what they needed to work on.

Self-management and sensemaking are frequently found to be essential parts of career progression, particularly in professional organisations (Grey, 1994; Bévort & Suddaby, 2016). Self-management is the ability to manage your emotions, particularly in stressful situations, and maintain a positive outlook despite setbacks. Sensemaking is the process by which people give meaning to their experiences.

After becoming senior leaders, many reflected on how far they had come, how far they should embrace the stereotypical leader identity, how to balance their work and personal lives, and how to give back to the next generation of Asian-Australians. They were more comfortable and relaxed with who they were as individuals. Most enjoyed their independence, freedom, and control in their leadership roles. As Andrew, a senior Big 4 partner remarked, 'I've got control over what I do, I feel like I'm… at last actually really good at everything I do, and I feel like I've got everything in equilibrium'.

THE CRITICAL ENABLER – SECURE AND SAFE BASES

How aspiring culturally diverse leaders step up into leadership positions, negotiate identity conflicts, and manage their anxieties in the liminal state varies significantly. Frequently, self-esteem and relationship support protect individuals from these anxieties.

One aspect that stood out to me was that I sensed that some culturally diverse leaders could contain (or repress) their emotions better than others. In these cases, they were not impulsively or outwardly emotional but would seek collaborative input from others and work hard to overcome the challenges they faced. Those who can contain their emotions through invisible boundaries such as team silos (Cilliers & Greyvenstein, 2012), or have a secure family base outside of work and have the capacity to reflect, manage their anxieties better. However, those who can't contain their emotions are more likely to exhibit individual and group defence mechanisms.

Having access to sponsors as a 'secure base' is one of the most critical aspects of whether someone makes it to leadership. However, not all leaders had access to sponsor or mentor relationships. Those with less access generally had a more difficult journey into leadership roles.

There has been increasing recognition that access to 'transition spaces' and 'holding environments' facilitates professional and personal transitions that support identity transitions in recent years. This recognises that not all social settings are equally favourable for developing leaders' identities (Ibarra et al., 2014).

Developed by Donald Winnicott in 1965, the holding environment construct was initially created to describe the nature of effective caregiving relationships between mothers and infants and eventually between individuals and organisations (Kahn, 2001).

A 'holding environment' is a 'social context that reduces disturbing effects and facilitates sense making' (Petriglieri & Petriglieri, 2010, p. 50), allowing both 'containment' and 'interpretation' as well as safety and protection. 'Containment' is the ability to internally manage troubling throughs, feelings, and behaviours – the contained – that arise so that they can be worked with.

Employers should create inclusive 'holding environments' to better support the leadership development of their aspiring culturally diverse leaders. However, they need to recognise that the needs of employees will differ depending on how they react in situations of stress.

Allowing aspiring leaders access to 'felt security' through holding environments requires employers to support them in two areas. These are access to sponsors, mentors and coaches, and leadership development programmes.

Access to sponsors, mentors, and coaches

Giving aspiring culturally diverse leaders access to sponsors, mentors and coaches is vital to supporting career progression.

In times of stress, they provide aspiring leaders with a secure holding environment that encourages them to try new things (Kahn, 2001).

One aspect that some leaders said was critical in supporting their development was having a leadership coach. These are coaches from outside their organisation who help them achieve their goals and become more effective leaders. In addition, to support their progression, coaches were instrumental in assisting leaders to be more aware of their vulnerabilities in their roles. One example cited by an interviewee was helping them overcome a fear of looking stupid if they spoke up in meetings where there were many people and how to overcome them.

Rebecca didn't have any problems developing her business case for promotion to partner. However, she said that having a personal coach really supported her in learning more about herself. She was fortunate that a partner mentor suggested that she do a session with his personal coach to help her understand more about herself and what was important to her. 'It was amazing. He broke me down', Rebecca said.

Her coach helped her to realise that authenticity was vital both at work and personally for her. She said,

> As long as you tell your story in that way, people can really connect with you. And I think that's so true for personal connections, but also for business and work. If you can really connect to people, then that's how you know you build rapport, how you build that network of people, and a one-on-one connection, where people feel like they can trust you and talk to you about things, including their work problems, their business problems. So, for me, that was a huge, huge revelation.

James was in a different situation. He got a coach at a time when he was asked to take on a significant new role. As a result, he used to speak to his coach frequently on various matters, which he found beneficial.

'I really adopted that learner side of things because I was in such a vulnerable position as a new leader of a team, not only just with my staff but within the firm', he shared. He still speaks to his coach from time to time today.

Access to leadership development programmes

Second, there is a role for investing more in leadership development programmes for aspiring leaders. This provides them with an environment of psychological safety and allows them the time and space to learn and reflect.

Some of the leaders I spoke to said that such programmes were in place when they became leaders. However, unfortunately, some organisations have since stopped them.

Elizabeth, who did a leadership development course before becoming a partner, found that it was instrumental in helping her understand more about herself and how to step up as a leader. 'I think that a lot about the development course... [was] around understanding who you are as a person and what you value. I swear to God, without that, I wouldn't be where I am right now', she revealed. The course helped her to understand how her early life experiences shaped her.

Chapter summary

- Early in their careers, culturally diverse leaders learn to deal with role and task anxieties and balance paradoxes. As their careers progress, they experience increasing individual, group, system, and organisational tensions and anxieties.
- How aspiring leaders negotiate their new roles, deal with identity conflicts, and manage these anxieties in the liminal transition period varies significantly. Leaders who can contain their emotions and have the capacity to reflect manage their anxieties internally better.
- To better support the leadership development of aspiring culturally diverse leaders, employers need to create 'holding environments' that allow them the time and space to reflect and develop. They also need to recognise that individual employees' needs differ depending on how they react to stressful situations.
- Employers should give aspiring leaders greater access to sponsors, mentors, and coaches and increase their availability to leadership development programmes.

Questions to ask yourself and your team members

Yourself

- If I am under stress, what are some of the behavioural patterns I am more likely to exhibit? What type of activities trigger them?
- How am I likely to react when I feel anxious in a group at work?
- Do I take the time to reflect, sensemake, and re-apply my learnings at work?
- How can I better support aspiring leaders that work for me by giving them the time to reflect, learn and sensemake during their career journeys? Are they given equal access to executive coaches and leadership development programmes?

Your team members

- How would we describe our team or organisational dynamics, especially when we are under stress? Do we tend to default to certain types of group defences, such as dependency or fight/flight? Or even ambivalence?

NOTE

1 © 2015, from Defences against anxiety in the law, by J. Stokes in D. Armstrong & M. Rustin, *Social Defences Against Anxiety: Explorations in a Paradigm*. Reproduced by permission of Taylor & Francis Group, LLC, a division of Informa plc. This permission does not cover third party copyrighted work which may appear in the material requested. User is responsible for obtaining permission for such material separately from this grant.

REFERENCES

Anderson-Gough, F., Grey, C., & Robson, K. (2001). Tests of Time: Organizational Time-Reckoning and the Making of Accountants in Two Multi-national Accounting Firms. *Accounting, Organizations & Society,* 26(2), 99–122. https://www.sciencedirect.com/science/article/abs/pii/S0361368200000192

Ashforth, B., Rogers, K., Pratt, M., & Pradies, C. (2014). Ambivalence in Organizations: A Multilevel Approach. *Organization Science,* 25(5), 1453–1478. https://doi.org/10.1287/orsc.2014.0909

Bévort, F., & Suddaby, R. (2016). Scripting Professional Identities: How Individuals Make Sense of Contradictory Institutional Logics. *Journal of Professions and Organization,* 3, 17–38. https://doi.org/10.1093/jpo/jov007

Cilliers, F., & Greyvenstein, H. (2012). The Impact of Silo Mentality on Team Identity: An Organisational Case Study. *SA Journal of Industrial Psychology,* 38, 1–9. https://doi.org/10.4102/sajip.v38i2.993

Coffey, A. J. (1994). 'Timing Is Everything'; Graduate Accountants, Time and Organizational Commitment. *Sociology,* 28(4), 943–956. https://doi.org/10.1177/0038038594028004009

Cohen, L. (2015). Interplay of Professional, Bureaucratic, and Entrepreneurial Career Forms in Professional Services Firms. In L. Empson, D. Muzio, J. Broschak, & B. Hinings (Eds.), *The Oxford Handbook of Professional Services Firms* (pp. 351–373). Oxford University Press. https://doi.org/10.1093/oxfordhb/9780199682393.013.19

Czander, W. M. (1993). *The Psychodynamics of Work and Organizations.* The Guildford Press.

Edmondson, A. (2021, December 20). Psychological Safety in Theory and in Practice. *The Anxious Achiever.* https://hbr.org/podcast/2021/12/psychological-safety-in-theory-and-in-practice

Empson, L. (2017). *Leading Professionals: Power, Politics, and Prima Donnas.* Oxford University Press. https://doi.org/10.1093/oso/9780198744788.001.0001

Foldy, E. G., & Buckley, T. R. (2017). Reimagining Cultural Competence: Bringing Buried Dynamics Into the Light. *Journal of Applied Behavioral Science*, 53(2), 264–289. https://doi.org/10.1177/0021886317707830

Gill, M. (2013). Elite Identity and Status Anxiety: An Interpretative Phenomenological Analysis of Management Consultants. *Organization*, 22(3), 306–325. https://doi.org/10.1177/1350508413514287

Grey, C. (1994). Career as a Project of the Self and Labour Process Discipline. *Sociology*, 28(2), 479–497. https://doi.org/10.1177/0038038594028002007

Hirschhorn, L. (1989). Professionals, Authority, and Group Life: A Case Study of a Law Firm. *Human Resource Management*, 28(2), 235–252. https://doi.org/10.1002/hrm.3930280209

Ibarra, H. (2000, March). Making Partner: A Mentor's Guide to the Psychological Journey. *Harvard Business Review*, 78(2), 146–155. https://hbr.org/2000/03/making-partner-a-mentors-guide-to-the-psychological-journey

Ibarra, H. (2015, January). The Authenticity Paradox: Why Feeling Like a Fake can be a Sign of Growth. *Harvard Business Review*, 93(1–2), 52–59. https://hbr.org/2015/01/the-authenticity-paradox

Ibarra, H., Day, D. V., Petriglieri, G., & Wittman, S. (2014). Leadership and Identity: An Examination of Three Theories and New Research Directions. In D. V. Day (Ed.), *The Oxford Handbook of Leadership and Organizations* (pp. 285–301). Oxford University Press. https://doi.org/10.1093/oxfordhb/9780199755615.013.015

Kahn, W. A. (2001). Holding Environments at Work. *Journal of Applied Behavioral Science*, 37(3), 260–279. https://doi.org/10.1177/0021886301373001

Kets de Vries, M. F. R. (2005, September). The Dangers of Feeling Like a Fake. *Harvard Business Review*, 83(9), 108–116. https://hbr.org/2005/09/the-dangers-of-feeling-like-a-fake

Kets de Vries, M. F. R., & Cheak, A. (2016). Psychodynamic Approach. In P. G. Northouse (Ed.), *Leadership: Theory and Practice* (pp. 295–328). Sage.

Kets de Vries, M. F. R., Korotov, K., Florent-Treacy, E., & Rook, C. (2016). *Coach and Couch: The Psychology of Making Better Leaders* (2nd ed.). Palgrave Macmillan.

Layton, G. (2021, July 28). The Inner Chief in 204. Vivek Bhatia, CEO of Link Group, on Lifelong Learning, Going Beyond Your Job Description, and Having Your Antenna On. https://theinnerchief.libsyn.com/204-vivek-bhatia-ceo-of-link-group-on-lifelong-learning-going-beyond-your-job-description-and-having-your-antenna-on

Lupu, I., & Empson, L. (2015). Illusio and Overwork: Playing the Game in the Accounting Field. *Accounting, Auditing & Accountability Journal*, 28, 1310–1340. https://doi.org/10.1108/AAAJ-02-2015-1984

Petriglieri, G., & Petriglieri, J. L. (2010). Identity Workspaces: The Case of Business Schools. *Academy of Management Learning & Education*, 9(1), 44–60. https://doi.org/10.5465/amle.9.1.zqr44

Pratt, M. G., & Crosina, E. (2016). The Nonconscious at Work. *Annual Review of Organizational Psychology and Organizational Behavior and Human Decision Processes*, 3, 321–347. https://doi.org/10.1146/annurev-orgpsych-041015-062517

Rathie, K. (2020, October 8). *Woman of Influence: In Conversation with Katrina Rathie* [Interview]. Professional Development Forum. https://www.youtube.com/watch?v=GG5QLuPXli0

Reynolds, E. (2016). Asian-Australians 'Can't Be Themselves' If They Want to Succeed. *News.com.* https://www.news.com.au/finance/work/careers/asianaustralians-cant-be-themselves-if-they-want-to-succeed/news-story/265a6aedb58893fe9563d3dc6f3fb69a

Shongwe, M., & Cilliers, F. (2020). The Systems Psychodynamic Experiences of Professionals Appointed in Acting Capacities. *South African Journal of Industrial Psychology,* 46, 1–9. https://doi.org/10.4102/sajip.v46i0.1785

Shragai, N. (2021). *The Man Who Mistook His Job for His Life: How to Thrive at Work by Leaving Your Emotional Baggage Behind.* Penguin.

Stokes, J. (2014). Defences Against Anxiety in the Law. In D. Armstrong (Ed.), *Social Defences Against Anxiety: Explorations in a Paradigm* (pp. 222–235). Routledge. https://doi.org/10.4324/9780429480300

Visholm, S. (2021). *Family Psychodynamics in Organizational Contexts.* Routledge. https://doi.org/10.4324/9781003164913

Yun, J. (2021, March 8). The Bamboo Ceiling 2021: The 'Double Whammy' Asian Women Face in Their Careers. *Yahoo Finance.* https://au.finance.yahoo.com/news/bamboo-ceiling-iwd-2021-023047411.html

Seven

INTRODUCTION

I find it fascinating to learn how prominent organisations shaped the early career experiences of successful C-suite leaders who worked for them.

One of these organisations is McKinsey, whose alumni include Sundar Pichai of Google, Sheryl Sandberg of Facebook, Jane Fraser of Citigroup, and James Gorman of Morgan Stanley.

Another is Citibank, which has been the training ground for many successful bankers worldwide, particularly in Asia-Pacific, and has a strong history of international mobility. Its alumni include Piyush Gupta, Group CEO of DBS Bank in Singapore.

Similarly, speak to the alumni of many large professional services firms (PSFs) or technology firms. They will speak fondly of their early experiences in these organisations and the networks of friends they started working with. Intriguingly, people working in a sector can tell which company someone started their career at. It's similar to how we often know which high school or university someone attended without asking them.

Are certain people attracted to particular organisations, or does the organisation 'mould' a person in a certain way? I actually think it is a bit of both.

Up to this point, I have mainly focused on how culturally diverse leaders take up leadership roles in organisations – in other words, an inside-out perspective.

This chapter will recap identities in organisations, explore 'institutional illogics', and how they influence culturally diverse leaders' experiences on their career journeys.

HOW DO ORGANISATIONS IMPACT THE CAREER JOURNEYS OF ASPIRING CULTURALLY DIVERSE LEADERS?

After holding senior roles in business, Emma was recruited by the Australian arm of a global services organisation to be its Chief Operating

DOI: 10.4324/9781003291237-9

Officer in her early 30s. 'They embraced my Asian background, as well as being younger and female – they actually wanted that profile in the management team'.

Instead of feeling the need to conform to corporate norms, Emma became more open about expressing her culture 'This was probably the first moment where I really started to embrace who I was in the workplace and use it as a real advantage, and an asset, rather than it be something in the background.'

She credits her husband and male boss for their strong support and encouragement. Further, she also realised that embracing workplace diversity requires more than just policies.

> Not only do you need, from a policy setting perspective, no discrimination and [to] have open policies, you need strong mentors and support from leaders... You need people to actively encourage you, [and] to embrace who you are. It's got to be strong and proactive, not just "we don't discriminate against anyone".

*****

Organisations undoubtedly have a considerable impact on the career journeys of aspiring leaders.

Having the right organisational culture that embraces diversity and inclusion helps aspiring culturally diverse leaders thrive in their organisations.

However, in more challenging corporate cultures, aspiring leaders need to learn how to manage their individual and group anxieties when managing their identity transitions.

For instance, some culturally diverse leaders I spoke to split/projected in situations of anxiety, describing someone negatively compared to themselves. Others described group defences – sharing that they did not enjoy having to fight with colleagues for revenue and staff – and ambivalence. Finally, a few felt that they were made scapegoats by partners 'past their use-by date', who split off and projected feelings of inadequacy and vulnerability (Stokes, 2014)[1] onto them.

Realising that there are few culturally diverse leaders, many became passionate and motivated to increase their firms' cultural diversity or to be a role model to young staff – possibly, if unconsciously, to reduce anxiety – such as Helen, who said, 'throughout my journey… I think that what actually drives me [is] to be successful and to be a role model for them'. Others sought a secure base among their culturally diverse peers and networks. As a result, some felt somewhat isolated or even left their firm.

The extent to which leaders 'internalised' the system they worked in varied depending on the organisation they worked for.

The internalisation of the system was relatively strong for Big 4 firm partners. By way of illustration, on thriving in chaotic situations, one Big 4 partner I spoke to said, 'that's because I've become that person through the environment. I don't know whether I was always that – I'm not sure'.

For the Big 4 partners who joined their firms early in their careers and 'grew up' in the system, I sensed that they generally understood how the partnership system operated. They recognised that they had to work within the system. Several flagged that other partners 'in the club' were skilled at gaming the system – this thought possibly being a defence mechanism (Visholm, 2021). In contrast, others who joined a PSF directly as partners had different views of the system and questioned the 'pedestal' upon which junior staff members put partners.

One explanation for the experiences across these different groups was that junior staff members often internalise the Big 4 firm system identity through 'introjected identification' (Stokes, 2014, p. 234).[2] This may be due to the 'associative unconscious' (Long & Harvey, 2013, p. 7), where thoughts are social rather than individual and can override an individual's autonomy in a system. I sensed that PSF professionals who remain in the PSF system could balance their individual and organisational identities. Those who struggle to maintain this balance typically leave their organisation.

So, what could be leading to these varied experiences in organisations? Institutional illogics help us to answer some of these questions.

EXPERIENCES IN THE SYSTEM – THE INFLUENCE OF INSTITUTIONAL ILLOGICS

In earlier chapters, we observed that identity work had become more challenging as our working lives have become more fluid.

Accordingly, identity work has become an increasing area of interest by researchers who have explored areas such as personal engagement, growth, authenticity, and organisations as permanent or temporary settings that allow people to define themselves at work (Petriglieri et al., 2018).

Many studies that explore identity work examine it through the lens of SIT, and highlight that people pursue self-esteem and protection from social anxiety through their identification with an organisation. Another group of scholars, with a more critical lens, have focused on 'organisations' exploitation of members' existential anxiety to impose identities that promise to keep it at bay' (Petriglieri et al., 2018, p. 127). Other researchers have explored how organisations confer social identities on their employees yet constrain the expression of personal ones; and how psychological safety helps employees express themselves at work and craft their desirable selves (Petriglieri et al., 2018).

With this context, I investigated the experiences of culturally diverse leaders at work. I examined leaders' encounters, which allowed me to understand the rational side of how institutions operate and the unconscious elements, referred to as 'institutional illogics'.

But, before discussing this further, it is worth briefly recapping some of the critical assumptions of the systems psychodynamics approach as applied to organisations.

System psychodynamics – a recap

The systems psychodynamic perspective focuses on the interplay between the management of emotions and tasks. It helps us to understand inter- and interpersonal dynamics.

Like individuals, organisations being groups of people, experience unconscious anxieties, which they try to defend themselves against.

There are three main concepts to grasp here. First, there are unconscious dynamics linked to the emotional impact of organisational roles and relations. Second, 'social defences' are created by organisations to manage their painful anxieties and fears. Lastly, there is an unavoidable interaction between emotions and power relations (Vince, 2019).

So, what are 'institutional illogics'?

Most of us have been in a group situation where the actions of other individuals didn't make sense, given our knowledge of them individually.

The way individuals behave in systems is often due to 'institutional illogics', a term coined by Russ Vince of the University of Bath.

Institutional illogics explain how dynamics can shape people's lives in organisations beyond reason. It also explores how these underlying forces are embedded in the social structures of organisations (Vince, 2019).

Vince defines two types of 'logics' within organisations, which he describes as two opposite sides of a coin. They are:

- Institutional logics – the 'rules of the game' that both regularise/normalise behaviour and provide opportunities for agency and change.
- Institutional illogics – the underlying unconscious forces that have both structuring and disturbing influences on the 'rules of the game'. These underlying assumptions can be defensive, deceptive, or irrational despite feeling normal (Vince, 2019).

Illogics operate at the interface between a person and an organisation. They are a vital part of our lived experience of institutions. To cope with these stresses that we feel and understand, we defend ourselves against these organisational anxieties and unknowns and consciously and unconsciously create fantasies through how we relate to others.

Illogics can be identified through language slips, projective relations, and irrational practices. In addition, they can be captured through visual methods (such as drawings), storytelling), and researcher fantasies and imaginative interpretation to pinpoint key themes (Vince, 2019).

It is essential to learn to accept and relate to unconscious dynamics within an institutional setting to understand our relationships within organisations.

HOW DO CONTEXT AND SYSTEMS AFFECT US AT WORK?

Applying a systems theory lens helps us understand the context in which behaviours occur in the workplace.

Systems theory explores how systems relate to each other within more extensive and more complex systems. Together with psychodynamics, it allows us to bring emotions alongside reason as a vital source of understanding.

If we take a step back, we all operate in various social systems. Each system has its own boundaries, and people have authority (whether formal or informal) to take on roles with them, and tasks. These include our family, local community, and country. Each of these systems has its own cultures, languages, and rules. We generally fit in, and there are certain expectations of us.

These systems both simultaneously influence and constrain our personal development through various conscious and unconscious rules, cultural patterns and networks (such as schools, work, and other social groups) that push and pull us (Long, 2016a).

Similarly, the place where we work (our work system) is set up for a purpose. This typically is to produce goods or services – bringing together our personal needs and desires and the needs and desires of others. Thus, a system's purpose generally relates to its (external) context.

Connecting with an organisation through our role supports our pursuit of self-esteem and protects us from social anxieties. It ideally provides us with an environment of psychological safety where we can express who we want to be and shape who we want to become through our 'identity work'. We feel proud to be associated with the organisation.

However, as most of us spend so much of our time at work, it can shape and even constrain our identity work.

The influence of the primary task on workplace dynamics

Reflecting on organisational cultures and using the analogy of Star Wars, why do some organisations have a Jedi-like philosophy of wisdom, kindness, and patience? And how can our organisations avoid succumbing to a Sith culture based on fear, arrogance and anger, and organisations that produce clones of themselves?

All organisations are set up with a particular primary task influenced by the external environment. This is generally the organisation's task to survive (Petriglieri & Petriglieri, 2020). For instance, most large organisations' primary task is to generate cash and create value for their shareholders.

Each employee has a role that supports the primary task. A leader's role is to discern and articulate the purpose of the system within its context (the why). This allows its members to know why they do what they do (Long, 2016a; Roberts & Bazalgette, 2016). Management's role is to achieve the system's primary task, including managing the individual and group tensions within the system.

Nevertheless, individual employees within organisations sometimes believe, consciously or unconsciously, that their organisation has other primary tasks. The influence of different stakeholders – such as regulators, investors, and customers – on company employees to focus on more than just shareholders – may be a key reason why some leaders and managers today find it challenging to achieve the organisation's primary task.

When an organisation's members disagree on its primary task, it is frequently believed to lead to a primary risk or anxiety (Hirschhorn, 1999). This guides people to act differently and exhibit basic assumptions behaviours, such as dependency and fight/flight responses which we discussed in Chapter 6.

Many organisations in today's increasingly complex and boundaryless world operate in environments with anxieties.

Case study – the influences on the primary task of banks

Banks sometimes have a challenging time managing their various stakeholders, including shareholders, customers, and regulators. Unfortunately, some banks face more challenges such as rogue trading, mis-selling, and money laundering incidents than others.

Traditionally, the primary task of a bank was to borrow and lend money and keep customer money safe. However, management and stakeholders may not all have the same views on the purpose of a bank. For instance, shareholders may want the bank to maximise its shareholder value and/or distribute high dividends. In contrast, governments may expect banks to serve the underbanked. In addition, regulators may expect banks to satisfy other requirements, such as preventing money laundering or providing sustainable finance.

Further, some employees may feel more aligned to the primary task of their business units, such as increasing market share. In contrast, other individuals may be focused on maximising their own bonus, influenced strongly by their personal motivation needs.

(Continued)

As a result, banks, their boards, leaders, and employees are often subject to informal unconscious assumptions and beliefs. These influence how the bank acts, perceives, and feels through its representatives (Long, 2016b), and its projections enacted through basic assumptions thinking, group-think or informal psychodynamic roles (Visholm, 2021). In other words, the collective emotions of the board members, leaders, and employees influence their behaviours.

This can become complicated when many leaders simultaneously wear multiple 'hats' in a matrix structure, such as a team leader, professional, and industry role. The different contexts in which various business units operate may also lead to variations in the behaviours between the employees in other business areas; how private bankers think and act is very different to investment bankers. This will then be moderated by how individuals are incentivised and motivated.

To contain the anxieties, organisations employ 'social defences' – ways to protect themselves from various fears, which I will explain shortly.

All organisations have some defensive features that provide them with a sense of stability. Yet, as groups have naturally regressive forces, the people in them tend to cling to familiar routines, structures, narratives, and attachments that provide meaning and belonging (Jarrett, 2021).

These defences can induce conformity and limit the organisation's ability to transform and change (Petriglieri & Petriglieri, 2020). People in organisations often collectively have hidden competing commitments – 'big assumptions' that are deeply ingrained opinions about themselves and the world around them (Kegan & Lahey, 2001). Moreover, in some corporate cultures, individual defence behaviours such as self-protection, denial, splitting, and projection become the norm. Outsiders are often blamed and become scapegoats.

Michael Jarrett of INSEAD argues that even if such patterns are recognised, they may not be easy to erase. Awareness training or tactical changes may make situations more bearable but won't address a culture's deep basic assumptions.

He contends that political correctness can become a substitute for genuine change and that formalised training programmes can undermine long-term change. Without appropriate interventions, continued defensive patterns fuelled by anxiety and threats of change can restrict our ability to think in more humane ways. They may instead elicit unconscious feelings and thoughts. This can further increase stress, lead to interpersonal and intergroup conflicts, reduce workplace productivity, stifle creativity, and reinforce dysfunctional relationships (Jarrett, 2021).

The more complex an organisation is, the more likely its members will have different views on its primary task. This may increase the social defences it puts into place to protect itself, and lead to basic assumptions behaviours being exhibited. This is common in hierarchical or matrix organisations, where silos may exist, creating boundaries between members and teams.

In summary, organisations can be viewed as 'the source for and container of people's emotional experiences of work' (Petriglieri et al., 2018, p. 127), shaping how they are expressed.

UNCOVERING INSTITUTIONAL ILLOGICS

Institutional illogics can be exposed through understanding three interrelated dynamics: social defences, disavowed assumptions, and structuring fantasies (Vince, 2019).

We can use Vince's framework to understand how institutional illogics play out in organisations by analysing the experiences of aspiring culturally diverse leaders.

The impact of social defences at work

The influence of the system visibly affected the behaviours of culturally diverse leaders as they become more senior and move into leadership positions.

As they progressed towards partnership, some of the partners in Big 4 firms felt like they needed to remain on the 'treadmill' to compete and be promoted. If they didn't, they thought that they would not be valued. This arose from the influence of the apprenticeship and tournament models.

Further, after making it to partnership, some partners continued to feel stressed as 'the pressure is relentless' (Jenny). Some partners thought they were starting at the bottom again, such as Kim: 'The mountain is after you get through – that's the mountain, it's not the admission process'.

Others expressed concerns about juggling the competing needs of clients, staff, firm, family, and their own interests. The leaders were increasingly subject to the pressure of group system dynamics beyond their control (Long, 2016b).

Jenny, who has held senior roles both in and outside of Big 4 firms, described her partner experiences as challenging. 'I refer to it as like mental gymnastics; [it] mentally challenged me more than any of my other roles'.

Why was this the case? I sense that the leaders were feeling the impact of the social defences put in place by their organisations. Let me explain this further.

Every system has a life of its own – sometimes called its group, organisational or societal culture (Long, 2016a).

In companies, corporate culture is generally defined as the pattern of shared unspoken beliefs and behaviours that guide how employees perceive, think, and feel in relation to various organisational external and internal interactions.

Suppose that we were to think about the corporate culture of an organisation we have worked in. We would tend to focus on its artifacts (the visible organisational structures and processes) and its espoused values (the strategies, goals, and philosophies). However, corporate culture also includes its (basic) underlying assumptions. These are the unconscious, taken-for-granted values, perceptions, ideas, and feelings that are ultimately the source of values and behaviours in an organisation (Schein, 2009). If we were to imagine an organisation's culture as an iceberg, its assumptions would be the significant hidden (and immovable) elements below the water's surface.

Organisational culture is an essential element of any organisation, aligning its overall vision to its performance. Every organisation feels different due to its culture, even if it has a similar mission, strategy, operations, products, or services as other organisations. For example, compare your experience shopping at Lululemon and Nike. Both sell some similar products. However, the 'smell of the place' – as the late Sumantra Ghoshal has described culture, are very different.

Leaders in high-performing organisations play an essential role in managing the practices, behaviours, and competencies they want of their people. They need to balance their performance and people as their organisation's key asset.

A challenge of corporate cultures today is that their strong focus on performance can create inner conflicts that are difficult to resolve. Aideen Lucey believes that 'the superficiality of the performance culture is a significant aspect of social defence systems in contemporary organizations, creating a kind of systematic blindness' (Lucey, 2014, p. 221).

To manage the tensions and protect themselves from anxieties, leaders and managers put in place various social defences or unconscious organisation-level defence mechanisms against anxiety (Krantz, 2010). These are group and organisational structures and processes organised at an unconscious level designed to protect employees from fears in their tasks.

Case study – social defences in PSFs

PSFs are paradoxical,[3] so they are controlled through various processes (Empson, 2017). A balance they need to manage is to allow their professionals to feel that they have a relatively high level of autonomy and independence, yet implement strategies that enable them to manage the paradoxes they face.

As a result, PSFs implement social defences to help manage their organisations. These include socialisation, structures, systems, and their legal structures form. They include:

- *The apprenticeship model.* The foundations of many PSFs started with the apprenticeship model. This is a socialisation process whereby junior professionals observe partners and managers, and learn appropriate technical, interpersonal skills, and the 'rules of the game'. When recruiting staff, firms consider their short-term productivity needs and look for future partners (Cohen, 2015). Various 'controls' such as time-sheets, financialisation, and mentoring lead professionals to internalise these rules in pursuing their careers (Grey, 1994). Reporting lines are also hierarchical. The work of many professionals is procedural and subject to significant regulation.
- *The tournament 'up-or-out' model of promotion.* While not used by all firms, the tournament model ensures the stability and robustness of the

(Continued)

partnership. The remuneration packages of younger professionals tend to be lower, increasing as they become more senior (Cohen, 2015). The model, however, increases the personal survival anxiety of both partners and aspiring leaders – the fear of not surviving in the organisation. How a professional's value is recognised is often translated into the amount of revenue they earn, the number of chargeable hours they bill or their salary and bonus. This fear sometimes increases anxieties about being good enough.

- The 'partnership ethos'. The partnership ethos is a philosophy that exists within PSFs and seeks to balance partners' individual and collective interests. When partners talk about what partnership means to them, they will generally refer to the 'ethos'. As owners of firms, partners have a clear imperative to maximise their individual autonomy. However, as partners, they also have a financial imperative to operate collectively and mentor and support each other personally and professionally. This inevitably leads to tensions among the partners between those who prefer to focus more on individual interests and those who believe the focus should be on collective pursuits (Empson, 2007). Therefore, various mechanisms are put in place to balance the paradoxical interests of the individual partners and the partnership as a collective. This includes the partner remuneration process, which aligns individual and collective interests (Stokes, 2014; Empson, 2017)[4] and seeks to balance rewarding long-term loyalty and shorter-term performance.

Some believe that this 'regulation' of workers' identities to conform with the norms of the organisation (Cohen, 2015) leads professionals to subsume their own identity in the profession and the organisation and form new occupational identities as their careers advance (Costas & Grey, 2014; Empson, 2017).

Social defences can help support organisational wellbeing and bring individuals together as a collective.

However, while social defences protect organisations, they also can inadvertently increase the pressures within the organisation, leading to regressive behaviours, such as splitting, projection and denial. In addition, these obstacles can modify the organisation's ability to accomplish tasks and adapt to change.

Further, their extensive use can lead to unintentional consequences when anxiety levels rise. While social defences help people understand who they are, they can also lead people to *avoid* understanding their own underlying feelings (Petriglieri & Petriglieri, 2010). These anxieties can be exacerbated when there are insufficient opportunities to discuss and work issues through.

Social defences sometimes present themselves as symptoms of complex organisational problems (Armstrong & Rustin, 2014), the nature and origin of which individuals may not understand (Lucey, 2014). For instance, the traditional 'system-wide' working identity of PSFs that demands that people conform with the system or quit is not necessarily aligned with increasing their organisational diversity.

Could diversity initiatives create illusions?

Irene Padavic, Robin Ely, and Erin Reid (Padavic et al., 2020) demonstrated that organisational arrangements to support greater diversity sometimes reinforce dominant discourses. They found that, in a PSF, the work-family narrative sustained workplace inequality. Their study uncovered how the firm's policies and practices enacted unconscious social defences that hampered women's advancement. However, *everyone* believed the illusion that work-family balance was a woman's problem rather than a casualty of the firm's gruelling 24/7 work culture.

Disavowed assumptions

Defences can increase power relations and patterns of domination in organisations.

Making an explicit link between unconscious dynamics and power in institutions helps us understand whether and how certain values or assumptions may be denied (or 'disavowed') but continue to impact an organisation's behaviours. This is because unconscious dynamics and political values can lead to irrational practices. An example is that the psychological contract between employers and employees is linked to the interests of the powerholders (Vince, 2019).

Power dynamics can be more challenging in multicultural groups than in homogenous ones due to historical context leading to differences in privilege and marginalisation (McRae & Short, 2010).

While I did not address power relations directly as part of my research, it was evident from the leaders that these unconscious dynamics influenced their organisations. For instance, some thought that some leaders benefit more than others from being part of the inner circle or the 'club', and by understanding and playing the game – 'I think if you're politically active as a partner, you probably have a few more safeguards', said one PSF partner.

Structured fantasies

'Fantasy' describes how the unconscious is collectively expressed in organisations, as well as its structuring or political effects.

According to Vince, these are ideas that are personally or politically useful to hold people together in groups. They help explain how a person's inner world is linked to both organisational and institutional structures of conformity or control. People invest in fantasies that allow them to maintain functional order yet contain and limit the emotional intensity within systems (Vince, 2019).

An example could be the collective view of an organisation's members' ideal 'organisation in the mind', which I explored in Chapter 4.

WHAT SHOULD YOU WATCH OUT FOR WHEN IMPLEMENTING DIVERSITY INITIATIVES?

Organisations play a powerful influence on our identities at work. We, in turn, also affect the organisations we work in.

When we think about organisational dynamics, we often focus on what we can see. However, frequently people exhibit individual defence mechanisms and group basic assumption behaviours such as fight/flight or dependency. When these ways of dealing with challenges become the norm in organisations, they can become dysfunctional and emotional.

In today's globalised, technological age with fewer boundaries in organisations, anxieties are increasingly prevalent in organisations and employees. Many of them arise because of their organisation's focus on performance, which has been exacerbated by crises such as COVID-19.

Whilst organisations may feel that it is appropriate to put into place new policies and procedures to manage these external anxieties, they can inadvertently hinder organisations from making the critical changes they need to be agile and innovative in the future. Further, certain initiatives such as increasing the cultural diversity of leadership may conflict with the organisation's primary task. Leaders responsible for diversity initiatives need to be aware of these dynamics when planning change programmes that support greater leadership diversity.

Further, aspiring leaders need to learn how to manage themselves in work systems. The challenges they will experience may not necessarily relate to dealing with task and role-related pressures (although these are extensive). Instead, they will relate to managing the tensions between themselves and their work systems.

A helpful exercise undergoing organisational change is to obtain data on the views of leaders, managers, and employees to understand their unconscious perspectives of their organisations.

Chapter summary

- Organisations strongly influence the group and individual behaviours of individuals who work in them. Consequently, the extent to which an individual internalises an organisational identity can affect their career experiences.
- Individuals at work need to balance various paradoxical tensions (including individual and collective interests, harmony and conflict, insecurity, and confidence) and manage their anxieties.
- Organisations have their own pressures and unconscious dynamics that have both structuring and unsettling effects on how they operate.
- As people in organisations often have different opinions on the primary task of an organisation, they act in different ways, sometimes unconsciously. These 'institutional illogics' can arise from social defences, disavowed assumptions, and structured fantasies within organisations.
- Career progression can be an emotional experience, depending on how individuals cope with the system pressures. Institutional illogics may also inhibit organisations from making the critical changes they need to make to be agile and innovative in the future.
- Organisations need to consider these dynamics when planning their diversity initiatives. Aspiring leaders also need to learn to manage themselves given these work dynamics.

Questions to ask yourself and your team members

Yourself

- How would I describe the culture of my organisation? To what extent does it focus on performance elements (such as competitiveness, results-orientation, and stakeholder management) vs people matters (such as respect, trust, teamwork and learning environment)? How does the culture support (or hinder) fostering culturally diverse leadership?
- How has my organisational system influenced my professional identity at work? How did it make me feel and act?

Your team members

- How would our people describe the culture of our team/organisation, particularly its values and basic underlying assumptions? How strong is our culture?
- What is the primary task of our team/organisation? To what extent do we agree (or disagree) on the task?
- What is really taking place in our team or organisation 'below the surface'?
- How do power relations play out in our team/organisation and influence its dynamics?
- What are some of the 'embedded' processes and protocols that influence our employees' thinking and working in our team/organisation? To what extent do these help or hinder our organisational culture change?

NOTES

1 Copyright © 2015, from Defences against anxiety in the law, by J. Stokes in D. Armstrong & M. Rustin, Social Defences Against Anxiety: Explorations in a Paradigm. Reproduced by permission of Taylor & Francis Group, LLC, a division of Informa plc. This permission does not cover third party copyrighted work which may appear in the material requested. User is responsible for obtaining permission for such material separately from this grant.
2 Copyright © 2015, from Defences against anxiety in the law, by J. Stokes in D. Armstrong & M. Rustin, Social Defences Against Anxiety: Explorations in a Paradigm. Reproduced by permission of Taylor & Francis Group, LLC, a division of Informa plc.

This permission does not cover third party copyrighted work which may appear in the material requested. User is responsible for obtaining permission for such material separately from this grant.

3 Paradoxes that PSFs face include autonomy and control, individual and collective interests, harmony and conflict, insecurity and confidence, and ambiguity and clarity (Empson, 2017).

4 Copyright © 2015, from Defences against anxiety in the law, by J. Stokes in D. Armstrong & M. Rustin, Social Defences Against Anxiety: Explorations in a Paradigm. Reproduced by permission of Taylor & Francis Group, LLC, a division of Informa plc. This permission does not cover third party copyrighted work which may appear in the material requested. User is responsible for obtaining permission for such material separately from this grant.

REFERENCES

Armstrong, D., & Rustin, M. (2014). Extreme Work Environments: Beyond Anxiety and Social Defence. In L. Hirschhorn & S. Horowitz (Eds.), *Social Defences Against Anxiety: Explorations in a Paradigm* (pp. 189–212). Routledge. https://doi.org/10.4324/9780429480300

Cohen, L. (2015). Interplay of Professional, Bureaucratic, and Entrepreneurial Career Forms in Professional Services Firms. In L. Empson, D. Muzio, J. Broschak, & B. Hinings (Eds.), *The Oxford Handbook of Professional Services Firms* (pp. 351–373). Oxford University Press. https://doi.org/10.1093/oxfordhb/9780199682393.013.19

Costas, J., & Grey, C. (2014). The Temporality of Power and the Power of Temporality: Imaginary Future Selves in Professional Service Firms. *Organization Studies*, 35(6), 909–937. https://doi.org/10.1177/0170840613502768

Empson, L. (2007). Your Partnership – Surviving and Thriving in a Changing World: The Special Nature of Partnership. In L. Empson (Ed.), *Managing the Modern Law Firm: New Challenges, New Perspectives* (pp. 10–36). Oxford University Press.

Empson, L. (2017). *Leading Professionals: Power, Politics, and Prima Donnas*. Oxford University Press. https://doi.org/10.1093/oso/9780198744788.001.0001

Grey, C. (1994). Career as a Project of the Self and Labour Process Discipline. *Sociology*, 28(2), 479–497. https://doi.org/10.1177/0038038594028002007

Hirschhorn, L. (1999). The Primary Risk. *Human Relations*, 52(1), 5–23. https://doi.org/10.1177/001872679905200102

Jarrett, M. (2021, March 22). The Darker Side of Organisational Life. *INSEAD Knowledge*. https://knowledge.insead.edu/blog/insead-blog/the-darker-side-of-organisational-life-16306

Kegan, R., & Lahey, L. (2001, November). The Real Reason People Won't Change. *Harvard Business Review*. https://hbr.org/2001/11/the-real-reason-people-wont-change

Krantz, J. (2010). Social Defences and Twenty-First Century Organizations. *British Journal of Psychotherapy*, 26(2), 192–201. https://doi.org/10.1111/j.1752-0118.2010.01173.x

Long, S. (2016a). The Transforming Experience Framework. In S. Long (Ed.), *Transforming Experience in Organisations: A Framework for Organisational Research and Consultancy* (pp. 1–14). Routledge. https://doi.org/10.4324/9780429484254

Long, S. (2016b). The Transforming Experience Framework and Unconscious Processes: A Brief Journey Through the History of the Unconscious as Applied to Person, System and Context with an Exploratory Hypothesis of Unconscious as Source. In S. Long (Ed.), *Transforming Experience in Organisations: A Framework for Organisational Research and Consultancy* (pp. 29–106). Routledge. https://doi.org/10.4324/9780429484254

Long, S., & Harvey, M. (2013). The Associative Unconscious. In S. Long (Ed.), *Socioanalytic Methods: Discovering the Hidden in Organisations and Social Systems* (pp. 3–22). Routledge. https://doi.org/10.4324/9780429480355

Lucey, A. (2014). Corporate Cultures and Inner Conflicts. In D. Armstrong (Ed.), *Social Defences Against Anxiety: Explorations in a Paradigm* (pp. 213–221). Routledge. https://doi.org/10.4324/9780429480300

McRae, M. B., & Short, E. L. (2010). *Racial and Cultural Dynamics in Group and Organizational Life: Crossing Boundaries.* SAGE Publications, Inc. https://doi.org/10.4135/978145 2274751

Padavic, I., Ely, R. J., & Reid, E. M. (2020). Explaining the Persistence of Gender Inequality: The Work–Family Narrative as a Social Defense Against the 24/7 Work Culture. *Administrative Science Quarterly*, 65(1), 61–111. https://doi.org/10.1177/00018392198 32310

Petriglieri, G., Ashford, S. J., & Wrzesniewski, A. (2018). Agony and Ecstasy in the Gig Economy: Cultivating Holding Environments for Precarious and Personalized Work Identities. *Administrative Science Quarterly*, 64(1), 124–170. https://doi.org/10.1177/ 0001839218759646

Petriglieri, G., & Petriglieri, J. L. (2010). Identity Workspaces: The Case of Business Schools. *Academy of Management Learning & Education*, 9(1), 44–60. https://doi.org/10.5465/ amle.9.1.zqr44

Petriglieri, G., & Petriglieri, J. L. (2020). The Return of the Oppressed: A Systems Psychodynamic Approach to Organization Studies. *Academy of Management Annals*, 14(1), 411–449. https://doi.org/10.5465/annals.2017.0007

Roberts, V. Z., & Bazalgette, J. (2016). Daring to Desire: Ambition, Competition, and Role Transformation in "Idealistic" Organisations. In S. Long (Ed.), *Transforming Experience in Organisations: A Framework for Organisational Research and Consultancy* (pp. 135–153). Routledge. https://doi.org/10.4324/9780429484254

Schein, E. H. (2009). *The Corporate Culture Survival Guide – New and Revised Edition.* Jossey-Bass.

Stokes, J. (2014). Defences Against Anxiety in the Law. In D. Armstrong (Ed.), *Social Defences Against Anxiety: Explorations in a Paradigm* (pp. 222–235). Routledge. https://doi.org/10.4324/9780429480300

Vince, R. (2019). Institutional Illogics: The Unconscious and Institutional Analysis. *Organization Studies*, 40(7), 953–973. https://doi.org/10.1177/0170840618765866

Visholm, S. (2021). *Family Psychodynamics in Organizational Contexts.* Routledge. https://doi.org/10.4324/9781003164913

Eight

INTRODUCTION

When I studied economics at university, and even when I did my MBA, the critical underlying assumption of all our studies was that people at work are rational. As a result, many ideas about how the world operated were explained using simple charts, formulae, and frameworks.

Mind you, I did my MBA nearly twenty years ago, when many current ideas on leadership development and organisational behaviour were less developed. As a result, my studies didn't help me understand the dynamics of my organisation and my clients. Instead, I was more likely to learn about work dynamics from reading *Dilbert* or watching *Yes Prime Minister*.

As employees, the work stress we experience increases as we move up the career ladder. Some of us cope better than others. As a partner in a Big 4 firm, I found that the work dynamics I had to deal with were highly demanding. While I was a competent client service partner leading major assignments for clients, I also had to learn how to survive in the partnership.

Many Big 4 firm partners I spoke to felt that becoming a new partner was like starting from scratch again. As Ian told me, 'It's like you are starting out again – you're at the bottom of the rank, and you go, "Well, now what do I do? How do I get to the next level of partnership?"' What they were referring to wasn't that they couldn't handle their clients' work. Instead, it was pressure from dealing with the various stresses of being a leader and balancing this with different and sometimes dysfunctional group dynamics as both a senior professional and a business owner.

How we navigate our careers frequently differs from our colleagues even though we have undergone similar journeys.

This chapter introduces the psychological concept of attachment theory which helps explain why the experiences of career progression of leaders differ.

DOI: 10.4324/9781003291237-10

HOW WE RELATE TO EACH OTHER – ADULT ATTACHMENT STYLES

When seeking to understand how culturally diverse leaders succeed, I was intrigued by the views of Laura Empson of Bayes Business School at the University of London, who researches professional organisations. Her book, *Leading Professionals: Power, Politics and Prima Donnas* was reviewed by the *Financial Times* in 2017 in an article with a catchy headline that suggested that many professionals are 'insecure overachievers' (Hill, 2017). An overachiever always discounts their success and keeps searching for more.

I could relate to the concept of insecure overachievers from my professional life in a Big 4 firm. I worked extremely long hours throughout my career, was efficient, and prided myself in providing superb service to my clients. However, I always felt that I was not good enough – and I was regularly disappointed with my annual performance rating. So, after being fascinated with the article, I quickly ordered her book and devoured it from cover to cover.

Empson suggests that insecurity in professional organisations arises from the interaction of three forms of insecurity – professional, organisational, and individual. She believes that insecurity is inherent in the kinds of people attracted to the challenges and status of elite professional organisations. Further, she highlighted that elite professional organisations might amplify professional insecurities, with many grappling with imposter syndrome. Insecure achievers often work in medicine, engineering, academia, professional services, consulting, and investment banking (Empson, 2017) – all professions that many culturally diverse leaders work in.

According to Manfred Kets de Vries, some insecure overachievers are from dysfunctional families. Their parents are overinvested in achievement and lack human warmth. This often produces children prone to 'neurotic imposture' – who suffer from 'imposter syndrome' or 'feeling like a fake' (Kets de Vries, 2005).

So, I wondered – is it true that partners in professional services firms (PSFs) are insecure achievers? Does a person's security type help to explain the puzzle around how culturally diverse leaders succeed in leadership?

In the case of Ben and Michael, the successful partners in PSFs I introduced in Chapter 1, could their styles and paths to leadership have been influenced by their security styles? I decided to explore this further.

What is attachment theory?

Attachment theory, one of the best-established psychological theories of relationships, guided my research. Initially used to understand the bond between infants and their caregivers, John Bowlby's well-known theory of attachment – that individuals seek emotional ties with an attachment figure – has been used to explain how people observe, respond to, and manage stress from interpersonal interactions (Mikulincer & Florian, 1995) through internalised working models.

In his theory, Bowlby described the dynamics of interpersonal attachment as an attachment behavioural system. This innate psychological system prompts us to seek support from others in times of need. Our attachment behavioural system regulates how we select, activate, and terminate our behaviours to attain protection and support from others (Mikulincer & Shaver, 2009).

Key propositions of attachment theory

1. *Our attachment behavioural system is activated by perceived threat or stress.* This prompts various emotional and relational responses to regulate the sense of threat. If we receive social support as 'felt security' in response to stress, deactivation occurs. However, if help is absent or inconsistent, our attachment behavioural system can become hyper-activated or suppressed.
2. *Our early relationship with our caregivers leads us to develop internal working models of relationships, our attachment style.* Attachment styles are cognitive-affective (beliefs and emotional) representations of self and others in interactions that are formed from our early caregiving relationships. They can shift over time with regular exchanges with other adults (Yip et al., 2018).

Our attachment styles simultaneously reflect two distinct working models – self and others. Our working model of self is our belief of self-worth in receiving support from others. In contrast, our working model of others is our belief concerning the openness and availability of other people in times of need.

Traditionally, attachment styles have been used to explore close relationships, such as romantic partners. However, applied to workplace scenarios, these have been found to predict people's feelings and behaviours towards their work and employment relationships. They also help to explain the extent to which individuals can cope with stress in the workplace (Richards & Schat, 2011; Johnstone & Feeney, 2015).

Taking Bowlby's idea of working models, Mary Ainsworth subsequently defined attachment styles initially as either secure or insecure (Ainsworth et al., 2015). She found that children generally form a secure attachment when their caregiver is trustworthy. However, when their caregiver is unpredictable or rejecting, they may develop an insecure attachment. For the latter, children adopt one of two possible patterns:

- *Avoidance* – where they minimise contact with their caregiver, reflected in discomfort with closeness and dependency; or
- *Anxious* – where they submissively cling to their caregiver and feel worried about potential rejection and abandonment.

How do I determine my adult attachment style?

We can use numerous models to determine our adult attachment style. These generally involve three primary types – interviews, self-report typologies, and self-report dimensional questionnaires. One of the more straightforward tools is the Relationship Questionnaire of Bartholomew and Horowitz (see Table 8.1).

Table 8.1 What is my attachment style? Assess which one best describes or is closest to the way you are?

Attachment style	How I am most likely to describe myself
Secure	• I am relaxed when I become emotionally close to others • I am comfortable depending on others, and having others depend on me • I am not concerned about being on my own or when others don't accept me
Insecure-anxious	• I want to be very emotionally close with others • Others are often hesitant to get as close as I would wish • It is awkward for me if I don't have close connections • I am occasionally concerned that others don't respect me as much as I respect them

Insecure-avoidant	• I am relaxed if I don't have close emotional interactions
	• It is vital for me to feel independent and self-reliant
	• I would prefer not to rely on others or have others depend on me
Fearful	• I avoid getting too near to others
	• I want emotionally close relationships, but it is not easy for me to rely on others entirely or depend on them
	• I am concerned that I will be disappointed if I let myself get too close to others

Source: Adapted from Bartholomew and Horowitz (1991)

People with *secure attachment* are generally more optimistic, have positive views of the self and others, and are confident that help will be accessible if required. In addition, they can usually manage and express their feelings and have good social skills. As a result, they have high self-esteem, others like them, and they build friendships quickly.

Individuals who have *insecure attachment* styles tend to have more negative views, often formed from negative experiences in childhood. This leads them to use defences such as denial and repression to cope. They also tend to blame others (projection) for their problems (Kets de Vries, 2013).

Those who are *insecure-anxious* have a positive view of others and a negative view of self. They tend to perceive themselves as unworthy, unlovable, and inadequate, so they have low self-esteem and feel helpless and powerless. As they seek love and care, they are 'clingy', which may scare others away. As a result, they may appear to be 'high maintenance', provoking conflict with people in positions of authority to gain their attention.

Individuals with *high avoidance patterns*, being either insecure-avoidant (those with low anxiety) or fearful (those with high anxiety), have negative models of others. They perceive others as not available and untrustworthy, so they find it difficult to relate to others.

Those who are *insecure-avoidant* have a positive view of self, so they strive for behavioural and emotional independence, preferring to be by themselves than forming personal relationships with others. As such, they may appear to lack empathy and be viewed by some as infuriating (Kets de Vries, 2011; Yip et al., 2018).

Those who are *fearful* have negative views of both themselves and others, so they want human interaction and contact but are afraid of rejection (Kets de Vries, 2014).

Some believe that attachment patterns can be passed down from one generation to the next, as children learn how to connect with parents and caregivers and, in turn, teach the next generation. However, others have found that attachment styles can vary within and between cultures and based on the region of origin, acculturation, and ethnicity (van Ujzendoorn & Kroonenberg, 1988; Agishtein & Brumbaugh, 2013).

In the workplace, academics have applied attachment theory to understand interpersonal relationships, explain social relationships, and predict individual outcomes (Leiter et al., 2015). It has also been used to examine career exploration, decision-making and aspects of career and leadership behaviour (Blustein et al., 1995; Harms, 2011; Mikulincer & Shaver, 2016), dyadic relationships in organisations between leaders and followers, co-workers in groups, sponsors and mentors (Mikulincer & Shaver, 2016; Yip et al., 2018), and organisational behaviour. Studies have also explored the relationship between attachment styles and leadership styles, including transformational leadership and authentic leadership/followership (Hinojosa et al., 2014; Underwood et al., 2016).

Scholars have also explored the attachment styles of perpetrators of discrimination. While it has been used less in the past to examine the targets of discrimination, more recent studies have investigated how felt security moderates the impact of racism and cultural distress (Mikulincer & Shaver, 2021).

HOW ADULT ATTACHMENT STYLES INFLUENCE OUR CAREER JOURNEYS

Our needs for attachment, affiliation, exploration, and assertion significantly impact how and why we take up work roles, including becoming leaders. As part of my exploration of the career journeys of culturally diverse leaders, I found that their attachment styles influenced their career progression.

In Chapter 1, we explored the stories of Ben and Michael, the successful partners in PSFs who both had similar backgrounds. Yet, their styles and paths to partnership differed. Ben, who has a largely independent style and tends to be more self-sufficient, is more likely to display an insecure-avoidant attachment style in times of stress. On the other hand, Michael, who turned a potential conflict into an opportunity and is more at ease in emotional situations, is more likely to have a secure attachment style.

Through actual relationships or internal models, the experience of security plays a crucial role in career development (Blustein et al., 1995). Attachment theory helps explain the types of dyadic relationships that culturally diverse leaders have with their sponsors, their relationships with other leaders and mentors, and how they manage the tensions and anxieties they experience on their way to becoming leaders. Its use can also be extended to analyse whether people attach themselves to their organisations (Cardona, 2020). Finally, it illuminates why individuals had different journeys and experiences of becoming leaders.

The leaders I spoke to adopted different relating styles, individual defence mechanisms, and basic assumptions behaviours in groups depending on their adult attachment styles.

Our preferred relating styles

As noted in Chapter 5, culturally diverse leaders took three crucial steps to progress their careers: experimenting with new things; building, enhancing, and maintaining relationships with sponsors; and building trusted relationships with others, in addition to improving business skills.

Being a leader requires individuals to balance several paradoxical tensions. This could be between their individual and collective interests, harmony and conflict, insecurity and confidence, and commercial and professional interests (Empson, 2017). These tensions, which increase as their careers progress, can lead them to default to their individual working models of relationships.

I found an association between these three critical elements of the career progression of culturally diverse leaders and their adult attachment styles. In addition, their attachment styles as followers influenced how they related to their leaders. Finally, their styles also explained why certain professionals build stronger ties with sponsors and mentors than others along their career journeys. As shown in Figure 8.1:

- Culturally diverse leaders with *secure or insecure-anxious* attachment styles had a *positive* view of *others*, and preferred to work with sponsors, mentors, and other leaders.
- Leaders with a *negative* view of others (*insecure-avoidant* or *fearful attachment* style) chose to work more independently.

- Leaders with *insecure* attachment styles (*anxious* or *avoidant*) were more likely to mention that they felt *imposter syndrome* than those with *secure* attachment styles.

Further details on the preferred actions of those who worked in Big 4 firms are below and summarised in Table 8.2:

Secure: Culturally diverse leaders with a secure attachment style were more likely to adopt both independent (such as working hard and planning/focusing) and dependency behaviours (including leveraging secure bases including sponsors, coaches/mentors, iconic leaders, and their families).

Insecure-anxious: Leaders with an insecure-anxious attachment style were more likely to mention that they built strong relationships with

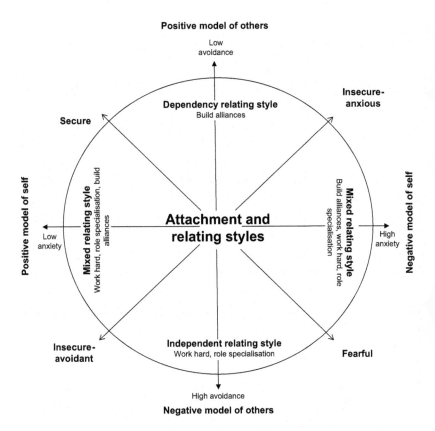

Figure 8.1 Attachment and relating styles

Source: Adapted from Bartholomew and Horowitz (1991)

clients and internally were strong client service leaders. They also showed a strong attachment to their organisation. They preferred to adopt a dependency relating style (enhancing and maintaining relationships) in groups, with their clients, the leaders they worked for, and their staff.

Insecure-avoidant or fearful: Leaders who have an insecure-avoidant or fearful attachment style tend to be in more technical roles. They focused on doing good work and letting their results do the job. Leaders who were insecure-avoidant were more independent and less likely to have sponsors, take risks and collaborate with others. They also tended to work hard on their own, with less support from others. On the other hand, fearful leaders were both less likely to have sponsors and to try new things.

Table 8.2 Most likely behaviours by relating styles

Adult attachment style	Experimenting with new things	Build, enhance and maintain relationships with sponsors	Build trusted relationships with others
Secure	• Learns new things • Tries things never done before/take risks • Works hard • Pushes self • Plans; focused	• Has sponsors • Has coaches and mentors • Works with iconic leaders • Has a supportive family	• Builds support network • Teamwork and collaboration • Recognised and promoted
Insecure-anxious	• Tries things never done before/take risks • Learns new things • Works hard • Adapts • Pushes self	• Has sponsors • Has coaches and mentors • Works with iconic leaders	• Builds support network • Teamwork and collaboration • Recognised and promoted
Insecure-avoidant	• Learn new things • Plans; focused • Works hard • Plans; focused	• Has coaching and mentoring • Has sponsors	• Builds support networks
Fearful	• Tries things never done before • Pushes self • Learns new things	• Has coaching and mentoring	• Builds support networks

Source: Own research.

Adult attachment styles influence the type of individual defence mechanisms that culturally diverse leaders use in situations of anxiety. Researchers have found strong systemic links between defence and attachment processes (Mikulincer et al., 2009).

Attachment-related security has also been found to reduce the harmful emotional effects of the experience of prejudice and discrimination. However, more research needs to be done to determine the extent to which felt security can mitigate this (Mikulincer & Shaver, 2021).

Table 8.3 aggregates my analysis of the leaders' adult attachment styles, preferred relating styles, defence mechanisms, and group basic assumptions behaviours for the culturally diverse leaders I interviewed who worked in Big 4 firms.

When interviewing the leaders, I did not ask them specific questions on whether their ethnicity impacted their career journeys positively or negatively. However, I was particularly interested in hearing if they mentioned any ethnicity-related incidents that activated their attachment behavioural system (evidenced by splitting, projection, or projective identification) (McRae & Short, 2010).

Table 8.3 Summary of adult attachment styles and behaviours

Adult attachment style	View of others	View of self	Preferred relating style with others	Individual defence mechanisms exhibited	Group basic assumptions behaviours exhibited
Secure	Positive	Positive	Dependency	Various; less than other attachment styles	Highlighted increase competition and politics
Insecure-anxious	Positive	Negative	Dependency	More likely to idealise, introject	Dependency
Insecure avoidant	Negative	Positive	Independent	More likely to split/project, fight/flight, repression, projective identification, regression	Fight/flight Awareness of increased competition and politics. More likely to mention that they fought with others
Fearful	Negative	Negative	Independent	Various; more than other attachment styles	As for insecure-avoidant

Source: Own research.

Lessons from Those Who Smashed the Bamboo Ceiling — 160

In relation to incidents involving their ethnicity, some culturally diverse leaders faced challenges managing identity triggers and threats concerning their ethnicity, which increased their anxieties and defence mechanisms. Insecure-avoidant or fearful leaders were more likely to describe incidents (and split/project) where they felt excluded or discriminated against in their childhood and/or work due to their ethnicity. However, when those who were secure or insecure-anxious experienced similar situations (generally in childhood only), they were generally more optimistic. They sometimes used the opportunity to build relationships with the majority.

The secure and insecure-anxious leaders had less difficulty making it into senior leadership positions than their insecure-avoidant or fearful counterparts. However, the latter were more likely to mention an incident involving their ethnicity and split/projection at work. In addition, they experienced more anxieties as leaders. This supports findings that people with a positive self-image (secure and insecure-avoidant) can access more mature defence mechanisms than those with a negative self-image (Laczkovics et al., 2020).[1]

Interestingly, of the partners in Big 4 firms, a much larger proportion of the leaders who spent most of their careers in Big 4 firms and were promoted from within the firm had a more secure attachment style than those promoted from outside the firm. In addition, partners with a secure adult attachment style were more likely to stay in the partnership longer than those with an insecure attachment style.

How our ethnicity and acculturation affect our attachment styles

Ethnicity and acculturation levels also influence the attachment styles of culturally diverse leaders.

Whilst attachment theory was developed primarily to understand social relationships, it cannot be separated from cultural factors. Although most research on attachment theory is from Western nations, there has been growing cross-cultural research exploring its applicability to other cultures and subgroups, such as ethnicity and religion.

Research on cultural backgrounds and attachment styles has generally concluded that people with East Asian backgrounds typically have higher attachment insecurity. In contrast, people with South Asian backgrounds have been found to have lower levels of attachment anxiety (Agishtein & Brumbaugh, 2013). This is believed to be due to their culture's rich assimilation of both collectivism and individualism tendencies.

While comparative information on attachment styles in Australia is less readily available, a meta-analysis by Marinus van Ujzendoorn and Pieter Kroonenberg (1988) found that 75% of people in the UK, where many Australians have their origins, have a secure attachment style, 3% were insecure-anxious, and 22% were insecure-avoidant. By way of comparison, the results for China were that 50% had a secure attachment style, 25% were insecure-anxious, and 25% had insecure-avoidant attachment styles.

Studies have also found an association between attachment and acculturation levels. In line with the larger body of research showing a positive relationship between acculturation and emotional well-being, higher levels of identification with a dominant culture were related to lower anxiety. In addition, higher levels of identification with *any* culture (home or host) were related to lower avoidance (Agishtein & Brumbaugh, 2013).

Interestingly, approximately two-thirds of the Big 4 partners I spoke with, who did all their high school in Australia, had a secure attachment style. Many of these leaders, who spent most of their lives in Australia, described incidents at the age of twelve when they were aware of being culturally different and wanted to fit in at school. During their adolescence, they became more used to segmenting roles (Ashforth et al., 2000) and straddling different aspects of their identities.

Most leaders with secure attachment styles had a positive attitude, took calculated risks, and viewed challenges as opportunities (Little et al., 2011). However, I sensed some repression of thoughts that many described as 'resilience', although dealing with being uncomfortable was necessary for them to transition to leadership. Some described incidents in their childhood where they overcame identity threats involving their ethnicity. These made them more aware of dealing with those situations as adults, often through being more confident, possibly to resist the fear of harmful incidents (Cardona, 2020). Oliver was one of these, noting that 'one of the things that helped me assimilate and actually click over in confidence was actually doing a lot more sport'. Others described being at a crossroads or ambivalence.

However, the leaders who moved to Australia during high school, university, or work were more likely to have an insecure attachment style, reflecting the extent of their acculturation in Australia.

A large proportion of those who moved to Australia in their adolescent years to complete high school or to go to university were more likely to have an insecure-avoidant attachment style.

On the other hand, a reasonably large proportion of the leaders who grew up overseas and moved to Australia as adults had an insecure-anxious attachment style. These leaders were more likely to leverage their relationships to succeed, explaining how they overcame cultural challenges and thrived in Australia.

There is an opportunity to research further the relationship between adult attachment styles, people with culturally diverse identities, and organisational systems in multicultural nations.

An interesting observation was that several leaders did not mention cultural diversity concerning their leadership progression, which may be due to identity denial (Cheryan & Monin, 2005). But, on the other hand, they may also have managed their boundaries well by (consciously and unconsciously) keeping their personal and professional identities separate. A psychodynamic view of this that INSEAD's Gianpiero Petriglieri suggests is that identity is a fabrication (Petriglieri, 2020), the search for which may be a partial defence against anxieties about the self.

Many leaders recognise that bringing one's whole self to work is vital in today's environment. However, most realise that the work environment has changed extensively since they started work. Some wished they could have been more open about celebrating their cultural diversity at work earlier in their careers. They managed these elements at work through various coping strategies and having their families and other sponsors, mentors, and friends as a secure base.

LEVERAGING SECURE BASES TO SUPPORT CAREER PROGRESSION

Having a secure base has been proven to support a person's career progression at work. This sense of security can come from dyadic relationships such as leader-follower relationships, mentoring relationships, and groups and organisations as attachment figures (Yip et al., 2018). It can also come from family and spouses (Petriglieri & Obodaru, 2018).

Those who are less secure and become senior leaders may face challenges at work, particularly in forming dyadic relationships such as gaining support from sponsors and mentors. In addition, the negative emotions that insecure leaders experience may negatively impact their leadership emergence. However, many of them can and do make leaders but need to work harder and focus on task completion (Yang et al., 2020).

It can be difficult, although not impossible, to change our attachment styles, which extend beyond the work environment (Johnstone &

Feeney, 2015). However, positive new life encounters and interventions can spur changes in relationship patterns (Kets de Vries, 2014). Furthermore, given the pervasive effects of attachment insecurities on stress and coping aspects, researchers suggest there are benefits to helping insecure individuals cope with stress (Johnstone & Feeney, 2015) in a safe and secure environment.

As Francesca Cardona, a London-based coach, has observed, forming attachments and having support structures is critical for healthy and meaningful commitment to our work (Cardona, 2020).

Understanding our attachment styles, how they are triggered, how to deactivate them to prevent them from being hyperactivated or suppressed, and how to 'feel secure' on our career journeys are essential lessons for us to learn to become more effective leaders.

One measure is to leverage 'holding' structures (which will be explored further in Chapters 9 and 10) that provide us with 'felt security'.

Chapter summary

- Adult attachment styles influence individuals' relationships during their lives and shape how they negotiate anxieties and tensions. Bowlby's attachment theory – that individuals seek emotional ties with an attachment figure – explains how people observe, respond to, and manage stress from interpersonal interactions through internalised working models.

- Adult attachment styles can vary between cultures and are influenced by acculturation. However, they unconsciously impact dyadic relationships, leader-follower dynamics and predict individual behaviours at work.

- When people are aware of their attachment styles and triggers (such as how they are triggered and how to deactivate them to prevent them from being hyperactivated or suppressed), they are able to understand their preferred relationship patterns, coping mechanisms when under stress and how they appear to others when anxious at work better.

- Accessing sponsors, mentors, and families can support aspiring leaders to feel secure. In addition, learning how to cope with stress by modifying their relationship patterns helps people become more effective leaders.

Questions to ask yourself and your team members

Yourself

- How do I feel if I experience an identity threat, such as racism or bias? What do I do, and who do I turn to?
- How am I likely to react if I am in a group and feel under pressure?
- How do I balance my identity at home and work? To what extent are my behaviour patterns similar, and when do they differ?

Your team members

- In our team/organisation, do we prefer that our leaders/aspiring leaders exhibit certain types of behaviours over others? Are there specific practices that we don't like in leaders/aspiring leaders?
- To what extent and how do we seek to minimise the stresses and anxieties at work in our team/organisation?

NOTE

1 More mature defence mechanisms include intellectualisation and sublimation, where unwanted urges or impulses such as anger are transformed into socially acceptable actions or behaviours, such as competitive sports (Laczkovics et al., 2020).

REFERENCES

Agishtein, P., & Brumbaugh, C. (2013). Cultural Variation in Adult Attachment: The Impact of Ethnicity, Collectivism, and Country of Origin. *Journal of Social, Evolutionary, and Cultural Psychology, 7*, 384–405. https://doi.org/10.1037/h0099181

Ainsworth, M., D. Salter, Blehar, M., C., Waters, E., & Wall, S. N. (2015). *Patterns of Attachment: A Psychological Study of the Strange Situation.* Psychology Press. https://doi.org/10.4324/9780203758045

Ashforth, B., Kreiner, G., & Fugate, M. (2000). All in a Day's Work: Boundaries and Micro Role Transitions. *Academy of Management Review, 25*, 472–491. https://doi.org/10.5465/AMR.2000.3363315

Bartholomew, K., & Horowitz, L. M. (1991). Attachment Styles Among Young Adults: A Test of a Four-Category Model. *Journal of Personality & Social Psychology, 61*(2), 226–244. https://doi.org/10.1037/0022-3514.61.2.226

Blustein, D., Prezioso, M., & Schultheiss, D. (1995). Attachment Theory and Career Development: Current Status and Future Directions. *Counseling Psychologist, 23*, 416–432. https://doi.org/10.1177/0011000095233002

Cardona, F. (2020). *Work Matters: Consulting to Leaders and Organizations in the Tavistock Tradition.* Routledge. https://doi.org/https://doi.org/10.4324/9780429317439

Cheryan, S., & Monin, B. (2005). Where Are You Really from? Asian Americans and Identity Denial. *Journal of Personality and Social Psychology, 89*(5), 717–730. https://doi.org/10.1037/0022-3514.89.5.717

Empson, L. (2017). *Leading Professionals: Power, Politics, and Prima Donnas.* Oxford University Press. https://doi.org/10.1093/oso/9780198744788.001.0001

Harms, P. (2011). Adult Attachment Styles in the Workplace. *Human Resource Management Review, 21,* 285–296. https://doi.org/10.1016/j.hrmr.2010.10.006

Hill, A. (2017, October 2). Insecure Overachiever? You Are Perfect for the Job. *Financial Times.* https://www.ft.com/content/ba0c9234-a2d7-11e7-9e4f-7f5e6a7c98a2

Hinojosa, A. S., Davis McCauley, K., Randolph-Seng, B., & Gardner, W. L. (2014). Leader and Follower Attachment Styles: Implications for Authentic Leader–Follower Relationships. *The Leadership Quarterly, 25*(3), 595–610. https://doi.org/10.1016/j.leaqua.2013.12.002

Johnstone, M., & Feeney, J. A. (2015). Individual Differences in Responses to Workplace Stress: The Contribution of Attachment Theory. *Journal of Applied Social Psychology, 45*(7), 412–424. https://doi.org/10.1111/jasp.12308

Kets de Vries, M. F. R. (2005, September). The Dangers of Feeling Like a Fake. *Harvard Business Review, 83*(9), 108–116. https://hbr.org/2005/09/the-dangers-of-feeling-like-a-fake

Kets de Vries, M., F. R. (2011). *The Hedgehog Effect: The Secrets of Building High Performance Teams.* Wiley.

Kets de Vries, M. F. R. (2013). *The Attachment Imperative: The Kiss of the Hedgehog.* INSEAD Working Paper No. 2013/51/EFE. https://papers.ssrn.com/sol3/papers.cfm?abstract_id=2253284

Kets de Vries, M. F. R. (2014, February 3). Self-Secure Leaders and the Role of Attachment. *INSEAD Knowledge.* https://knowledge.insead.edu/leadership-management/self-secure-leaders-and-the-role-of-attachment-3143

Laczkovics, C., Fonzo, G., Bendixsen, B., Shpigel, E., Lee, I., Ramskogler, K., Prunas, A., Gross, J., Steiner, H., & Huemer, J. (2020). Defense Mechanism Is Predicted by Attachment and Mediates the Maladaptive Influence of Insecure Attachment on Adolescent Mental Health. *Current Psychology, 39,* 1–9. https://doi.org/10.1007/s12144-018-9839-1

Leiter, M. P., Day, A., & Price, L. (2015). Attachment Styles at Work: Measurement, Collegial Relationships, and Burnout. *Burnout Research, 2*(1), 25–35. https://doi.org/10.1016/j.burn.2015.02.003

Little, L. M., Nelson, D. L., Craig Wallace, J., & Johnson, P. D. (2011). Integrating Attachment Style, Vigor at Work, and Extra-Role Performance. *Journal of Organizational Behavior, 32*(3), 464–484. https://doi.org/10.1002/job.709

McRae, M. B., & Short, E. L. (2010). *Racial and Cultural Dynamics in Group and Organizational Life: Crossing Boundaries.* SAGE Publications. https://doi.org/10.4135/9781452274751

Mikulincer, M., & Florian, V. (1995). Appraisal of and Coping with a Real-Life Stressful Situation: The Contribution of Attachment Styles. *Personality and Social Psychology Bulletin, 21,* 406–414. https://doi.org/10.1177/0146167295214011

Mikulincer, M., & Shaver, P. (2016). *Attachment in Adulthood. Second Edition: Structure, Dynamics, and Change*. The Guildford Press.

Mikulincer, M., Shaver, P., Cassidy, J., & Berant, E. (2009). Attachment-Related Defensive Processes. In J. H. Obegi & E. Berant (Eds.), *Attachment Theory and Research in Clinical Work with Adults* (pp. 293–327). The Guilford Press.

Mikulincer, M., & Shaver, P. R. (2009). An attachment and Behavioral Systems Perspective on Social Support. *Journal of Social and Personal Relationships*, 26(1), 7–19. https://doi.org/10.1177/0265407509105518

Mikulincer, M., & Shaver, P. R. (2021). Enhancing the "Broaden-And-Build" Cycle of Attachment Security as a Means of Overcoming Prejudice, Discrimination, and Racism. *Attachment & Human Development*, 1–14. https://doi.org/10.1080/14616734.2021.1976921

Petriglieri, G. (2020). A Psychodynamic Perspective on Identity as Fabrication. In A. D. Brown (Ed.), *The Oxford Handbook of Identities in Organizations* (pp. 169–183). Oxford University Press. https://doi.org/10.1093/oxfordhb/9780198827115.013.22

Petriglieri, J. L., & Obodaru, O. (2018). Secure-Base Relationships as Drivers of Professional Identity Development in Dual-Career Couples. *Administrative Science Quarterly*, 64(3), 694–736. https://doi.org/10.1177/0001839218783174

Richards, D., & Schat, A. (2011). Attachment at (Not To) Work: Applying Attachment Theory to Explain Individual Behavior in Organizations. *The Journal of Applied Psychology*, 96, 169–182. https://doi.org/10.1037/a0020372

Underwood, R., Mohr, D., & Ross, M. (2016). Attachment Style, Leadership Behavior, and Perceptions of Leader Effectiveness in Academic Management. *The Journal of Leadership Education*, 15, 100–116. https://doi.org/10.12806/V15/I4/R7

van Ujzendoorn, M. H., & Kroonenberg, P. M. (1988). Cross-Cultural Patterns of Attachment: A Meta-Analysis of the Strange Situation. *Child Development*, 59(1), 147–156. https://doi.org/10.2307/1130396

Yang, Y., Wang, Y., Lu, H., & Tan, L. (2020). Too Insecure to Be a Leader: The Role of Attachment in Leadership Emergence. *Frontiers in Psychology*, 11(3120). https://doi.org/10.3389/fpsyg.2020.571401

Yip, J., Ehrhardt, K., Black, H., & Walker, D. O. (2018). Attachment Theory at Work: A Review and Directions for Future Research. *Journal of Organizational Behavior*, 39(2), 185–198. https://doi.org/10.1002/job.2204

PART III

A Roadmap for Fostering Culturally Diverse
Leadership in Organisations

Nine

INTRODUCTION

Sundar Pichai is not your conventional CEO. Born in Tamil Nadu in India, his family didn't have a telephone until he was ten years old. His first flight on a plane was when he left India to attend graduate school at Stanford University. Pichai became the CEO of Google at the age of forty-three.

Likewise, John Chen from Hong Kong was the CEO of Sybase from 1998 to 2012 and is now the CEO of Blackberry. And outside of the tech industry, Indra Nooyi, from Chennai in India, was the CEO of PepsiCo from 2006 to 2018.

All three are examples of success stories of new immigrants who rose through the ranks of their organisations. They have led some of the most successful and admired companies in the world. They are recognised for their personal attributes, not just their technical skills.

For instance, on taking risks, Pichai has been quoted saying, 'You might fail a few times, but that's OK. You end up doing something worthwhile which you learn a great deal from', and 'Wear your failure as a badge of honor!' Likewise, in a LinkedIn post, John Chen said that his best career advice is not to be a superstar – be as unselfish as possible (Chen, 2015). And, in a LinkedIn interview in 2019, Nooyi's top advice for aspiring leaders included developing a human 'hip pocket' skill and having a set of ethics and the courage and skill to communicate them (Petrone, 2019).

Career progression is never easy, even for the best of leaders. It requires us all to balance our different identities with the organisation's identity. This can be more complex for people with culturally diverse backgrounds, who may already be challenged juggling their different identities between home and outside work.

As we become more senior, our work stresses and pressures increase, making us more likely to use individual defences to fend off anxieties. Some leaders can manage these tensions well. However, others find this more challenging and may even become narcissistic leaders.

Being culturally different nevertheless shouldn't hold you back. In a Professional Development Forum webinar in September 2021, Chin Tan, the

DOI: 10.4324/9781003291237-12

Australian Race Discrimination Commissioner, shared his career advice with young, culturally diverse professionals. His personal view is that cultural intelligence should be viewed as a competitive advantage regardless of a person's background. In addition, people of culturally diverse backgrounds shouldn't use the race card to get ahead – people still need to be highly competent for a role. They also need to understand how to sell themselves and their competitive advantage to prospective and current employers. Finally, no matter where someone was born or how they moved countries, they should understand what it means to be a citizen or resident of their country. They should leverage their cultural intelligence to bring all the other benefits of diversity to their country's multiculturalism (Tan, 2021).

Before continuing, take a few moments to ask yourself the following questions (Table 9.1):

Table 9.1 Are there things I should do to super-charge my career?

	Yes	No
If people were to describe me at work honestly, would anything they say about me surprise me?		
Do I have any blind spots I am not aware of?		
When experiencing stress, do I react impulsively based on my gut feel? Or, do I sometimes appear to lack self-control or have extreme emotions?		
Do I have challenges with self-esteem?		
Do I use work as an excuse to avoid personal relationships?		
At times, do I appear to lack empathy or seem negative?		
There are few sponsors who advocate for me at work		
There are few people I can turn to if I need support at work when and where I need them for career and emotional support		
I don't have family support (spouse, relatives) and friends I can turn to for help		
When faced with challenging black-and-white issues, I prefer to choose one response rather than a compromise answer.		
I prefer to resolve challenging and uncomfortable issues quickly rather than leave them unresolved.		
I prefer to stick to things I know rather than try new things.		
I tend not to try new things, as I don't have the time.		
I frequently don't clear my annual leave, as I am too busy.		
I don't sponsor or mentor younger staff at work, as this is not part of my job scope.		

Source: Own research.

If your answers to any of these questions are yes, then keep reading.

This chapter covers my critical recommendations on super-charging your career based on my research and own career experiences.

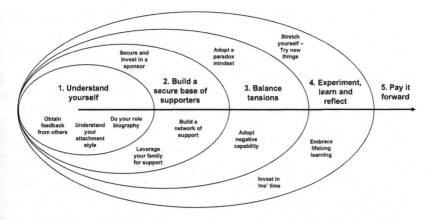

Figure 9.1 Keys to super-charging your career
Source: Own research

To succeed, aspiring culturally diverse leaders need the 'capacity for containment, attachment, and taking risks' (Cardona, 2020, p. 80). They need to understand themselves and become more aware of their vulnerabilities in situations of stress. They need strong relationships with supporters who help them achieve aspirations, understand the paradoxical challenges of being a leader, and make them aware of the journey ahead. They also need a secure base of family and friends to support their journey, and to be able to balance their various tensions. They should be open to experiential learning, taking risks and learning from mistakes, even in cases where they are uncomfortable. And finally, they should pay it forward (Figure 9.1).

1. UNDERSTAND YOURSELF

Leadership is all about leading a group of people or an organisation – in other words, leader-follower relationships. Becoming a leader requires us to understand and be aware of how we relate to others. This includes being more self-aware of how our 'inner conflicts' can become interpersonal ones through elements such as projective identification. These conflicts can have both positive and negative implications (Pratt & Crosina, 2016).

In earlier chapters, we learnt more about how our experiences in the family system and attachment styles play a crucial role in influencing who we are, even unconsciously. Here are a few things you may wish to try.

Obtain feedback from others
Understanding how others see us allows us to recognise our strengths, weaknesses and blind spots and become more self-aware (Kets de Vries, 2014).

A common and helpful way to do this that a number of the leaders I spoke to use, is to obtain 360-degree feedback from supervisors, work colleagues, direct reports, and clients. Like putting a mirror to ourselves, this feedback will provide you with invaluable insights about you and your leadership actions. Further, through greater self-awareness, it will support you in becoming a better and more effective leader who can better adapt and embrace change.

Many tools are available in the market that can help you with this. Alternatively, your organisation may run assessments that you can leverage. Reflect on the comments you are provided with and the actions you can take to improve yourself.

Remember – your colleagues want you to become a better version of yourself, so make the most of their views as an opportunity to develop.

Better still, consider obtaining independent feedback from family or friends you trust. You will be surprised by what they see and say about you. Additionally, seek feedback regularly, especially if you take on a new role.

360-degree feedback as part of lifelong learning

If undertaken using a well-thought-through and trusted approach, together with group coaching, regular 360-degree feedback can benefit all professionals.

A few years back, as part of a board education programme, I obtained 360-degree feedback in the context of my board roles. My feedback was from my class colleagues, the people I sit on boards with, facilitators who observed me in board simulations, socioanalytic drawings, and group coaching. I found it insightful to hold up a mirror to myself to understand how others saw me, as I was relatively new to board roles.

I undertook a similar exercise as part of my recent Executive Master in Change at INSEAD. Using role biography and 720-degree feedback (from both colleagues in my work roles and family and friends) and group coaching, I was given invaluable feedback on how I come across to others and operate both in my family and my work system, which at times will be different. It was clear that my family understood me much better than my colleagues at work. This feedback allowed me to reflect on who I am as a person, and at work.

Table 9.2 Examples of signs and symptoms of attachment problems

Insecure-anxious	Insecure-avoidant
• Challenges with self-esteem	• Difficulties with authority figures
• Idealises and devalues relationships	• Over self-reliance
• Possessive/needy/clingy behaviour	• Sensitivity to criticism
• Impulsive	• Perceives others as unreliable
• Fails to take personal responsibility for tricky circumstances	• Uses work as an excuse to avoid personal relationships
• Feels underappreciated/wronged	• Difficulties in expressing emotions
• Lacks self-control/has extreme emotions	• Apparent lack of empathy
• Sensitive to rejection	• Negative view of people and society

Source: Adapted from Kets de Vries (2013).

Understand your attachment style

Be mindful of your attachment style and how it may impact how others view you.

Understanding your attachment style helps you understand why you react in certain ways in times of anxiety and allows you to recognise potential blind spots (refer to Table 9.2). While these may not have stopped you from progressing so far, they may lead to challenges later.

For instance, suppose you have an insecure-anxious attachment style, and your boss has an insecure-avoidant attachment style. Consequently, you may both find it challenging to work with each other. However, suppose you are aware of your attachment style. In that case, you may become more mindful of self-managing and modifying your responses when working with them.

There are many tools and self-questionnaires available online and in leadership books that you can use to identify your attachment style. One of the simplest is by Bartholomew and Horwitz (refer to Table 8.1 in Chapter 8). In addition, it may be worth reaching out to someone you trust, such as a coach, to work through the findings.

Becoming more self-aware

Valerie Khoo, the Australian Writers' Centre CEO, believes that building relationships is vital for career success. Interpersonal skills are essential, but they take time to perfect. However, she notes that it is also essential to be aware of how people perceive you. '[It] is

(Continued)

not just about your immediate manager, [it] is about how you're perceived by the senior management, by people outside the organisation, by those around you and by, you know your peers and your staff and everyone else as well', she says.

Valerie thinks some people may not have 'good awareness' and may not be wired to know how they are perceived. She highlighted an example of someone she knew who was unaware that they appeared abrupt and said things that others might think very direct. Having recognised this, that person sought coaching support, then worked with a set of rules. For example, when listening, she would use listening behaviour (such as leaning forward in a video call). She might also have had a rule to send a thank-you email after a particular kind of meeting. She may not actually genuinely have felt those things, but she had enough awareness to know that these rules helped people feel better about their interactions with her (Khoo, 2020).

Do your role biography exercise

Are there certain types of roles you tended to be attracted to in your life? Roles you prefer not to do? Each of us prefers certain types of roles that we have previously played in relationships – starting with our family and friends.

So, what is meant by the 'work roles' in our lives? In my case, examples which others may call me are:

- Independent first-born to my parents
- Bossy big sister to my brother during childhood
- Studious, obedient nerd at school
- Reliable and hardworking team member
- Bossy leader
- Event organiser in social settings
- Trustworthy consultant to my clients

These are not formal titles or official responsibilities but social and psychological patterns manifested in various situations.

Our behavioural and emotional patterns, which can arise due to our adult attachment styles, often play out in how we interact with these people, somewhat like an unconscious drama. They can also hold us back. Knowing what activates our emotions can help us to avoid these patterns. Undertaking a role biography exercise is a helpful way to assist us in understanding this.[1]

Our role biography has been described as being like our own unique fingerprint. It shows how our experiences in life shape how we are inclined to take up roles in the present. It also helps us to identify triggers and recurrent patterns.

Understanding your role biography will help you know whether and why you want to step into a leadership role. In addition, it will aid you in answering questions such as what are you looking for/your goals in life. Further, in terms of organisations and roles you prefer, it will assist you in understanding the type of culture, values, and people you like to work with. Lastly, it will allow you to understand the anxieties and tensions you experienced in these situations and how you dealt with them.

Role biography can also be used in teams. When working in psychologically safe spaces, they will allow people to understand each other.

How to carry out your role biography

- Take a large piece of paper and draw something you remember or a critical incident involving you as you progressed through life – for example, at the ages of six, sixteen, twenty-six, thirty-six and so on – to where you are today.
- Note that this is not a test of artistic skill; in fact, it is not a test at all. So be playful with this, and have fun – use colours, images, and no words!
- After completing the drawings, share the following information at each age with a colleague.

  - Who are the people involved?
  - What is the system (or organisation)? What is the context?
  - What were the high points in the role?
  - What were the low points in the role?
  - What were the challenges in the role, and how did you approach these challenges?
  - What did you learn in that role that is still with you? Or, what is the link between this role and your current work role?

  Source: Adapted from Long (2013).

2. BUILD A SECURE BASE OF SUPPORTERS

Being a leader at the end of the day is about relationships and relationship management; it's the ability of an individual to influence, motivate and enable others to contribute to the effectiveness and success of the organisation. Strong networks are often cited by first-generation professionals as one of their most crucial career success factors (Maldonado & Burwell, 2020). Further, collaboration skills have become increasingly critical in today's hybrid world, as we frequently don't have the opportunity to meet people in person at the water cooler easily.

Getting into leadership is not easy, and you may feel uncomfortable. You will need to leverage your relationships with people around you to support you – sponsors, mentors, coaches, family and friends – to help you as your secure base. Think about building your own personal 'advisory board' – a trusted network of connections you can tap into for advice, support, and a helping hand to succeed. Further, leveraging a diverse network of people helps you in different ways.

The importance of having an 'advisory board'

Kathrina Lo, NSW Public Service Commissioner, believes that it is vital to have a group of trusted advisors and supporters. These are people to whom you can go to for a second opinion and moral support. 'I have a group of senior women that I have breakfast with every month. I call them my girl squad', she said.

We pump up each other's tyres up when any of us is going for an interview. We boost each other up. We vent to each other. We confide in each other things that we couldn't confide to other people, knowing that they remain in the cone of silence. It's a really safe and supportive environment. So, I think it's just really important to have a group of people that have your back.

(Lo, 2021)

Here are some tips to think about.

Secure and invest in a sponsor

Vivek Bhatia, CEO and Managing Director of Link Group credits his leadership success to having strong sponsors that supported his career.

One of the biggest insights that I have learned through my career is to make sure that I make the effort to develop a strong relationship with my boss and my manager... They are the ones who are paying for services. They are the ones who have bought me into the organisation. And if you don't deliver what they expect of you, then you're not fulfilling your role.

He added: 'Build a relationship; build a connection – people work with people' (Layton, 2021).

A sponsor is worth securing and investing in. Sponsors will be the ones who believe in your potential and are willing to advocate for you as your career progresses.

You will need to earn your sponsorship relationship. Then, work to maximise it and make it fulfilling and long-lasting, as a sponsor relationship is a two-way street. Unfortunately, sponsorship relationships don't happen on their own.

When looking for a sponsor, Jovina Ang suggests that a sponsee should take the following actions:

1. *Gain and obtain a sponsor* – Establish a solid performance track record, demonstrate leadership potential and qualities, and ask for sponsorship.
2. *Boost your relationship with your sponsor* – At work, take the initiative, and support your sponsor's achievements. In addition, have a strong home support system.
3. *Take your sponsor relationship to the next level* – Repay and build on your relationship (Ang, 2019)

Remember to build a broad range of sponsors who are not like you. Almost all of the Asian-Australian leaders I spoke to did not have an Asian-Australian sponsor at work in Australia, as there were few Asian-Australian leaders in senior roles above them. Having non-Asian-Australian sponsors allowed them to understand better how to work with other leaders.

Jackson Lu of MIT Sloan has found that, in the US, regardless of their ethnicity, people with ethnic backgrounds who bond with people of other ethnic backgrounds are more likely to emerge as leaders (Lu, 2021).

For those of you who have an East Asian ethnicity, be particularly mindful of building relationships with people of other ethnicities. People with East Asian backgrounds have been found to have a higher propensity to socialise with other people with East Asian backgrounds compared to people of other ethnic backgrounds. This translates into differences in leadership attainment (Lu, 2021).

Further, consider finding sponsors early in your career in your organisation, even if you don't think you need one.

Many of the leaders I spoke to started to get to know their sponsors very early in their careers – they were often a few levels more senior than them. So, if you hold off finding a sponsor until you recognise that you need one, it may already be too late.

Build a broad network of support

Some of my best supporters have been people I met in the first few years of my career in my company. They saw me 'grow up' at work; they trusted me, and I trusted them. They taught me new skills and broadened my perspectives. Some of them also become sponsors. Others are mentors or informal coaches to me.

Good leaders recognise that it is essential that you build a network of sponsors both within your organisation and outside (industry leaders or clients). This will also reduce your over-reliance on one sponsor and the risk if your sponsor disappears.

Some leaders I spoke to specifically sought to work for leaders from whom they could learn or support in areas where they have skill gaps.

John's advice for aspiring leaders is not only to find a sponsor.

> Find someone that you can learn off and who's willing to cultivate. And it's not just someone you can learn off – there's a lot of people that you can learn off... look for someone that you can see that there're certain qualities that they have that you aspire to be.

These qualities may come from several people in the firm, not just one person. However, he also cautioned that these relationships are two-way – and that aspiring leaders should be prepared to give before they receive. 'Be prepared to work hard and not receive anything first... And then be prepared to be able to give more away, give more back than anything else'.

Also, don't be shy to ask for approaching people for help, suggests Vivek Bhatia.

> I have never felt shy of actually approaching someone and saying, "would you be OK to give me some time? Every couple of months, every

quarter - can I spend an hour with you just talking through things and listening to [your] ideas?" And what I have found is that people have been very generous.

Vivek says that speaking to others has helped him grow personally and professionally, as he can learn from them as they all bring different perspectives. Further, he feels that if the other person says no, don't take it personally (Layton, 2021).

Bear in mind that not everyone will want to be your best buddy, nor you theirs. Keep some relationships purely professional – although others will more naturally become more personal. Keep in touch with colleagues – alumni, clients, university friends and others. You never know when they can help you, when you can help them, or will be asked for their views on you.

Finally, remember that while sponsors will be there to back you, detractors may also want to block your promotion. It may only take one detractor to cast doubt on your abilities, even if you have multiple sponsors. Therefore, the more backers you have who support you, the more likely you will get support for your promotion.

Who are you as a person?

When I was a senior manager, I worked extremely long hours on some fantastic assignments with brand-defining clients. Unfortunately, while my client revenues and chargeable hours were high, I didn't spend much time in the office walking the corridors. As a result, the first time I was considered for partnership, I didn't make it. One of the reasons given was that other partners said they didn't know me as a person.

In a professional services firm (PSF), it's tempting to think that you will be made a partner if you bring in the revenue. In some cases, that may be true. However, being a partner in a PSF involves being granted admission to a leadership group where you all collectively share in the rewards and risks. In other words, your fellow partners really need to trust that you will do the right thing.

I decided to give partnership another go. I spent more time getting to know people in the office at various social events, even

(Continued)

though I was exhausted from my client work. Fortunately, the following year, I was promoted to partnership.

Given the collaborative and global nature of PSFs, where I worked on cross-border audits and transactions with colleagues in other offices throughout my seventeen years as a partner, it was crucial for me to maintain close friendships with my fellow partners around the world.

Leverage your family for support

Leadership is demanding – physically and emotionally. So, we need all the help we can get, especially at home.

Today's working lives are particularly challenging, as most households have dual-career couples. Jennifer Petriglieri of INSEAD, who researched dual-career couples, believes that to succeed at work, it is essential that we have a secure, dependably supportive relationship with our spouse that encourages exploratory behaviour and enhances our professional identity development (Petriglieri & Obodaru, 2018).

Yet, in households with more Asian cultural influences, support from the broader extended family system, including parents, aunts, uncles and cousins and beyond, may also be the key to success.

Having your family as your cheer squad

To understand whether the obstacles faced by Asian female leaders along their career journeys differed from those of women in the West, Jane Horan, author of *How Asian Women Lead – Lessons for Global Corporations*, interviewed several Asian female leaders. One crucial observation she made was that for many Asian women, family support is critical to success.

Horan discusses the concept of Asian women leaders embracing the value of 'harmony' – the idea of having inclusive networks that operate like an 'integrated web'. This web emphasises harmony between the diverse communities that the leader may use across, such as team, church, sports, family, and work. If any of the elements are out of sync, the entire web is impacted. This focus on harmony reflects the collectivist values adopted by many in Asia (Horan, 2014).

Caroline, an Asian-Australian leader credits having supportive relationships as the key to her career success – particularly with her husband. 'For me, the support networks around you are so fundamental for what you can achieve in your career, whether that's your parents, whether that's your partner, whether that's your friends, whether that's your bosses, whether that's your children... Everyone's got a different cheer squad, but you need a cheer squad', she shared. She added,

I've been very lucky – I've always had a cheer squad – my parents, my teachers, my bosses, my husband... I think that's been crucial to where I'm at, but also the choices that I've made in terms of how I focus my time.

It's essential to experiment with what works for you.

Another challenge for many people from culturally diverse backgrounds is that their parents often don't have networks in, or the technical knowledge of other professions. In the case of Australia, the parents of many aspiring culturally diverse leaders moved to Australia as skilled migrants – frequently in specialised areas such as medicine – or as part of family sponsorship programmes.

Some of the leaders I spoke to said that their parents could not provide them with relevant input and insight on their chosen profession. An example was where or how to apply for internships, which is particularly important for professionals in PSFs. As a result, some leaders felt that they were at a disadvantage compared to their peers they were competing with, whose parents may already be professionals and had broader networks they could tap on for advice.

In my case, fortunately, my parents asked our family accountant if I could work at their firm for three months at the end of my first year of university. That experience helped me get a vacation employment role with a Big 4 firm at the end of my second year at university. Similarly, Greg's brother-in-law, a partner in a law firm, advised him on which law firm to join after he finished university.

It is crucial to access a broader network of people beyond your immediate family to help you early on for career advice outside of work. So don't be scared to ask for help.

3. BALANCE TENSIONS

Feeling stressed from time to time is expected. Sometimes it motivates us to do more; at other times, we feel overwhelmed and can't concentrate on anything. Pressure can be positive and encouraging, but it can also be destructive, and cause anxiety and longer-term health problems.

When we experience too much stress, it can trigger particular behaviours depending on our attachment style. This may lead us to use individual and group defence mechanisms, sometimes unconsciously, to protect ourselves. We need to be mindful of this when it occurs and consider whether these are the right reactions in that circumstance.

The challenge we face at work is that the more senior we become, the more complexity we are expected to handle. Conversely, when we are more junior, we tend to be expected to resolve more logical and straightforward issues.

Leadership can be a lonely experience. Many senior positions involve dealing with emotions and politics much more than at junior levels, making them significantly more challenging to manage. In addition, people often expect you to know all the answers. As a result, talking to your clients, people in your team, or people around you about things you don't know the answers to can be confronting. Further, you may not know who to speak to for advice on a day-to-day basis because you feel insecure.

When we face these challenges, it's always easy to follow our gut instinct and default to our natural style under stress. We then act quickly and rush decisions rather than thinking things through carefully and taking the time to consider and reflect. Sometimes, however, following our gut isn't the right option and may not lead to the best outcome. If we are not careful, our strong feelings can interfere with our ability to think clearly, read a situation correctly and focus on our work (Shragai, 2021).

Adopt a paradox mindset

One of Caroline's lessons from her early days as a leader was that she was probably too black-and-white in her thinking. 'I [now] approach things with, there's not a right or wrong. There's not a 'your view' or 'my view'. We want to get to 'our view'. We want to use the skills of really deeply listening, and really hear[ing] what's important to people, then finding solutions that work for everyone, rather than trying to win from your perspective, or from the perspective that you think is right for the organisation', she mentioned.

*****

Today's working life is paradoxical. We need to deal, consciously or unconsciously, with numerous tensions and decisions. As our careers progress, we need to manage the pressure of deciding whether to be ourselves and do what we wish or to follow the expectation of the majority. As leaders, we also experience the tension of managing ourselves and other relationships.

Adopting a paradox mindset involves considering the world with a 'both/and' approach instead of an 'either/or' one. In today's challenging times, we must do many tasks simultaneously. Therefore, we need to feel comfortable with discomfort – as these obstacles aren't going away (Miron-Spektor & Smith, 2020).

Unfortunately, when we experience tensions and anxieties under pressure, we often react defensively with an either/or zero-sum approach. This is because we sometimes feel a sudden drive to respond to an 'impulse'. We prioritise one answer with this approach, creating certainty and consistency.

Adopting a paradox mindset suggests an alternative standpoint – accepting and learning to live with the tensions associated with competing demands. It recognises that these conflicting needs are not resolvable, as they can't be eliminated entirely, and is beneficial in many areas of our business and personal lives.

To give you an idea, we may decide to focus on work or family. Or in a business situation, we may seek to be profitable or socially and environmentally oriented. However, particularly for tensions of a personal nature, whichever we choose, there is always a feeling in the back of our minds that we are missing out on something. As a result, we tend to feel blame, guilt, or shame. This can lead to negative spirals and vicious cycles, creating harmful emotions.

One paradox that we need to manage is what Herminia Ibarra calls the 'authenticity paradox'. Her research suggests that career advancement requires all of us to move way beyond our comfort zones. While we may feel uncomfortable and wish to protect our identities, we often fall back on actions and patterns we are most comfortable with. Instead, we should also use these moments to learn how best to lead effectively through trial and error. This requires courage; the times when we struggle the most are when we need to take charge in unfamiliar circumstances, sell ourselves and our ideas, and process less positive feedback. To overcome this, we should adopt 'a playful frame of mind' – to be open to learning from diverse role models, work on becoming better, and stick to our narrative (Ibarra, 2015).

Another paradox is balancing between our work and life outside work. In reality, our work and family life will continue in different ways, regardless of our choices. Having a paradox mindset means moving the spotlight away from the need to decide between work and family and instead, replacing it with learning how to continuously balance these challenges over time (Miron-Spektor & Smith, 2020).

Ways to resolve a paradox mindset include reframing the question; accepting the tension and developing comfort with the discomfort; and distancing ourselves and searching for new possibilities (Miron-Spektor & Smith, 2020).

Adopt negative capability

So, how can you become more comfortable with discomfort and not act impulsively when our natural impulse is to jump to a conclusion?

A crucial skill worth cultivating to manage work tensions is negative capability, a term first coined by poet John Keats and applied by psychoanalyst William Bion. This generally refers to the ability to live with and tolerate ambiguity and paradox; to hold or contain – not just react to – the pressure to act from one's own ego impulses (French, 2001).

Negative capability is negative, as it is the ability not to do something – to be attentive and patient without reacting. It's like pressing the pause button to allow you to stop and reflect on what is really important. In contrast, positive capability is what we do as part of our roles and usually involves taking decisive action.

When we have negative capability, we can manage something painfully real without yielding to fear, blame or denial. Other ways used to describe this are having patience, reflexive inaction, composure, poise under stress, trust, or courage (Simpson et al., 2002; Guerin, 2018).

How does negative capability help you? According to Marisa Guerin, a former consultant, being more attentive means that you are more likely to observe what is happening in complex and stressful circumstances. As a result, you will have the mental and emotional space to fully comprehend the situation around you, allowing new insights to emerge that support the basis for decisive action. Second, in times of stress or tension, others around you will be less anxious, encouraging discussion, problem-solving and thinking. This is not easy, as frequently, the first thing we lose when anxiety strikes is the ability to think clearly (Guerin, 2018).

Having negative capability and being aware of our feelings isn't easy in all situations. We are often swayed by the moment's emotions and act impulsively when heightened risks occur. Further, it requires time and can create uncertainty or ambivalence (Shragai, 2021).

For me, my default style is to respond to requests quickly and trust my gut feel. This works in some situations but sometimes leads to others having a misguided impression of me. At times, spontaneous actions may not lead to the best possible outcome.

As leaders, we are often expected to be positive and take decisive action (Simpson et al., 2002). However, at times it may be better to wait until further information or resources are available or relationships develop. In addition, it requires us to develop greater self-awareness and to become more curious about how our past may affect us, bringing our unconscious drives to consciousness (Shragai, 20201).

Ways we can cultivate negative capability daily include journal writing, going for a walk, or run, taking time to reflect or even mediation.

Journaling as a tool to cultivate negative capability

James was asked to take on a new and unexpected leadership role as a new partner. In addition to being assigned an external coach, he kept a journal of his reflections during this period.

He found this beneficial during his earlier leadership years and still uses it today. 'I just wrote copious notes about tips from people. When I was having negative thoughts, I used to write them down, and I used to write down a lot of positive stuff. [It] wasn't a journal or a diary so much, but it was just my way of just trying to keep on top of things', he said.

4. EXPERIMENT, LEARN, AND REFLECT

Gone are the days when your formal education stopped once you finished university or completed your professional exams. Traditionally, you could acquire all the knowledge you needed for work on the job.

Today, internal and external pressures require us to learn more regularly. In addition, we are likely to undergo various identity transitions throughout our working lives.

As a result, it's vital that we continuously experiment, learn and reflect about ourselves, who we are and who we want to be, and why with a growth and not a fixed mindset, as was the case for some of the leaders.

As Kate said,

> You need to know what your goal is, and what motivates you, and work towards it. If you amplify the barrier in your mind, it's not necessarily [going to] do you any good in terms of adding extra pressure... I perceive the barrier as a learning opportunity, rather than being something I'm frustrated about, because what I believe is frustrating is not going to get you anywhere. It's about the actions and what you do.

Here are my tips based on the lessons from Asian-Australian leaders.

Stretch yourself – try different things

Think about what you did as a kid – a time when you went through a lot of identity transitions – and all the fun you had trying out new things. Identity transition is sometimes described as 'trying new roles on' and acting yourself into a role.

Yet, to some, this may sound completely inauthentic and uncomfortable. Occasionally, all we want to be is ourselves. That is natural, as being ourselves is comfortable and easy. Often, what holds us back is that we fear failing or embarrassing ourselves. Trying to be in control is often a defence we use when we feel anxious.

However, all identity transitions involve trying things out to see how they feel, whether we like them or not – in other words, experimenting, learning and sensemaking. We do a lot of this during our identity formation, particularly in adolescence. However, as adults, we frequently lose our sense of curiosity, and we are too scared to take risks and fail. We like to take the safe option and cling to old ways of doing things.

One of Jenny's pieces of advice for aspiring leaders was to take a chance – have self-belief and the courage to put yourself forward.

Just be courageous. Take a chance. These days, no question is really a dumb question. If it's external, maybe it's different [as] you['ve] got to be a little bit more prepared when you go to the client. But internally, just be curious and ask questions. Have the courage to ask questions and keep learning.

So, what's stopping you now as an adult – and what do you have to lose?

The power of lifelong learning – Piyush Gupta, Group CEO, DBS

Piyush Gupta, who grew up in India, has been the CEO of DBS Group Holdings, Singapore, South-East Asia's largest bank, for twelve years. In 2019, *Harvard Business Review* named him one of the world's one hundred best-performing chief executives. In addition, DBS has won various awards for the World's Best Bank over the years.

Piyush spent twenty-seven years at Citibank (Citi). In his final role, he was the CEO for South-East Asia, Australia, and New Zealand at Citi. He speaks fondly about his early career experiences at Citi and how they shaped him.

'When I started, I was given tremendous scope [and] variety [of work]. In my 27 years at Citi, I wound up doing 22 different assignments. I did [stints in] Human Resources [and] learned [about] technology, strategy, planning, and sales, so the variety was immense. [I was also given] the opportunity to move around in different countries and markets. [I] worked in six or seven different countries over the years', he shared.

Now, that variety and scope [means that] you're constantly learning and reinventing yourself. That's obviously hugely important in keeping the passion alive…[Your] passion stays alive when you know that you're making a difference, you're growing yourself, and you're able to grow with [your] people. So, these are the things that you need to be able to find, or better still create, in all that you do.

(Gupta, 2021)

One way to start off is to observe role models across a broad role of personality types within and outside your organisation. See how they behave, observe what styles work for them, and understand why.

Stuart owes his success to various role models he encountered during this career. 'I've had such a great opportunity to work with a lot of wonderful people that I've learned so much from' he said. He learned various things from the numerous people he worked for over the years in different situations – the way they approached problems, thought, behaved in challenging times, and coped with adversity.

> When you meet people, and work with them, you get to know them. You take bits and pieces from everybody you think are great and discard the bits and pieces you don't like. And you think, "Well, I can't do those things. But I'd love to do that attribute of that person."

Try some of the ideas you see in others yourself and see how you feel. You won't know what something is like unless you try something out.

Another suggestion is to hone your skills, experiences, and networks outside of your own organisation, especially if you are in a specialist field and have less exposure to general management concepts. This is essential today, given the speed of business change. Join or volunteer for groups outside of your organisation that excite you. Examples that I highly recommend are joining a not-for-profit to learn about corporate governance, board dynamics, different management disciplines, sectors, and people that you may not be exposed to at work; or a committee associated with the professional bodies you are a member of.

Embrace lifelong learning

Sometimes, after studying for so many years, we decide that's it – no more study. In the past, we may have thought that our organisations' training would give us sufficient knowledge to get our work done. That might have been the case in the past, but it is unlikely to be enough in today's rapidly changing world.

Much of our professional development at work today, especially in our first few years, is geared towards what we need to know to accomplish our work tasks. Structured programmes and professional groups are definitely important early on in our careers. However, they can narrow the lens we use to look at problems. Here are my suggestions:

1. *Don't limit yourself to technical learning.* Many people with culturally diverse backgrounds already have strong technical knowledge; however, they are not as strong in people and workplace navigation skills (Maldonado & Burwell, 2020). As such, be open to experiential learning. Consider learning about other areas that will help you develop your leadership, such as communications, conflict management, networking skills, and navigating office politics. Have coffee with someone you have never met before. Improve your elevator pitch, presentation skills and network by joining a Toastmasters Club.
2. *Learning should be fun, not a chore* – it should engage and challenge you in different ways. Perhaps, your experiences at school evoke bad memories for you, as earlier in your career, you studied something for the sake of getting a qualification, rather than because you really wanted to do it. Choosing something different will let you see things from different perspectives and meet people you would never have met. This will enable you to add value to your organisation and also make you more interesting.
3. *Study at institutions where you will meet different people.* Many learning formats and courses are available today that don't require you to do exams and sit in lecture theatres. Instead, consider arrangements that leverage innovative learning methods. With e-learning platforms and Zoom, you are not even limited to studying in your own country.

Invest in 'me' time

When I finished university, it wasn't common for people to take a 'gap' year between finishing full-time studies and starting work. However, I was keen to commence work straight away, get my first pay-cheque, and save up enough to go on a holiday, buy a car, and put a deposit on a property. As a result, I started my full-time employment at twenty and became a partner at thirty-three.

I have a different view of this today. Careers are now very long. Many of us will work well into our 50s and more commonly into our 60s – often for forty years or longer. So, taking some breaks – whether sabbaticals or regular holidays – during your career isn't really going to make a big difference over the long term. And if you don't, you may find yourself being anxious, feeling out of date, burned out, having health issues, and wanting to stop work earlier than you need to.

When you feel stressed – work less

Tim received two pieces of advice when he worked in a PSF from some senior partners about managing his long-term career sustainability.

First, enjoy the moment when you have downtime, such as when you are on leave.

Second, when you feel stressed, you should work less. In the PSF where he worked, where everyone was working long hours, his partner advised him that working five hours a week less would not impact the quality of his work and ensure that he could work for many years longer.

'In a career, sustainability is an important aspect because sometimes you can work so hard and be focused on something that you get burnt out. I think that's a great danger for a lot of people, myself included', Tim said.

After receiving advice from the senior partners, Tim has incorporated it into his life.

'I still have a crazy job, but now I'm able to manage it a little bit better', he said. 'I think they've helped guide me throughout my career not to not to burn out… If you're feeling stressed out or burnt out, just work less.'

It's also essential to take the opportunity to experiment and reflect during your career journey.

However, trying to do this in a work environment is becoming increasingly challenging. The boundaries between home and work have blurred, and our working lives have become more fast-paced.

It may be necessary for you to spend time away from work to 'take stock' with people outside your regular work circles and networks.

Try to explore different ways that will allow you to invest in yourself. Resting and reflecting between intensive periods is vital. Allow yourself the time to figure out what you want to do and plan the steps you need to take to reinvent yourself.

Case study – INSEAD's Executive Master in Change (EMC)

INSEAD's EMC programme is an eighteen-month programme that I have completed, integrates a business education with a range of psychological disciplines. It has an intense focus on the identity development of yourself and others and how you can use that knowledge to create more effective organisations.

The programme uses a mixture of methods. These include traditional lectures, simulations, socially mediated methods (including mentoring, group coaching, and peer interactions) and written narratives.

It concurrently seeks to maintain liminality for its students in a safe transitional space; facilitates mental and emotional data generation and sensemaking to support increasing self-awareness and identity experiences; helps participants take a meta-view of their own growth processes; and supports them in applying this learning to their organisations.

One of the critical successes of the programme is its experiential learning. It allows students to have a psychologically safe educational 'holding environment' where rules are suspended. Instead, students have opportunities for 'play' that enable them to explore, reflect and undertake identity experimentation.

Key benefits of the programme included that it enhanced our individual and personal development, broadened our theoretical knowledge, and improved our people and leadership skills.

Source: Florent-Treacy et al. (2013)

What we do at the beginning of our careers frequently looks nothing like what we are doing at the end, even though we may be in the same organisation in the same industry. If we don't feel that we can take the time to invest in ourselves, who else will?

5. PAY IT FORWARD

Leadership is about being a leader to followers. So, don't forget to pay it forward to the next generation of leaders.

As a leader, you are responsible for supporting others following behind you. What is your legacy? Here are my three tips.

First, sponsor, mentor, and coach the next generation of leaders. Encourage your other work colleagues to do so.

Second, do what you can in your own organisation to bring to consciousness the underlying reasons for some of the emotions within organisations that may inhibit true diversity.

Finally, encourage your organisation to develop holding spaces for all people (particularly aspiring culturally diverse leaders) to support their reflection and leadership development.

Chapter summary

Career progression is challenging even for the best of leaders, as it requires them to balance their multiple identities. However, being culturally different should not hold people back. To succeed, aspiring leaders need to take risks and yet be able to contain their anxieties.

Five steps aspiring leaders can take to super-charge their careers are:

- Understand themselves and become more aware of their vulnerabilities in stressful situations.
- Have strong relationships with sponsors, mentors, and family who support their aspirations, understand the paradoxical challenges of being a leader and make them aware of the journey ahead.
- Adopt a paradox mindset and negative capability.
- Be open to experiential learning, taking risks and learning from mistakes, even when uncomfortable.
- Pay it forward to the next generation of leaders.

Questions to ask yourself, or for your team members to ask themselves

- If people were to describe me at work, what would they say about me? Would it surprise me? Are there any blind spots I am not aware of?
- Who are my secure bases of people I can turn to both in my work and personal lives to support me at work?
- When experiencing stress, how do I react? Do I take the time to take a step back and work out what is happening and why? Or do I act intuitively, based on my gut feel?
- Am I open and taking the time to learn and experiment? If not, what is holding me back?

NOTE

1 Role biography is a term used to describe a biography of the person-in-role as described through the various work roles they have taken up throughout their lives. This is distinguished from 'role history', a history of an organisational role shaped over time by its various incumbents, especially the original or foundation role-holder. Both role biography and role history, taken together, give the current role-holder a strong sense of how the past might unconsciously influence their current behaviour in the role (Long, 2013).

REFERENCES

Ang, J. (2019). *The Game Plan of Successful Career Sponsorship: Harnessing the Talent of Aspiring Managers and Senior Leaders.* Emerald Publishing. https://doi.org/10.1108/9781787562950

Cardona, F. (2020). *Work Matters: Consulting to Leaders and Organizations in the Tavistock Tradition.* Routledge. https://doi.org/10.4324/9780429317439

Chen, J. (2015). *Best Advice: Don't Be a Superstar.* https://www.linkedin.com/pulse/best-advice-dont-superstar-john-chen

Florent-Treacy, E., Guillen, L., & Van de Loo, E. (2013). *It's About Time You Asked: Participants' Assessment of Learning Experiences in an Executive Development Journey.* INSEAD.

French, R. (2001). 'Negative Capability': Managing the Confusing Uncertainties of Change. *Journal of Organizational Change Management,* 14, 480–492. https://doi.org/10.1108/EUM0000000005876

Guerin, M. (2018). Paradox: "Negative Capability" Is a Very Good Thing. https://www.guerinconsulting.com/post/paradox-negative-capability-is-a-very-good-thing

Gupta, P. (2021, September 6). *The Purpose-Driven Leader: Paige with Piyush Gupta* [Interview]. https://open.spotify.com/episode/0fvvmLJbgsAFSOQEwe7w5O

Horan, J. (2014). *How Asian Women Lead: Lessons for Global Corporations.* Springer.

Ibarra, H. (2015, January). The Authenticity Paradox: Why Feeling Like a Fake can be a Sign of Growth. *Harvard Business Review,* 93(1–2), 52–59. https://hbr.org/2015/01/the-authenticity-paradox

Kets de Vries, M. F. R. (2013). *The Attachment Imperative: The Kiss of the Hedgehog.* INSEAD Working Paper No. 2013/51/EFE. https://papers.ssrn.com/sol3/papers.cfm?abstract_id=2253284

Kets de Vries, M. F. R. (2014, October 23). Take a Look at Yourself in the Leadership Mirror. *INSEAD Knowledge.* https://knowledge.insead.edu/leadership-management/take-a-look-at-yourself-in-the-leadership-mirror-3651

Khoo, V. (2020, October 5). *Interview: 5 Career Lessons I Wish I Knew Earlier – with Valerie Khoo* [Interview]. Professional Development Forum. https://www.youtube.com/watch?v=63PsDjgiWtc&t=1s

Layton, G. (2021, July 28). The Inner Chief in 204. *Vivek Bhatia, CEO of Link Group, on Lifelong Learning, Going Beyond Your Job Description, and Having your Antenna On.* https://theinnerchief.libsyn.com/204-vivek-bhatia-ceo-of-link-group-on-lifelong-learning-going-beyond-your-job-description-and-having-your-antenna-on

Lo, K. (2021, July 12). *PDF Webinar: Women in Leadership: Conversation with Kathrina Lo* [Interview]. Professional Development Forum. https://www.youtube.com/watch?v=GBTsVYu7vjs

For Individuals

Long, S. (2013). Role Biography, Role History and the Reflection Group. In S. Long (Ed.), *Socioanalytic Methods: Discovering the Hidden in Organisations and Social Systems* (pp. 227–236). Karnac. https://doi.org/10.4324/9780429480355

Lu, J. G. (2021). A Social Network Perspective on the Bamboo Ceiling: Ethnic Homophily Explains Why East Asians but Bot South Asians Are Underrepresented in Leadership in Multiethnic Environments. *Journal of Personality and Social Psychology,* Advance online publication. https://doi.org/10.1037/pspa0000292

Maldonado, B., & Burwell, M. (2020). *First Generation Professionals.* https://firstgentalent.org/

Miron-Spektor, E., & Smith, W. (2020, May 5). Overwhelmed? Adopt a Paradox Mindset. *INSEAD Knowledge.* https://knowledge.insead.edu/leadership-organisations/overwhelmed-adopt-a-paradox-mindset-14026

Petriglieri, J. L., & Obodaru, O. (2018). Secure-Base Relationships as Drivers of Professional Identity Development in Dual-Career Couples. *Administrative Science Quarterly,* 64(3), 694–736. https://doi.org/10.1177/0001839218783174

Petrone, P. (2019). *How to Become a CEO, According to Indra Nooyi: Focus on These 3 Things.* https://www.linkedin.com/business/learning/blog/career-success-tips/how-to-land-your-dream-job-according-to-indra-nooyi-focus-on

Pratt, M. G., & Crosina, E. (2016). The Nonconscious at Work. *Annual Review of Organizational Psychology and Organizational Behavior and Human Decision Processes,* 3, 321–347. https://doi.org/10.1146/annurev-orgpsych-041015-062517

Shragai, N. (2021). *The Man who Mistook his Job for his Life: How to Thrive at Work by Leaving Your Emotional Baggage Behind.* Penguin.

Simpson, P., French, R., & Harvey, C. (2002). Leadership and Negative Capability. *Human Relations,* 55, 1209–1226. https://doi.org/10.1177%2Fa028081

Tan, C. (2021). *How Your Diverse Heritage Is an Asset in the Workplace* [Interview]. Professional Development Forum. https://www.youtube.com/watch?v=UtmZPV9a0ew

Ten

INTRODUCTION

There is no doubt in my mind that a coordinated ecosystem effort is required to foster culturally diverse leadership in organisations. It will require contributions by all ecosystem partners – particularly business organisations.

In many countries, societal leaders have increasingly recognised the importance of having culturally diverse leadership. In Australia, the DCA and the AHRC have each released several reports emphasising the importance of leveraging culturally diverse talent over the past decade. Additionally, one of the five recommendations of the Asia Taskforce, an initiative of the Business Council of Australia and Asia Society, was 'championing our rich Asia talent' (Asia Taskforce, 2021). Further, aspiring culturally diverse leaders are willing and eager to step up. The successful Asian-Australian Leadership Summit (AALS) 40 Under 40 Awards demonstrates Australia's wealth of culturally diverse talent.

However, more companies need to step up and play their part. Organisations and their leaders play a significant role in reducing the barriers that lead to aspiring culturally diverse leaders leaving their organisations faster than their colleagues from the cultural majority. This will require organisations to adopt more systematic approaches.

This chapter recaps the importance of leadership diversity and reminds us why diversity and inclusion programmes often fail. It provides a roadmap of the eight essential steps leaders can take to foster culturally diverse leadership in their organisations.

LEADERSHIP DIVERSITY – AN IMPERATIVE FOR SUSTAINABLE ORGANISATIONS

Every day, technology is disrupting business models. Organisations, nonetheless, still need to optimise their 'human' skills – innovation, emotions, and mobility/agility – to survive in the future. Leaders will need to be agile, adaptive, resilient, collaborative, and creative to succeed.

DOI: 10.4324/9781003291237-13

In addition, they will need to operate in another way, embrace a different mindset, and embrace lifelong learning.

On top of this, since the outbreak of the COVID-19 pandemic, employee anxiety has increased, further eroding the traditional psychological contract between employers and employees and leading many people to rethink the meaning of work. Moreover, the 'Great Resignation' has impacted the competition for and availability of talent. As a result, companies need to improve their employees' mental wellbeing. Having a human-centric culture has, therefore, become even more critical.

Tomorrow's high-performing organisations will be the ones that balance performance and people issues. They will achieve financial results, manage for the long term, integrate and align management structures, continuously improve, and treat their employees as their primary asset.

Studies have found that healthy organisations support the fundamental motivational needs of individuals, including their psychological safety, belonging, esteem, and self-actualisation. Likewise, they create an environment that promotes performance- and people-related elements that attract and retain diverse talent and embrace diversity and inclusion in their leadership.

WHY DO MOST DIVERSITY AND INCLUSION PROGRAMMES FAIL?

Changing external stakeholder views; and social, economic, and political forces means that many more organisations now embrace diversity and inclusion. As the importance of ESG grows, today's organisations are expected to satisfy many stakeholders. However, this situation is challenging as most were not established to serve multiple stakeholders or focus on diversity and inclusion.

Embedding diversity in talent management processes and having key performance indicators (KPIs) such as targets to improve diversity can help support cultural diversity. Yet, studies have shown that many diversity management practices can have an uncertain impact on workplace diversity in organisations.

Most diversity initiatives are significant change management interventions that aim to influence and change core organisational elements and challenge organisational and professional identities. They cover areas as broad as corporate culture and structures, human resource management policies and practices, and intergroup dynamics.

However, diversity organisational change initiatives are complex and difficult to implement. Change programmes challenge 'deeply held beliefs, practices and basic assumptions that bond insiders together and cast others out' (Jarrett, 2021, p. 1). Further, in the case of cultural diversity, they also aim directly at cultural identities, which are identities that are developed in young children and may be deeply rooted (Foldy & Buckley, 2017). If organisations are not careful, new initiatives can have unintended consequences and won't create sustainable change.

Ronit Nadiv and Shani Kuna suggest that there are three paradoxes of diversity initiatives (Nadiv & Kuna, 2020). These paradoxes are:

- *Long-term business goals vs short-term losses*, as most companies arguably focus most on the business case for cultural diversity in leadership. Unfortunately, this means that some diversity initiatives are reprioritised when companies focus on managing other external issues, such as COVID-19 challenges, and when business opportunities reduce.
- *Necessary change vs desire for stability*, as unconscious dynamics in organisations resist change.
- *Bureaucratic control vs flexible procedures*. Diversity and inclusion initiatives that add procedures without well-thought-out responsibility and accountability mechanisms can act as social defences and inhibit change. This is sometimes the case for many traditional diversity interventions, such as having employee resource groups (ERGs) or implementing flexible work policies. Many of these initiatives are designed to increase equality of opportunities at work and enlighten people on workplace challenges. However, they do not address the deep assumptions within their organisational cultures nor increase their leadership diversity.

In reality, many diversity programmes fail to have the impact that organisations hope. For many organisations, increasing diversity is not one of their top business issues but, instead, is a 'nice to have'.

While some companies focus on meeting legal requirements, others link diversity to customer opportunities. Many organisations use quotas or targets to drive accountability for change and implement well-meaning policies and procedures. Others focus on diversity training that can make things worse, not better. This is because they can exacerbate conflicts, activate bias and anxieties or fail to deal with underlying power issues. As a result, KPIs are missed, and organisations prioritise other business challenges over their diversity initiatives, having failed to achieve meaningful change.

Clearly, a few band-aids and tactical solutions won't move the dial in the long run. That is not to say that they shouldn't be undertaken. However, the interventions an organisation chooses need to be well thought through, closely managed and lead to sustained behavioural change.

Adopting rational solutions that only deal with institutional logics may not move the dial. On the contrary, if they don't get below the surface and deal with emotions, they may increase anxieties. Further, inertia and ambivalence can kill change in many organisations, particularly in cultures with an aversion to new ideas, multiple silos, and a lack of implementation skills (Jarrett, 2009).

Why is change so painful?

Most change programmes are hard work. According to Edgar Schein, the start of any change programme requires organisations to undergo a period of disconfirmation and overcome learning anxiety to change.

Disconfirmation is any information that shows that some of the organisation's goals are not being met or processes are not accomplishing what they are supposed to. Still, disconfirmation doesn't always motivate change until it evokes *survival anxiety* or guilt. Even when survival anxiety is felt, people often deny or repress their thinking, feelings or behaviours. Often disconfirmation data is accessible in organisations, but attention is not paid to it. This may be because leaders in positions to act may deny or repress the data for personal psychological reasons or because the information is available in the organisation but is suppressed.

Only when strong forces and survival anxiety are experienced can a change programme be launched. But, unfortunately, this often only takes place because of a scandal or a crisis.

Learning anxiety is where we resist change as it requires us to give up old habits and ways of thinking and learn new ones. Regrettably, people cannot discover new behaviours or adopt new attitudes when they fear losing their current position or group membership or lack self-esteem. This can lead to denial, scapegoating and manoeuvring.

As such, for any change process to be effective, first, survival anxiety or guilt must be greater than learning anxiety. And second, learning anxiety must be reduced rather than increasing survival anxiety.

Sources: Coutu (2002) and Schein (2017).

Before continuing, take a few moments to ask both yourself and your colleagues/team members the following questions (Table 10.1):

Table 10.1 Do we need to refine our diversity initiatives?

	Yes	No
Are our diversity initiatives and our organisational culture fully aligned?		
Do we truly understand the barriers/shared basic assumptions to greater cultural diversity across all levels of our organisation, including what may be 'under the surface' and 'unsaid' that inhibits change?		
Is our organisation ready for change?		
Do we believe that our organisation has an environment of psychological safety, which allows our people to speak up, take risks and challenge the status quo?		
Do we, as leaders, understand what is expected of us as part of our diversity initiatives?		
Do we leverage relationships across the whole organisation as part of our diversity initiatives?		
Do we solicit input from our teams on their points of view on our initiatives and provide them with timely feedback?		
Do we use a variety of interventions that involve both 'imitation and identification', as well as 'trial-and-error' learning?		
Is accountability for diversity initiatives, both individual and collective clear and understood?		
Are our measures for improvements in diversity long-term, directional, qualitative and quantitative, and consider improvements across the organisation?		
Do our aspiring culturally diverse leaders have equal access to sponsorship, mentoring, and coaching programmes? Do we use a combination of internal and external programmes?		
Do we ensure that aspiring culturally diverse leaders get access to a diverse range of sponsors, mentors, coaches and role models from across our organisation?		
Do we ensure that aspiring culturally diverse leaders are given equal access to leadership development programmes? Do they provide aspiring leaders with sufficient time and space to undertake identity work?		
Do we review and refine our diversity initiatives regularly?		

Source: Own research.

If your answers to any of these questions are no, then keep reading.

EIGHT STEPS TO FOSTER CULTURALLY DIVERSE LEADERSHIP IN YOUR ORGANISATION

Now that your organisation has decided that it needs to refine its initiatives to increase the cultural diversity of its leadership (Figure 10.1), what are some of the critical steps you need to take?

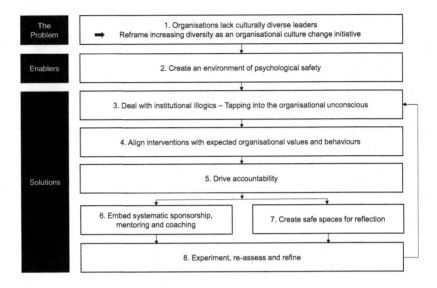

Figure 10.1 Eight steps to foster culturally diverse leadership in your organisation

Source: Own research

1. Reframe increasing diversity as an organisational culture change initiative

Embracing diversity in leadership requires organisations to balance their performance and people objectives. Additionally, they need to increase their diversity leadership and grow their talent pool simultaneously. Finally, it requires everyone to believe (both consciously and unconsciously) in diversity and inclusion and act inclusively at all levels. The glue that pulls this all together is the organisation's culture – which aligns the organisation's purpose and lived behaviours.

> **Why reframe diversity as an organisational culture change initiative?**
>
> You may be asking – why should we view increasing diversity in leadership as a culture change initiative? The reason is that there is a need to modify some of the shared basic underlying assumptions in the organisation, which determine behaviours, perceptions, thoughts, and feelings.

In Edgar Schein's well-known model for understanding and analysing organisational culture, one of the three levels is assumptions. Shared basic assumptions are unconscious, taken-for-granted beliefs and values in groups that explain what people focus on, what things mean, how people react emotionally to what is going on, and what they may do in different circumstances. Additionally, they provide group members with a sense of identity, inform members who they are, how to behave towards each other, and help them feel good about themselves (Schein, 2017).

There is clearly strength in companies having a strong organisational culture. Yet, shared basic assumptions tend to be non-confrontable and non-debatable, so they are difficult to change.

To change them requires revisiting closely held beliefs, which can destabilise individuals or groups and lead to anxiety. This involves managing large amounts of learning and survival anxiety and having an environment of (re)learning (Coutu, 2002; Schein, 2017; Burke, 2018).

Consequently, organisations and individuals should consider reframing the steps they take to address workplace diversity and inclusion as a form of organisational cultural change. It requires us to consider several questions (Table 10.2).

Table 10.2 Change questions to ask

Questions to ask	Possible considerations
What are our alternatives?	Increase leadership cultural diversity, maintain status quo
How are we going to change? (content)	Groom talent from in, recruit talent from outside
What is the process of change?	When, how fast, in which order
How are the recipients of change likely to act?	Resistant, supportive, ambivalent

Source: Adapted from Burke (2018).

Edgar Schein stresses that it is essential to be very clear about the change goals before undertaking a culture assessment. His views are that:

1. The change goal must be described in concrete behavioural terms, not as 'culture change'.
2. Old cultural elements can be destroyed by eliminating those who 'carry' those elements. New cultural elements can be only learned if the new behaviour leads to success and satisfaction over time.
3. Changes in the shared basic assumptions of a culture always require a period of unlearning that is psychologically painful.
4. The change will become perpetual as task complexity and systematic interdependency increase (Schein, 2017).

Where do you start?

Several change management frameworks could be applied when developing your programme. A typical evidence-based institutional change programme covers the following areas:

1. Collect the data.
2. Assess the organisation's 'changeability'.
3. Implement evidence-based change interventions.
4. Build up effective change leadership.
5. Develop and communicate a compelling vision.
6. Leverage your social networks.
7. Support implementation practices – empower others to act.
8. Promote small trials and experimentation.
9. Assess change progress and results over time.
10. Embed the change to sustain effectiveness (Adapted from Jarrett, 2009; Stouten et al., 2018).

Getting Steps 1 and 2 right is vital – it can make or break a programme. The programme should be based on a well-developed understanding of the problem.

- *Step 1: Collect the data.* Assess whether the change is needed. Obtain information across the organisation from multiple stakeholders, not just top management and human resources. Use qualitative and quantitative[1] information across all levels of the organisation (and possibly even from external stakeholders) and consider discrepancies between current assumptions and realities. From a qualitative perspective, be aware of:

- *Societal and historical context.* Recognise the influence of societal and historical contexts to avoid leaping to diagnoses based on individual or cultural inadequacies—instead, position processes and outcomes in the historical and social environment.
- *Power and authority.* Understand the group and organisational power dynamics in your organisation. These include which organisational members hold power (formal and informal) and why some of them may be more likely than others to be 'authorised' as leaders.

Do not get bogged down in collecting extensive 'spuriously accurate' quantitative data. Many organisations begin their diversity journey by attempting to determine the exact number of culturally diverse individuals throughout the organisation and then get stuck when they discover that they don't have this data going back in time. Random sampling can be employed to assist in gathering this longitudinal data on the number of culturally diverse individuals.

- *Step 2: Assess the organisation's readiness for change.* Consider external perspectives, internal capabilities, and leadership when assessing an organisation's readiness for change.

Most change management frameworks focus on institutional logics and increasing productivity. However, the approach adopted should focus both on logics (technical solutions) and incorporate illogics (or adaptive solutions) that get below the surface and deal with the messiness of the emotions of the change recipients.

Further, as every company's culture is different, organisations and their leaders need tailored approaches that balance the various paradoxes and tensions they face between their multiple stakeholder objectives. They also need to bring unconscious emotions that sustain inequities to the surface.

What about existing diversity initiatives?

By now, you may be thinking: what about all the other diversity initiatives we have already put in place?

Over the past ten years, many organisations have implemented various diversity interventions and measures. These include improving recruitment processes to reduce bias, unconscious bias training, mentoring, targets or quotas, and measuring pay equity.

Whilst it is necessary to consider interventions at many different levels, and have mechanisms in place to measure progress, your organisation's leaders should reflect on whether they genuinely understand what is inhibiting greater cultural diversity and whether the proposed interventions will lead to behavioural changes and progress in the right direction.

Furthermore, sometimes initiatives may not have a lasting effect, may not be deep enough, or if not well thought through or well implemented, could cause more harm than good.

Beware of jumping to conclusions and adopting solutions that may have worked for other organisations whose circumstances may differ. In addition, they may not work in the context of your organisation. Therefore, it is worth taking the time to plan upfront.

2. Create an environment of psychological safety

Diversity without inclusion can lead to exclusion. To feel included means that people feel socially accepted, have meaningful relationships, and feel they belong to the organisation.

As part of any change process, a key enabler is creating an environment of psychological safety. This is a situation where people are comfortable expressing and being themselves – where they aren't embarrassed, ashamed, or punished for their questions, concerns, or mistakes on the job. It is a group norm related to how group members believe others view them.

When there is psychological safety, team members feel accepted and respected. Both openness and vulnerability are welcome in the workplace. Psychological safety helps people overcome their defensiveness or 'learning anxiety' – it permits people to speak up, take risks and challenge the status quo (Edmondson & Lei, 2014). Further, it supports organisational learning for individuals, groups, and organisations. Leaders play a critical role in creating an environment for learning by acting in ways that promote psychological safety and reduce team fault lines and invisible barriers.

However, Harvard Business School's Amy Edmundson suggests that having an environment of 'psychological safety is not an "anything goes" environment where people are not expected to adhere to high standards or meet deadlines. It is not about becoming "comfortable" at work' (Edmundson, 2019, p. 17). Those organisations that adopt high-performance standards *and* high psychological safety will operate in a 'Learning and High-Performance Zone'. However, organisations that adopt low-performance standards and low psychological safety will be in an 'apathy zone'. Their people come to work, but their hearts and minds are elsewhere. Therefore, it is vital to ensure that employees do not become too comfortable or overanxious (Edmundson, 2019).

Leaders likewise need to remain mindful that power hierarchies can limit the effectiveness of communication and collaboration, silence weaker team members and inhibit teamwork. Moreover, if they are left unexplored and uncontested, misunderstandings may arise (Edmondson & Roloff, 2009).

Embracing cultural humility – welcoming emotions and anxiety into group discussions to improve cultural diversity

In today's environment of heightened sensitivity about race and ethnicity, many people in the majority may feel threatened. They may fear and avoid discussions about race and ethnicity at work. In addition, many of their thoughts and questions about diversity may become more repressed as people seek to be politically correct. As a result, people may become more likely to make assumptions about someone or something than ask questions about things they don't understand. This may not improve cultural diversity in the long run.

Many global organisations use cultural competence tools to support greater diversity and inclusion. These are designed to help

---

(Continued)

improve people's cultural intelligence. However, a view gaining more prominence is that we shouldn't depersonalise people's individual experiences (Foldy & Buckley, 2017). Instead, we need to embrace greater cultural humility and be more open to listening to each other.

As part of your initiatives, find ways to leverage small group discussions in safe spaces where people of all different backgrounds become more comfortable speaking about their own experiences without fear of unearthing what is below the surface.

Encouraging people to learn about each other's perspectives and feelings is an integral part of improving cultural diversity in organisations.

3. Deal with institutional illogics – tap into the organisational unconscious

As discussed in Chapter 7, institutional illogics can derail well-thought-through plans if not understood.

It is particularly important to understand this when seeking to support diverse leaders during their careers. A key success factor for aspiring culturally diverse leaders in any organisation is to build a foundation of competence, credibility and confidence during their careers. Specifically, an organisation's culture and context can reinforce or detract from whether someone is perceived to be credible. This perception of credibility is further enhanced by validation from influential sponsors and mentors. However, unsupportive environments may lack psychological safety, and may not encourage sponsors and mentors to support aspiring leaders (Thomas, 2001).

Therefore, as part of the change process, make sure that you tap into your employees' unconscious at all levels to understand 'what is under the surface' that may inhibit change.

Unfortunately, this step is often avoided. Pressure on leadership and their change teams means they are expected to show results. Hence, sometimes they use a 'stick' approach to change, which may have unintended consequences.

Leaders and change managers also need to pay attention to individual and group defence mechanisms, which are inevitable in any change process (refer to Table 10.3).

Table 10.3 Defence mechanisms that may be experienced during diversity culture change

Phases	Common defence mechanisms	
	Individual	Group
Initial diagnosis	Denial	Dependency
	Rationalisation	One-ness[a]
	Intellectualisation	
	Projection	
During change process	Denial	Fight/flight
	Projection	Pairing[b]
	Splitting	
	Projective identification	
	Scapegoating	
	Regression	

Source: Own research.

a One-ness is where group members form a powerful union with and absorb into an omnipotent force. They surrender themselves for passive participation and thereby feel existence, well-being and wholeness.

b Pairing is where the development of the group is frozen by the hope of being rescued by two members who will pair off and create an unborn leader.

Tools to spike into the organisational 'unconscious'

There are several ways organisations can tap into the unconscious of their people, some of which may warrant outside facilitation. It may be helpful to use a combination of data sources. These could include:

- *Group discussions that surface the 'unsaid'*. Focus groups are a common way to understand the views of organisational members. Most focus groups pay attention to what is 'said'. However, they should also focus on bringing *what is 'unsaid'* in the room to the surface. This can be done using group coaching techniques and tools that 'spike into the unconscious' to surface and address issues such as individual and organisational defence mechanisms. Consider leveraging observers who focus on understanding the unconscious group processes in groups. Encourage team members to go below the surface to unearth team dynamics that could impede group functioning. Tools that could be used are:

(Continued)

- *Night Vision cycle* – This tool, which uses a series of techniques from psychoanalysis and free association, encourages people to allow, communicate and discover whatever thoughts, images or emotions come to their mind when thinking about a problem or a situation (known as associations). The person or team is then encouraged to look for patterns in the associations and frame options informed by these associations (Lehman & van de Loo, 2016).
- *'Immunity to change' model* – This tool helps individuals in groups explore their hidden competing commitments to change (Kegan & Lahey, 2001).

- *Drawings.* Socioanalytic drawings are a valuable way of obtaining rich data about the conscious and unconscious experiences a person has about an organisation. They can facilitate challenging conversations and allow participants to think creatively and openly about their work, relationships, and individual and collective commitments to the organisation. They are frequently used when starting group discussions and drive debates on a collective viewpoint about an organisation's culture (Nossal, 2013). They can also be used with survey tools that explore an organisation's readiness to change.

Other commonly used tools include narratives, storytelling and understanding dreams.

Also, consider using the results of any recent organisational culture audits. A culture audit seeks to identify gaps between the organisation's espoused values and desired behaviours and practices and its actual lived behaviours and practices. The organisation's annual people surveys may also contain other valuable data on its culture. For example, analysing the grades, cultural background, business units, and written comments could provide additional information.

Don't forget about obtaining the views of the senior leadership group. Remember to take the time to understand how your leaders and HR feel about these initiatives.

As part of diversity initiatives, organisations need to welcome emotions into the workplace rather than denying them. Denying feelings can block learning, growth and change, and therefore innovation and creativity. Instead, encourage emotions to be surfaced and discussed is essential in the change process (Foldy & Buckley, 2017). These tools can also be used throughout the change programme to assess how the programme is progressing (or regressing) and determine what modifications need to be made.

4. Align interventions with expected organisational values and behaviours

Any proposed diversity interventions should focus on initiatives that support aligning actual behaviours and practices required to the organisation's desired values.

When planning for them, consider the organisation's external context, past and future values, and unconscious basic underlying assumptions (thoughts, perceptions, beliefs, and feelings) and group dynamics (such as leaders' and followers' behaviours).

So, how do you start? Some people have differing views on what comes first. Case in point – should organisations seek to change beliefs and values first, with behaviour change following then after? Or should they change behaviour first, and then beliefs and values will follow to justify the behaviour?

The key to remember is that behaviour change will only lead to culture change if a new behaviour is perceived to improve things and is adopted. If people are coerced and not involved in the change process, there is a risk they will go through the motions, but the culture won't change them. Table 10.4 suggests my dos and don'ts.[2]

Table 10.4 Dos and don'ts when selecting interventions

What you should do	What you shouldn't do
• Define upfront what is expected of people • Leverage relationships across the ecosystem • Ensure employees share their points of view and provide feedback throughout the process • Consider interventions that involve a combination of 'imitation and identification', and 'scanning and trial-and-error' learning	• Don't assign significant responsibility for driving diversity to junior staff • Avoid putting in place additional policies and procedures that act as social defences

Source: Own research.

What should you do:

- *Define upfront what is expected of people* if the change programme is successful (Schein, 2017).
- *Leverage relationships across the ecosystem* – In managing any diversity programme, recognise that it is essential to *leverage relationships*. Programme leaders should tap into their 'social networks' (such as influential leaders who act as positive role models) and teams in the organisation. Leverage their influence, recognising that change agent effectiveness is frequently created from personal skills and network ties. Building relationships and momentum is important but will take time. For instance, challenging the values and behaviours ingrained in people since childhood, and discussing ethnicity and race, may not be matters people are open to or comfortable speaking about.
- *Ensure that employees share their points of view, provide feedback throughout the process, and that leaders address it quickly and thoughtfully* (Stouten et al., 2018). Millennials and Gen Z will generally be the most open to adopting diversity initiatives, particularly if they wish for a healthier working culture. Therefore, it may be valuable to leverage them as part of transitional arrangements, such as experimenting with pilot projects and trying out bottom-up initiatives they propose.
- *Consider interventions that involve a combination of 'imitation and identification'* (imitate a role model and psychologically identify with that person) and *'scanning and trial-and-error' learning* (Schein, 2017).
- *Don't forget to make the learning experience fun, not a chore!* Fresh ideas using gamification, simulations and humour that promote experiential learning can make the experience more enjoyable.

Diversity nudges, not sludges

One tool frequently used to encourage behavioural changes are 'nudges'. These help individuals break addictions and form new habits. Various books, such as Chip Heath and Dan Heath's *Switch*, Daniel Kahneman's *Thinking Fast and Slow* and Richard H. Thaler and Cass R. Sunstein's *Nudge*, suggest how 'nudges' can be used.

A similar idea for encouraging innovative behaviours has been suggested by the consulting firm Innosight, which uses the term BEAN: Behaviour Enabler, Artifact and Nudge. The behaviour enabler is something like a checklist: a routine or a ritual that makes it easier to do new things. The nudge is an indirect way to encourage new behaviour. In contrast, the artifact is the connective tissue between the two – a type of digital or physical reinforcement to remind you to perform the new behaviour you are trying to follow. In aggregate, these can help overcome blockers to change and can encourage new innovative behaviours (Anthony et al., 2020).

While nudges are helpful when thinking through interventions, remember that you are also seeking to deal with institutional illogics. Therefore, nudges should be part of a broader programme of interventions used over a more extended period of time.

Beware, however, of 'sludges' – which Richard Thaler, the author of *Nudge*, defines as the opposite of a nudge. These are policies, communication or other artifacts that cause friction and get in the way of people taking action.

However, beware of the following:

- Don't assign significant responsibility for driving diversity to junior staff members, such as giving duties to ERGs. Many diverse staff may be happy to take on part-time volunteer roles. However, when the going gets tough, they will have to focus on their business responsibilities, and their focus on diversity may stop.
- Avoid putting in place additional policies and procedures that act as social defences. Whilst organisations will need some guidelines and programmes, these can inadvertently perpetuate issues by increasing survival anxiety and creating more defences. Instead, organisations need everyone who can influence diversity to support people proactively. Identify ways to encourage trust and psychological safety and reduce barriers and blockers, such as support groups where learning problems can be aired and discussed. Remove obstacles and build supporting systems and infrastructure. Have positive role models, resources, training, and involve the learner.

The role of talent management in supporting greater diversity

Some organisations put a cultural diversity lens on their talent management process. Their plans typically are across all human capital areas and include ensuring the following:

- *Recruitment* – All recruitment and succession planning processes include a diverse slate of candidates (including culturally diverse candidates) for all roles and identifying ways to incentivise the recruitment of candidates with a mix of styles and backgrounds into roles.
- *Retention* – Culturally diverse candidates are given equal opportunities to be sponsored/mentored by senior leaders, access to networks and role models, learning and development opportunities, and stretch assignments such as secondments.
- *Promotion* – Identify more culturally diverse staff with leadership potential. Monitor effectiveness of pipeline management through data analytics with a cultural diversity lens at the business unit level. Identify job levels/areas where the representation of culturally diverse talent drops off significantly and consider the need for additional interventions.

While it is crucial to put well-thought-through talent management initiatives in place to enhance cultural diversity in the workplace, leaders must be mindful that these actions alone won't move the bar.

Remember – more often than not, the day-to-day access that aspiring leaders can have with their sponsors, mentors and coaches is one of the most critical factors in people's career progression at work.

Source: Asia Taskforce (2020), own research.

5. Drive accountability

By now, you should have identified interventions appropriate for your organisation and started to roll them out. In addition, your senior leader should clearly understand and articulate why diversity is vital to the organisation.

The next questions to answer include who is responsible for driving improvements in diversity, and what should we measure?

Who is accountable?

Driving accountability for diversity in organisations is not easy. As a leader, the key focus of your initiatives will be to change the collective behaviours of your people towards embracing greater cultural diversity. Yet, each person will have their own perspectives on this. Some people will naturally be open and keen on change – it's crucial to find them and leverage their enthusiasm. However, others will exhibit inertia to change. Unfortunately, ambivalence is often a sign of conflicting tensions.

So, how do you drive accountability for improving diversity individually and collectively? While leaders can modify individual performance criteria and reward individuals who demonstrate inclusive behaviours, it is more challenging to move accountability collectively.

Driving collective accountability for progress in diversity

From my experience leading diversity initiatives, getting the governance and accountability for increasing diversity and having the right resources (both time and funding) from the start is critical. Consider the following:

- *Tone from the top* – The CEO and his leadership team should be responsible for the programme and be accountable for it to the board.
- *Assigning accountability for diversity to those responsible for talent management decisions* – Today, most organisations that operate using a matrix structure should also make business unit leaders accountable for the diversity of their units. This recognises that talent management decisions are generally the responsibility of each business unit. They can be supported by the diversity leader. They should report to the CEO on diversity matters given its strategic importance to the organisation.
- *Appointing a senior leader to coordinate the organisation's diversity efforts* (diversity leader) who also reports directly to the CEO and works closely with the business unit leaders. They should ideally be a member of the organisation's leadership team. In addition,

(Continued)

they should ensure that diversity is a regular agenda topic of the leadership team.

- *Aligning talent and diversity management.* The diversity leader should be involved with talent management oversight to ensure that a diversity lens is given to all talent management decisions. In addition, talent managers should be incentivised to consider diversity (in its broad sense) in all decisions.
- *Ensuring that adequate time and organisational resources are devoted to diversity.* The business unit leaders and the diversity leader should be given sufficient time allocation and budget for diversity matters if they are also responsible for other initiatives. Their performance assessment should consider their role in driving greater diversity across the organisation.
- *Align performance measures with improvements in diversity.* For example, explore whether it is appropriate to align leaders' and team performance measures (such as performance ratings and remuneration) with diversity measures and people engagement scores around diversity elements.

Another question I sometimes hear is, do we need a diversity leader, and what is their role?

When companies start their diversity journeys, they commonly assign responsibility for diversity to a relatively junior HR specialist. Others give responsibilities to internal volunteers. When the role grows, they may then recruit or assign a full-time resource to manage diversity and inclusion.

C-suite leaders need to ask themselves whether this is the best structure. Do they have the right people in charge to ensure that the organisation gives diversity the proper attention and priority? Do their diversity leaders have the conviction, gravitas and/or the experience to drive through the change? Ensure that your diversity leader is set up to succeed – not scapegoated when things get tough.

What should we measure?

The next question I often hear is – should we use quotas or targets?

Even though I am an accountant, I often cringe when people say 'what gets measured, gets done'. Many people conclude that they need to set a quota or target to improve diversity.

Using KPIs is becoming more common, especially as companies are under pressure to disclose their measurable progress in improving their diversity.

Yet, concentrating on meeting a few quantitative indicators fails to recognise that improving diversity should be part of a longer-term cultural journey. Ultimately, what needs to occur is that diversity and inclusion become embedded in the organisation's DNA.

Nevertheless, diversity measures and HR data analytics are helpful tools to track whether organisations are making improvements, provided they are used sensibly. They should focus on measuring progress, both inside and outside HR talent management processes. Here are some broad principles to consider:

- *Directional measures* – Consider using directional measures to assess the progress of the change programme. If targets are used, they should become the longer-term aspirations that the organisation wishes to work towards, not the programme's overall objective.
- *Individual and collective measures* – Use both individual and collective measures to assess whether longer-term improvements in leadership diversity have been made. Consider a balanced scorecard with both quantitative and qualitative measures that reward progress in making sustained behavioural changes over several years, recognising that improvements in diversity and inclusion take time.
- *Across the organisation, not just at the leadership level* – Measure diversity of the talent pipeline across the organisation, and at each key business unit level, not just at the leadership level. Understand the longer-term trend of annual people scores cut by demographics to understand how people think about diversity and inclusion, not just changes in the leadership profile and pipeline.

For instance, senior business leaders could be evaluated using a scorecard that tracks their organisations' and business units' progress in improving diversity for both quantitative and qualitative measures. The scorecard could use various quantitative data over a rolling multi-year period. The qualitative data could include assessing the maturity of the organisation's and each business unit's diversity initiatives against defined best practices across core categories. These categories could include the extent to which diversity is embedded in the business unit's strategy, leadership pipeline progress, talent management processes, learning and development, and client and market initiatives.

Given the increasing focus of organisations on ESG, some companies have been considering how they can best manage their diversity programmes together with their sustainability endeavours. In addition, supporting greater human rights and fairness is part of UN Global Compact Principle #6, which acknowledges that discrimination negatively influences individuals' greater contribution to society.

My view is that there should be coordination between diversity and sustainability efforts, particularly concerning external reporting and disclosure. However, the change initiatives needed to drive diversity are significantly different from sustainability. Therefore, combining all areas together may dilute the effectiveness of your diversity programme.

6. Embed systematic sponsorship, mentoring and coaching

Access to sponsorship, mentoring, and coaching is vital to supporting aspiring culturally diverse leaders to forge new identities as their careers progress. These relationships provide both career and emotional support to aspiring leaders. They are a vital element in the identity work of diverse leaders.

Sponsors, mentors and coaches allow aspiring culturally diverse leaders a diverse, interconnected social environment for personal and reflective learning about their leadership and individual identities. Further, they provide aspiring leaders with a psychological safety environment that encourages them to take interpersonal risks without fear or threat. Finally, they can allow aspiring leaders a safe place to overcome biases and traditional power structures (Murrell, 2022). Each has different benefits for an individual, depending on the circumstances. In particular, having access to sponsors can make or break the career of an aspiring leader.

In reality, most sponsor-sponsee arrangements grow organically, and their attachment styles influence their relationships. Further, people tend to be attracted to work with others similar to themselves. This means that aspiring culturally diverse leaders are less likely to find support organically than other colleagues, and are more likely to find it through professional networking (Maldonado & Burwell, 2020). Unfortunately, this often means that aspiring culturally diverse leaders may not have as many opportunities to bond with potential sponsors in their own workplaces as their colleagues.

Best in class sustainable sponsorship programmes cover selection and matching, engagement process, metrics and measures of success, and top management involvement aligned to their talent development strategy. In addition, sponsors are recognised for their efforts to sponsor diverse candidates. Finally, sponsors are provided with training on the why, what, and how of being a sponsor, and managing 'like me' bias. Specific roles that sponsors can take to help aspiring leaders to 'create a leader persona' include:

- *Access to a broad range of role models* – Help aspiring leaders to observe and work with a wide range of role models with different personalities. This will allow them to accumulate a more extensive repertoire of possible styles to choose from. Leaders can assist this process by sharing clearly what styles work for them and why.
- *Care under challenging conditions* – Take extra care to support young leaders at the most challenging moments in the process (Ibarra, 2000).

In addition to sponsorship programmes, forward-looking organisations recognise that a one-size-fits-all approach may not be the answer for aspiring leaders. So instead, they also use a variety of initiatives that go beyond the traditional relationships and combine different types of mentoring. These include one-on-one mentoring, peer mentoring, group mentoring, reverse mentoring, and purposefully safe spaces for identity work (see *Create safe spaces for reflections* below). One best practice example is inter-organisational one-on-one formal mentoring programmes by culturally diverse mentors, together with peer mentoring (Murrell, 2022).

Finally, given that East Asians have a higher tendency to socialise with other East Asians, sponsorship, mentoring and coaching programmes should ensure that they create opportunities for them to have more inter-ethnic interactions (Lu, 2021).

Don't forget about the men

As companies seek to increase the number of women in their leadership ranks and the cultural diversity of their leadership, it is easy for them to focus on supporting culturally diverse women, and 'kill two birds with one stone'.

When thinking of high-profile Asian-Australian leaders, I found it relatively easy to identify high-profile Asian-Australian women in senior roles. People that came to mind include Ming Long, Katrina Rathie, Kathrina Lo, Penny Wong (Minister for Foreign Affairs), Anna Lee (CEO of Flybuys), and several partners in the Big 4 accounting firms and law firms.

However, when identifying Asian-Australian men, I found that most Asian-Australian male C-suite leaders have a South Asian background. There are fewer C-suite leaders with an East Asian (including South-East Asian background) outside of the accounting and law professions.

When seeking to understand this through the lens of Asian-Australian men, some of them felt that they experienced a 'double-whammy' – feeling it was best not to speak up about their experiences as the diversity and inclusion agenda is so focused on gender that they could be targeted. Another view was that Asian-Australian men are more likely to start their own businesses and succeed that way.

From my interviews, the experiences and aspirations of Asian-Australian men do differ from those of women. Therefore, employers should understand in more detail the experiences of their Asian-Australian men *and* women as distinct groups to ensure they are better supported in the workplace.

---

7. Create safe spaces for reflection

Chapter 8 highlighted the importance of organisations creating safe holding environments and containers, which support identity transition and reflection. As noted in earlier chapters, organisations can often be the cause and container of people's emotional encounters at work.

In today's fast-paced working environments, some employees feel they are on a treadmill that they cannot get off. As a result, work is becoming more difficult for all employees, not just aspiring culturally diverse leaders. Consequently, there is a risk that many leaders may burn out due to the stress and anxieties they experience at work.

Various research has also shown that there are benefits for aspiring leaders having access to temporary identity workspaces. These create a safe space and time for them, providing them with relief from social validation, and legitimising exploration, which supports them in their identity experimentation.

Identity workspaces are institutions that serve as holding environments for identity work. These places offer a strong support network, a community and essential initiation processes that help individuals consolidate their existing identity or move to a new one (Petriglieri & Petriglieri, 2010). Temporary membership in an identity workspace, a place that promises short term-membership but a permanent transformation, can arouse commitment and allow members to reinvent and transform themselves. Furthermore, these experiences can be utilised across future roles and organisations over time (Petriglieri et al., 2017). Examples include pursuing an MBA programme.

Recent events like the COVID-19 pandemic and the Great Resignation have further weakened organisations' ties with their people. As such, there is arguably a greater need for organisations to create identity workspaces that support the career progression of their aspiring leaders.

Several Asian-Australian leaders I spoke to felt that identity workspaces (through participation in leadership programmes) played an invaluable part in preparing them for leadership positions. Unfortunately, not all leaders had access to such workspaces.

Many organisations have well-developed and elaborate leadership development programmes that focus on traditional teaching methods, such as lectures, readings, and case studies. However, leading organisations have created developmental programmes beyond the traditional 'classroom versus on-the-job' dichotomy of methods. These programmes allow participants experiences that enhance their reflections and experimentation in ways that blur the boundaries between the two 'worlds'. This allows learning that is more closely aligned to increased self-awareness (Florent-Treacy et al., 2013).

Unfortunately, some programmes have been modified to operate virtually or even been cancelled in more recent times due to funding concerns. Further, many organisations would prefer that aspiring leaders focus more on client-facing productive work during tough economic times. During times of crisis, my view is that organisations should be even more supportive of people through their leadership journeys and assist them in managing their transitions.

To support lifelong learning, these programmes should continue after people make it into senior leadership positions and comprise of both internally driven initiatives and external programmes.

Case study – building tomorrow's leaders: the role of transition spaces

In my second year as a partner, in 2004, I was fortunate enough to be selected as a member of a Global Emerging Advisory Leadership Team programme. It was a one-year programme with approximately twenty participants. We all benefited from meeting in person in New York for one week at the beginning of the programme. As a result, we had the opportunity to network with global leaders and other partners, understand more about the firm, and reflect more about ourselves. We also met in person a few times in different venues around the world.

In addition, in between these sessions, we worked on a virtual basis in smaller groups on a project where we sought to resolve a business issue for our Global Advisory Leadership Team (GALT). My small group had representatives from the US, Russia, Australia, and Singapore. At the time, there were no female leaders in our Global Leadership Team nor our GALT. The group was asked to investigate how to increase the diversity of our firm – a real-life problem that required us to examine it from different angles and perspectives. We not only considered gender but the rise of the BRICs (Brazil, Russia, India, and China) and the need for greater cultural diversity and cultural intelligence to support our clients. At the end of the programme, we presented our findings and recommendations to the GALT in person in New York.

There were several interesting outcomes of the programme. First, some of the partners in the programme are now very senior global or national leaders in their firms. Second, there is now, nearly two decades later, significantly more diversity in the partnership, including in leadership roles. Who would have thought that my exposure to the programme would have sparked my longer-term interest in diversity and inclusion?

I was not a natural choice for this programme – being female, Asian and from a smaller territory. I was fortunate that the Global Advisory Leader insisted that the candidates selected for the programme be diverse. I was lucky that the Global Financial Services Leader nominated me to attend the programme and gave me the opportunity.

8. Experiment, re-assess, and refine

All change programmes require organisations to experiment, learn and regularly revisit progress and outcomes in line with the broader change initiative. Many successful organisations adopt a 'growth' mindset. Some ideas include:

- *Promote small trials and experimentation.* Focus on creating small wins but be open to experimentation. Leverage failures as an opportunity for opportunities to learn. These should involve different groups of people (managers, junior staff) across the organisation.
- *Assess change progress and outcomes over time.* Consider appropriate use of metrics to gauge the progress of the initiatives across the organisations, leveraging smart data and analytics. Think about using both qualitative and quantitative tools and data that leverage different data sources and cut by business units and demographic groups to determine trends. These could include using people surveys, actual employee data and pipeline data (such as information on propionate promotions). As diversity improvements takes time to progress, don't overfocus on short-term statistics; instead, focus on longer-term trends. And remember to celebrate and communicate small wins!
- *Embed the change to sustain effectiveness.* Integrate diversity change initiatives into the larger systems of the organisation, including its governance, culture, and management systems. One example is ensuring that diversity considerations are embedded in all induction and milestone training programmes. Another is to align expected diversity

223 **For Organisations**

and inclusion behaviours with the organisation's values and performance assessment processes for individuals. Take care to ensure that the rollout of these changes is well thought through and communication plans aligned. Further, they should be flexibly managed and rolled out over time, so their implementation doesn't become bureaucratic and detract from the longer-term objectives of improving diversity.

Remember that all change projects require recalibration over time. Like identity transition for individuals, organisational change is an iterative process of experimenting and learning. Some of the best initiatives are often a result of trying something new, seeing if it works, and then re-assessing what we learned and trying again.

Chapter summary

- Fostering culturally diverse leadership is not easy for organisations. It requires them to balance their performance and people objectives. It also involves all their people to believe and act inclusively (both consciously and unconsciously) at all levels.
- The glue that pulls this all together is the organisation's culture – which aligns its purpose and lived behaviours. Thus, increasing leadership diversity requires embracing diversity to be part of an organisation's lived behaviours.
- Organisations should reframe improving cultural diversity as part of an organisational culture change initiative that supports better intergroup relations. They should go beyond typical approaches and adopt a different lens that gets below the surface and brings to the surface unconscious emotions that can sustain inequities.
- The change management model used to accelerate diversity-related initiatives needs to consider both rational and institutional illogics.
- The critical enabler is having an environment of psychological safety.
- Specific focus areas should include dealing with institutional illogics, aligning diversity interventions with expected organisational values and behaviours, driving accountability, embedding systematic sponsorship, mentoring, and coaching, creating safe spaces for reflection, experimenting, and re-assessing and redefining.

Questions to ask yourself and your team members

- What is our organisation's diversity change goal? What are our alternatives to change?
- How should we change, what process should we adopt, and how are our people likely to react?
- What does our initial data available tell us about our leadership diversity? What do our people think about our existing diversity initiatives to date? What other information might we need to understand our current position?
- Out of a scale of 5, with five being the highest, how would you rate our organisation's readiness for change?
- What could be holding increasing leadership diversity back in our organisation? What could be the conscious and unconscious inhibitors to change? What other issues could be at play?
- If we were to ask aspiring culturally diverse leaders of various levels of seniority about the organisation's culture, what would they say? How would they describe the environment in terms of allowing them to be themselves, say what they think and take risks?
- How does having greater leadership diversity align to our organisation's values and behaviours?
- Who is accountable for improving diversity in our organisation? How do we measure cultural diversity?
- How do we decide who is selected to attend leadership development programmes or participate in mentoring programmes? How do we ensure that these are tailored to the individuals, not just a one-size-fits-all initiative?
- How are aspiring culturally diverse leaders given the time and space to reflect, experiment, re-assess and refine during their careers?

NOTES

1 Quantitative considerations could include understanding the cultural profile of your workforce, your talent pipeline, data from people surveys, and other qualitative information from interviews and focus groups.

2 Various organisations have also made recommendations on how to increase cultural diversity in leadership, which are helpful reference guides for leaders. In Australia, these include the DCA, AHRC, and the Business Council of Australia and Asia Society Australia Asia Taskforce Sub-Committee on Asian-Australian and Diaspora (Asia Taskforce).

REFERENCES

AHRC. Australian Human Rights Commission. (2018). *Leading for Change: A Blueprint for Cultural Diversity and Inclusive Leadership Revisited*. https://humanrights.gov.au/our-work/race-discrimination/publications/leading-change-blueprint-cultural-diversity-and-0

Anthony, S., Painchaud, N., Parker, A., & Cobban, P. (2020). *Eat, Sleep, Innovate: How to Make Creativity an Everyday Habit Inside Your Organization*. Harvard Business Review Press.

Asia Taskforce. (2020). *A Forgotten Advantage: Enabling Australia's Asian-Australian and Diaspora Communities Asia Taskforce Discussion Paper*. Business Council of Australia and Asia Society Australia Asia Taskforce. https://asiasociety.org/australia/enabling-australias-asian-australian-and-diaspora-communities-asia-taskforce-discussion

Asia Taskforce. (2021). *'A Second Chance: How Team Australia can Succeed in Asia': How Team Australia can Succeed in Asia*. Business Council of Australia and Asia Society Australia Asia Taskforce. https://asiasociety.org/australia/second-chance-how-team-australia-can-succeed-asia-report

Burke, W. W. (2018). *Organizational Change – Theory and Practice*. Sage.

Coutu, D. L. (2002, March). The Anxiety of Learning. *Harvard Business Review, 80*, 100–106. https://hbr.org/2002/03/the-anxiety-of-learning

Edmondson, A. C. (2019). *The Fearless Organization: Creating Psychological Safety in the Workplace for Learning, Innovation, and Growth*. Wiley.

Edmondson, A. C., & Lei, Z. (2014). Psychological Safety: The History, Renaissance, and Future of an Interpersonal Construct. *Annual Review of Organizational Psychology and Organizational Behavior, 1*(1), 23–43. https://doi.org/doi.org/10.1146/annurev-orgpsych-031413-091305

Edmondson, A. C., & Roloff, K. (2009, Fall). Leveraging Diversity Through Psychological Safety. *Rotman Magazine*, 47–51. https://scholar.harvard.edu/files/afriberg/files/leveraging_diversity_through_psychological_safety_hbs_article.pdf

Florent-Treacy, E., Guillen, L., & van de Loo, E. (2013). *It's About Time You Asked: Participants' Assessment of Learning Experiences in an Executive Development Journey*. INSEAD.

Foldy, E. G., & Buckley, T. R. (2017). Reimagining Cultural Competence: Bringing Buried Dynamics into the Light. *Journal of Applied Behavioral Science, 53*(2), 264–289. https://doi.org/10.1177/0021886317707830

Ibarra, H. (2000). Making Partner: A Mentor's Guide to the Psychological Journey. *Harvard Business Review, 78*(2), 146–155. https://hbr.org/2000/03/making-partner-a-mentors-guide-to-the-psychological-journey

Jarrett, M. (2009). *Changeability: Why Some Companies Are Ready for Change and Others Aren't.* Pearson.

Jarrett, M. (2021, March 22). The Darker Side of Organisational Life. *INSEAD Knowledge.* https://knowledge.insead.edu/blog/insead-blog/the-darker-side-of-organisational-life-16306

Kegan, R., & Lahey, L. (2001, November). The Real Reason People Won't Change. *Harvard Business Review*. https://hbr.org/2001/11/the-real-reason-people-wont-change

Lehman, R., & van de Loo, E. (2016, October 10). The Value Lurking in Your "Leadership Unconscious". *INSEAD Knowledge*. https://knowledge.insead.edu/blog/insead-blog/the-value-lurking-in-your-leadership-unconscious-4974

Lu, J. G. (2021). A Social Network Perspective on the Bamboo Ceiling: Ethnic Homophily Explains Why East Asians But Not South Asians Are Underrepresented in Leadership in Multiethnic Environments. *Journal of Personality and Social Psychology*, Advance online publication. https://doi.org/10.1037/pspa0000292

Maldonado, B., & Burwell, M. (2020). *First Generation Professionals*. https://firstgentalent.org/

Murrell, A. J., & Onosu, G. O. (2022). Mentoring Diverse Leaders: The Necessity of Identity Work. In R. Ghosh & H. M. Hutchins (Eds.), *HRD Perspectives on Developmental Relationships: Connecting and Relating at Work* (pp. 175–195). Springer International Publishing. https://doi.org/10.1007/978[[sbn]]3[[sbn]]030[[sbn]]85033[[sbn]]3_8

Nadiv, R., & Kuna, S. (2020). Diversity Management as Navigation Through Organizational Paradoxes. *Equality, Diversity and Inclusion: An International Journal, 39*(4), 355–377. https://doi.org/10.1108/EDI-12-2018-0236

Nossal, B. (2013). The Use of Drawing as a Tool in Socioanalytic Exploration. In S. Long (Ed.), *Socioanalytic Methods: Discovering the Hidden in Organisations and Social Systems* (pp. 67–89). Routledge. https://doi.org/10.4324/9780429480355

Petriglieri, G., Petriglieri, J., & Wood, J. (2017). Fast Tracks and Inner Journeys: Crafting Portable Selves for Contemporary Careers. *Administrative Science Quarterly, 63*, 479–525. https://doi.org/10.1177/0001839217720930

Petriglieri, G., & Petriglieri, J. L. (2010). Identity Workspaces: The Case of Business Schools. *Academy of Management Learning & Education, 9*(1), 44–60. https://doi.org/10.5465/amle.9.1.zqr44

Schein, E. H. (2017). *Organizational Culture and Leadership* (5th ed.). Jossey-Bass.

Stouten, J., Rousseau, D. M., & De Cremer, D. (2018). Successful Organizational Change: Integrating the Management Practice and Scholarly Literatures. *Academy of Management Annals, 12*(2), 752–788. https://doi.org/10.5465/annals.2016.0095

Thomas, D. (2001, April). The Truth about Mentoring Minorities: Race Matters. *Harvard Business Review, 79*(4), 98–112. https://hbr.org/2001/04/race-matters

Eleven

INTRODUCTION

As the saying goes, 'it takes two to tango'.

As our lives progress, we all need help from others to succeed at what we do, whether at work, sport, or school. We learn from many people – our parents, teachers, and bosses. And, while our own passion, hard work and intelligence will help us get part-way there, we ultimately need to remember that being a leader is about leading and inspiring followers. Not only do we need to hone not own knowledge to do this, but also our skills and ability to work with others in the systems in which we operate.

Moreover, identity transitions are hard work, especially emotionally. As a result, we often need to unlearn to relearn new things. This requires us to be open, take risks and have the humility to learn from our mistakes.

In earlier chapters, I explored the concept of our identities at work. We also learned how our early experiences in our families, our caretakers influence our adult attachment styles, behaviours and the types of roles and organisations we are attracted to. We also covered the experimentation and learning career cycle of identity work that culturally diverse leaders undergo when undergoing identity transitions and the influence of organisational systems.

This chapter introduces the Career Progression Model for Culturally Diverse Leaders. It also suggests the actions that society, organisations and individuals should take to increase the proportions of culturally diverse leaders at work.

INTRODUCING THE CAREER PROGRESSION MODEL FOR CULTURALLY DIVERSE LEADERS

The development of the leadership identities of culturally diverse leaders involves a dynamic and continuous cycle of experimentation and learning (refer to Chapter 5). They experience increasing anxiety as they become leaders on their journeys. These arise from the tension and paradoxes they

DOI: 10.4324/9781003291237-14

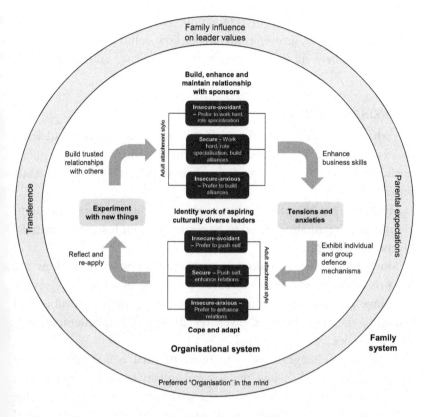

Family influence
on leader values

Build, enhance and
maintain relationship
with sponsors

Insecure-avoidant
– Prefer to work hard,
role specialisation

Secure - Work
hard, role
specialisation, build
alliances

Insecure-anxious
– Prefer to build
alliances

Adult attachment style

Build trusted
relationships
with others

Enhance
business skills

Transference

Parental expectations

Experiment
with new things

Identity work of aspiring
culturally diverse leaders

Tensions and
anxieties

Insecure-avoidant
– Prefer to push self

Secure – Push self,
enhance relations

Insecure-anxious –
Prefer to enhance
relations

Adult attachment style

Reflect and
re-apply

Exhibit individual
and group
defence
mechanisms

Cope and adapt

Organisational system

Family
system

Preferred "Organisation" in the mind

Figure 11.1 Career progression model for culturally diverse leaders

encounter as their careers progress, impacted by the organisational systems they work in (Chapter 7). These conclusions are summarised in Figure 11.1.

The experiences of culturally diverse leaders are significantly affected by a critical unconscious influence – adult attachment styles – that shape how they cope with and handle these anxieties and tensions, as explored in Chapter 8. Adult attachment styles are primarily influenced by their early interactions that people have with their parents and the extent of their acculturation. Further, their experiences within the family system – which I explored in Chapter 4 – influence their career choices, behaviours, and preferences.

While I took a different viewpoint and examined how culturally diverse leaders make it into leadership roles rather than focusing on the barriers to progress, this is not to say that a bamboo ceiling doesn't exist. Successful culturally diverse leaders do experience challenges along their career journeys that they overcome. Their attachment styles can inhibit their career progression if they cannot balance the various divergent tensions.

Few people, culturally diverse or otherwise, make it into leadership roles. However, greater awareness of how culturally diverse leaders succeed will help us to better support our aspiring culturally diverse leaders.

LINKING IT TOGETHER

So, what do we need to do to foster culturally diverse leadership in organisations? To date, companies, individuals and other public institutions have been working on various initiatives but frequently separately.

Figure 11.2 summarises some of the key considerations that individuals and organisations need to be aware of when fostering culturally diverse leadership.

Much of the focus of diversity management by organisations has been on 'above the surface' initiatives. Many organisations have sought to reduce potential discrimination by complying with regulations and changing the organisation's diversity climate by implementing additional policies.

Making the changes needed to move the dial will require a more significant focus on 'below the surface' initiatives. These should seek to positively influence intergroup relations and lead to behaviours that ultimately increase the number of culturally diverse leaders. This will require critical social groups and the organisations where aspiring culturally diverse leaders work to improve their underlying culture. Further, aspiring leaders should become more aware of how they react in work roles and groups. It requires an ecosystem approach.

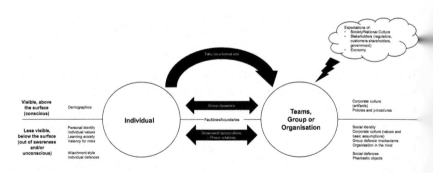

Figure 11.2 Areas that contribute to improvements in culturally diverse leadership

Source: Own research

KEY STEPS REQUIRED BY ECOSYSTEM PARTIES

Understanding the experiences of culturally diverse leaders within organisations has allowed me to suggest ways that individuals, organisations, and society can collectively create more inclusive environments that enable aspiring culturally diverse leaders to reach senior leadership positions. This will require initiatives that lead to changes both above and below the surface.

What aspiring culturally diverse leaders can do

Aspiring culturally diverse leaders in multicultural nations need to recognise that reaching the pinnacle of your organisation is not easy. The closer you get to the top, the more difficult it will become. It requires both efforts by you and the help of others. Everyone in a leadership role is successful in their own right. So, yes – you need to be motivated and work hard. However, you also need to be aware of the external environment you are operating in. Here are some suggestions.

- *Understand yourself.* The value you bring to an organisation includes your technical skills and being trusted to act respectfully. In line with changing societal expectations, organisations increasingly seek leaders who demonstrate sustainable performance – balanced with people. Become more aware of how you operate and appear in the eyes of others. Knowing your preferences will help you identify the types of organisations and roles you prefer and where you shine.
- *Understand your organisational culture.* Each organisation has its own culture. The more complex your organisation, the more challenging it can be to navigate. To succeed, you will need agility and adaptability to experiment and learn how to handle yourself, as there will be multiple stakeholders and perceptions to manage. Build solid relationships and visibility across the organisation, especially ones with people who can help you succeed.
- *Understand your environment.* External context and expectations play a part in shaping how people are evaluated. National cultures shape the expectations of who a leader is and how people expect them to operate. These expectations change over time, as it is a collective view. It is essential that you bear this in mind and embrace it at work, not fight against it.

What organisations and their leaders should do

A challenge for any programme that seeks to change an organisation's behaviours is that organisations and their people are frequently resistant to change.

Most programmes tend to focus on the rational and logical elements of the change process. However, anxieties exist in all organisations and are often demonstrated through unconscious individual defence mechanisms such as projection, regression or splitting, or externalised through practices such as groupthink or scapegoating, and group basic assumption behaviours. As a result, well-intended initiatives such as increasing leadership diversity and inclusion in organisations can be derailed if they are not well thought through.

Further, if they don't deal with emotions such as feeling threatened, anxious, and doubtful, these programmes may inhibit longer-term change. An example is where a firm's policies and practices create the illusion that work-life balance was a woman's problem rather than a result of the firm's gruelling 24/7 work culture (Ely & Padavic, 2020).

Increasing the number of culturally diverse leaders more systematically requires organisations to create a psychologically safe environment that supports them on their journey into leadership roles. It also needs each organisation to be brave enough to take the necessary steps to remove the unconscious inhibitions, blockers, and conflicts to more open intergroup relations.

It is vital that companies create environments where staff can feel safe, contain their emotions, and adopt negative capability.

Their national context will influence how companies deal best with these change initiatives.

Companies should also partner with government and industry bodies, professional organisations, and universities to share best practices and build collective momentum.

What should society do?

There are several actions societal groups can take to support increased cultural diversity in leadership. It will be crucial that they coordinate with each other to advocate for and drive change. While not within the scope of my research, the following are some suggestions.

- Governments have a role in developing coordinated national frameworks that support multiculturalism and ensure the appropriate representation of culturally diverse leaders. Governments should consider:

  - Establishing frameworks for measuring diversity and capturing data.

- Coordinating, participating in, or supporting partnership efforts and working groups, as appropriate to support dialogue and actions between government departments, companies and their senior leaders to increase cultural diversity in leadership, such as across industries/sectors. Clear responsibilities should be assigned for this.
- Supporting champion networks, advocacy and communication of case studies and profiling of role models.
- Developing and communicating well-thought through best practices in increasing cultural diversity.
- Increasing the diversity of the leadership in the public sector, government boards and committees.
- Offer funding, scholarships or incentives for appropriate organisations or individuals

- *Industry groups and professional organisations* play a crucial role in supporting their members through networking, education and sharing best practices. In addition, professional organisations have a role in supporting their members' career development and greater long-term sustainability, not just their short-term business needs.
- *Advocacy groups* play a role in supporting more culturally diverse leadership. They should continue to deepen their collaboration with companies, industry groups, professional organisations, and universities.
- *Education* – Universities and other educational institutions play a critical role in supporting greater cultural diversity in leadership through their research, advocacy and education initiatives.

In Australia, the Australian National University (ANU – see below), the University of Sydney (through various programmes such as the Dr John Yu Fellowship), and the University of Melbourne (including through Asialink) have launched a number of cultural diversity initiatives to date.

In particular, the success of the inaugural AALS in September 2019 led one of the Summit's co-convenors, the ANU, to initiate a national call-to-arms through the establishment of the ANU Centre for Asian-Australian Leadership (CAAL) in 2020. Its vision is to achieve greater Asian-Australian representation and cultural diversity leadership in Australia and break the 'bamboo ceiling' facing Asian-Australians. CAAL seeks to address the significant under-representation of Asian-Australians in leadership positions within Australian public institutions and major private-sector corporations. Since its establishment, CAAL has undertaken independent research and public policy development, targeted engagement and outreach initiatives. It is driving conversations at the national level to challenge existing leadership models to ensure Australian institutions better reflect the diversity of Australian society.

However, other organisations, particularly industry groups and professional organisations, can do much more to support the future sustainability of their organisations and members through these initiatives.

FOSTERING THE NEXT GENERATION OF CULTURALLY DIVERSE LEADERSHIP IN ORGANISATIONS

Most boards and C-suite leaders today agree that embracing greater diversity and inclusion in the workplace is right and makes business sense. Changing societal views require organisations to become more inclusive. However, despite the strong business case, most leadership teams in multicultural nations still lack cultural diversity. In the meantime, many talented and aspiring leaders are eager, willing, and ready to step up. How can we all work together to create a win-win situation for all?

Using a system psychodynamic lens and theories of identity development and attachment theory, in this book, I identify how culturally diverse leaders in Australia resolve the conflicts and contradictions between their multiple identities.

From their stories, I propose that fostering culturally diverse leadership in organisations will require an ecosystem approach. For cultural diversity to become a hallmark of leaders in multicultural nations will require a different 'change lens' to be adopted – by their people, organisations, government bodies and society. I suggest steps that aspiring culturally diverse leaders can take to super-charge their careers and propose a roadmap on how to foster culturally diverse leadership in organisations.

This book shares several new perspectives. First, taking a psychodynamic lens, I explain how individuals with culturally diverse backgrounds incorporate multiple identities and take up roles. Second, I contribute to identity work research in Australia, which has not been studied extensively previously. Third, I show how attachment styles influence identity work and explain why experiences differ. Finally, I show how hidden family dynamics play out in organisations.

*****

In September 2021, in support of the 'This Little Girl is Me' campaign, shared a post on LinkedIn that went viral, garnering over 850,000 views

This little girl is me

Figure 11.3 The author, age one, and her father
Source: Loon family collection

This little girl grew up in Tamworth, five hours by car from Sydney, in a small Australian city where there were few Chinese families and where she was always the only Chinese kid in her class (Figure 11.3).

She came home crying one day from primary school as the kids called her a Ching Chong Chinaman. She didn't realise that she was different to the other kids. Her mum told her to say that "sticks and stones will break my bones, but names will never hurt me". But deep down, they did.

Her parents worked super hard so that she and her brother could both go to private high schools. However, in high school, she never felt she fit it.

One day, her English teacher told her that her written English was like a foreign student in front of the whole class despite all her grandparents being born in Australia and that she only spoke English. She also didn't get the scholarship she really wanted to get to go to the UK.

Determined to prove them all better, she threw herself into her studies and got the marks she needed to get into a degree that would allow her to qualify as a Chartered Accountant. She was the first in her family to go to university.

(Continued)

This little girl loved her work at her Big 4 firm, where she got to work with some amazing people. She got double promoted after her first year, although she remembers hearing snide comments about her from male colleagues. So, she left Australia at twenty-five to work in Singapore and became a partner at a Big 4 firm.

She, however, often felt imposter syndrome – as if she was never good enough. So, she threw herself into her work to minimise the likelihood of being challenged. Fortunately, there were people who helped her in her journey and gave her a go, even though she was always the less conventional candidate for the role.

This little girl now wants to give back to others through boards and other roles. She is determined to ensure that the next generation of Asian-Australians has greater opportunities.

To all the little girls out there and younger Asian-Australians who feel that there are barriers to their career progression, be confident and positive, and always ask for help from sponsors and mentors. Don't let the pressure get to you when you don't feel like you belong. And follow your heart.

Many talented little girls and boys of all backgrounds out there, like me, have big dreams of making a difference in their nations.

As leaders and aspiring culturally leaders, we can all learn a lot from narratives of culturally diverse leaders who have thrived and smashed the 'bamboo ceiling' in their organisations. We are all shaped by our experiences with our parents in our families, and the various roles we have taken on in the past. Some of them have been able to negotiate our identity transitions better than others, depending on their early family experiences, attachment styles, and experiences at work.

Make sure you take the time to understand yourself, your journey so far, your aspirations and the system you work in. However, don't forget to remember that you are not alone in your career journey. Reach out to others to help you – family, colleagues, and friends – who all want to make sure that you succeed. A key success factor will be finding secure bases to support you in balancing the various tensions you will face. Adopting a paradox mindset and negative capability will help. Continue to experiment, learn, and reflect – but keep in mind that a career journey is a marathon and not a sprint. And finally, to be a leader, you need to have followers, so remember to give back to the next generation of aspiring leaders behind you.

*****

COVID-19 has reminded many of us how our feelings can play out at work. Many of us felt strong emotions, which we could not contain at times due to boundaries between home and work being dismantled. Some of us felt fear, which has played out in many ways, with people handling it differently. Yet many have also been reminded of the importance of secure bases – our family and relationships.

At the same time, recent reports of increased discrimination and anxiety by people of Asian backgrounds in many multinational nations suggest that understanding cultural diversity, identity work and emotions in the organisations in these countries cannot be ignored.

Many leaders are now much more aware of balancing between focusing on performance and people. To better support their people, leaders need to provide their people of all backgrounds to contain their emotions at work. Further, they need to create psychologically safe environments.

Many organisations are now at a tipping point. Their focus on ESG and COVID-19 has required them to revisit why and how they do business, including the right talent for their future sustainability. In addition, many are rethinking how they can better support attracting and retaining the right people for their organisations in the longer term. This will involve pivoting towards more human-centric organisations.

Tomorrow's world-class organisations will be the ones that ensure that their aspiring culturally diverse leaders will become the best they can be. First, they will provide psychologically safe environments. Their people will feel comfortable being themselves, sharing their vulnerabilities, and understanding each other's long-buried unconscious and emotional concerns. Their organisation's values and behaviours will be fully aligned, focusing on greater leadership diversity. They will also provide sponsorship and mentoring opportunities and create safe spaces for reflection for aspiring leaders. Finally, they will have appropriate accountability for progress and regularly experiment, re-assess, and refine their initiatives.

If you are a leader, now is the time for you and your organisation to take sustainable action to foster greater culturally diverse leadership. We all have a role in bringing the dreams of all little girls and boys to life.

Chapter summary

- The identity work of culturally diverse leaders, encapsulated in the Career Progression Model for Culturally Diverse Leaders, involves a dynamic and continuous cycle of experimentation and learning.
- On their career journeys, impacted by the organisational system, culturally diverse leaders face increasing anxieties as professionals then leaders that arise from the tension and paradoxes encountered as their careers progress. In addition, their experiences are significantly affected by a critical unconscious influence – adult attachment styles – which shape how they cope and handle these anxieties and tensions.
- Their adult attachment styles are influenced by their early interactions with their parents and their acculturation. Further, their experiences within the family system influence their career choices, behaviour, and preferences.
- The key to increasing cultural diversity in leadership is to recognise that unconscious dynamics are frequently at play in organisations, inhibiting intergroup relations.
- Efforts to improve intergroup relations, which consider both above and below the surface dynamics, can improve an organisation's culture and, ultimately, its cultural diversity.
- Accelerating cultural diversity in leadership requires an ecosystem approach, combining individual, organisational, and societal efforts. While some actions have been made to date, much more can be done.

Questions to ask yourself and your team members

Yourself

- What are the three steps that I am going to take to super-charge my own career and support the careers of aspiring culturally

diverse leaders behind me in my organisation? What is my timeframe, and what support do I need to complete the steps?
- What will I do to foster culturally diverse leadership in broader society? Examples could include mentoring aspiring culturally diverse leaders outside my organisation, or working with industry bodies, professional organisations and advocacy groups to promote greater cultural diversity in leadership?

Your team members

- How would we describe how people interact in teams in our organisation? For instance, are people comfortable being open and transparent about their thoughts and feelings? Or are there silos and side conversations, or no conversations at all?
- How would our employees describe the culture and behaviours in our organisation? Does it allow us the opportunity to grow collectively, as well as individually simultaneously?
- How does the external societal context (government, professional groups, advocacy groups) encourage or inhibit improvements in the cultural diversity of our organisation?
- What are the top three actions that we will take to foster culturally diverse leadership in our organisation? What is the timeframe by which we will complete them by? Who do we need help from?
- What will our team/organisation do to foster culturally diverse leadership in our broader society? Examples could include working with industry bodies, professional organisations and advocacy groups to promote greater cultural diversity in leadership?

REFERENCE

Ely, R. J., & Padavic, I. (2020, March). What's Really Holding Women Back? *Harvard Business Review*. https://hbr.org/2020/03/whats-really-holding-women-back

Appendix A

The study that forms the basis of this book is an extension of my thesis undertaken as part of my Executive Master in Change at INSEAD. My research interest was identifying how people with culturally diverse backgrounds become leaders in Australia. I felt that understanding how they became leaders would enable me to recommend to aspiring culturally diverse leaders how they could accelerate their careers, and to organisations how to foster culturally diverse leadership. Whilst working on my thesis, I became fascinated by the concepts of identity and identity work.

I decided to focus on Asian-Australians, given their growing presence and unique challenges in reaching senior leadership positions. Outside of the Asian-Australian cohort, the number of people with non-European backgrounds in Australia is small.[1] Many Asian-Australians have a preference to become professionals – particularly doctors, dentists, and lawyers.

In determining whom I should interview, I sought to identify Asian-Australians who had similar career patterns. To date, Australian researchers have explored the barriers to greater culturally diverse leadership in listed companies, academia, the legal profession, and media. However, academics have done little industry-wide research in the accounting profession, a sector where many Asian-Australian graduates and skilled migrants start their careers. As a result, I decided to focus on the accounting profession, and particular partners of Big 4 accounting firms. This was because the promotion processes of all Big 4 accounting firms to partner are broadly similar globally, and I would be able to identify a relatively large number of Asian-Australian partners in the Big 4 firms to whom I could speak to.

I used grounded theory to answer my research question, 'How do Asian-Australians become partners in Big 4 firms in Australia?'. Grounded theory is an appropriate method to use to identify how Asian-Australians reach leadership positions as it is a qualitative, bottom-up exploratory method that generates theory 'grounded' in data to explain a situation where participants have all undergone the same process (Creswell & Poth, 2018). Bearing in mind the considerations and recommendations of Creswell and Poth (2018) and Thomson (2011), I interviewed thirty current or former partners.

The partners I spoke to were relatively senior, with 37% over fifty, 40% between forty and forty-nine, and all aged at least thirty-five. There was a close to fifty/fifty mix of men and women. The partners also had diverse ethnic backgrounds (North Asian, South-East Asian, and South Asian ethnicities), and life experiences, with 60% of the partners doing all their schooling in Australia, and the remaining 40% moving to Australia in late high school or as working adults.

While a large majority of the interviewees joined a Big 4 firm as graduates, 27% joined a Big 4 firm as a direct-admit partner from a law firm, another consulting firm, or a corporate. The partners interviewed worked across all lines of service. Some held senior global roles, national and business unit leadership roles, and senior client service roles in their organisations.

I invited them to share with me details of critical incidents they remembered at the ages of twelve, twenty-two, thirty-two, and so on in their work roles using self-drawings to prompt their thoughts. At each age, they revealed to me the positives, negatives, challenges, and lessons that they learnt. I also asked them to tell me about their experiences making it to partnership. My focus was not just on the words they said but also on what was not said – body language, feelings, and how these made me feel 'from the balcony'.

As part of the interview process, I asked each of the participants to draw a critical incident they remembered at the ages of twelve, twenty-two, thirty-two, and so on in their work roles using mini-drawings of themselves. After completing the drawing, I explored the biography with them, asking them to describe the positives, negatives, challenges, and lessons learned from the role. If they did not do a drawing, I asked them to explain what came to mind from a role at each age.

For instance, twelve is when many people change schools and start their adolescent identity formation. At this age, the leaders described situations such as making new friends, learning who they could trust and realising that they were different to some of the other kids at school. These types of situations can be stressful and lead to anxieties. As for the age of twenty-two, many had just started work. At thirty-two, most were in middle management, had family commitments and were progressing towards senior leadership positions. At forty-two, most were senior leaders. At work, they often described situations where they had to deal with certain emotions, whether positive or negative, such as a promotion, an identity threat or making an important decision.

For the incidents described at twelve, I classified the leaders by attachment styles (being secure, insecure-anxious, insecure-avoidant, fearful), discussed further in Chapter 8. For two of the leaders, as their adult behaviours indicated that their attachment style had changed as an adult, I reclassified their attachment style determined at twelve. Finally, I analysed my interviews categorised by adult attachment styles to decipher any patterns that influenced their journeys into senior leadership roles. This iterative process of moving back and forth between my data, my emerging model, and the relevant literature on identity, identity work, and leadership development allowed me to develop my Career Progression Model for Culturally Diverse Leaders.

For this book, I interviewed an additional seven senior (predominantly C-suite or equivalent) Asian-Australian leaders of various backgrounds across the public and private sectors and various industries. I sought to understand where their experiences were similar or differed from those in the Big 4 firms. I also undertook additional research into cross-cultural identities and developed my roadmaps of recommendations through further research.

NOTE

1 Of the top twenty countries for foreign-born residents in 2016 based on data from the Australian Bureau of Statistics, the only countries not in Europe, the only non-Asian countries were New Zealand, South Africa, the US, and Lebanon. Other than people born in Lebanon, of which less than 100,000 live in Australia, the residents of these other countries are likely to have backgrounds similar to people born in Europe.

REFERENCES

Creswell, J. W., & Poth, C. N. (2018). *Qualitative Inquiry and Research Design: Choosing among Five Approaches* (4th ed.). Sage.

Thomson, S. (2011). Sample Size and Grounded Theory. *JOAAG, 5*. https://www.researchgate.net/publication/228513695_Sample_Size_and_Grounded_Theory

The Clinical Paradigm

Appendix B

The concept of the Clinical Paradigm, promulgated by Manfred Kets de Vries, is a helpful framework through which we can understand how people behave in organisations.

The starting point of the Clinical Paradigm is that 'the key to growth and happiness lies in knowing and accepting oneself' (Kets de Vries et al., 2016, p. 19). As such, leadership development is an exploration of and by the leader. This is undertaken by making sense of our deepest wishes and fantasies, and then understanding how these fantasies influence our behaviour in the organisational world (Kets de Vries & Cheak, 2016). Understanding ourselves can help us reveal blind spots we are unaware of, impacting our longer-term career progress.

The Clinical Paradigm has four basic premises.

The four basic premises of the Clinical Paradigm

1. *There is a rationale behind every human act* – a logical justification, even for actions that appear irrational. All our behaviours have a reason. However, trying to uncover this can be tricky and mysterious, as it links with our unconscious needs and desires.

2. *What we see isn't what we get.* We all have blind spots. A great deal of our emotional life – feelings, fears, and motives – lies outside of conscious awareness but influences our conscious reality and even physical wellbeing. Even the most sensible people have aspects they can't see about themselves – a dark side that they don't know and don't want to know. Our human unconscious affects (and in some instances even dictates) our conscious reality. Often, we may not always be aware of what we are doing, much less why we are doing it.

3. *Nothing is more central to who we are than the way we express and regulate our emotions.* During our lives, we develop different ways of communicating and regulating our emotions. In parallel, our intellectual thinking side becomes more sophisticated. Our cognition and emotions together eventually determine what we do and don't do. By delving into our feelings, we can access the more concealed parts of our identity.

4. *The past is the lens through which we can understand the present and shape the future.* We are all the result of our previous encounters with others. These incidents, including the early developmental experiences with our parents, continue to impact us throughout our lives.

Source: Kets deVries and Cheak (2016).

So, why is this the case? First, we inherit 'motivational need systems' – our 'operational code' that determines our personality when we are born. At a most fundamental level, these include our physiological needs, such as food and water. In addition, our need for attachment/affiliation and exploration/assertion impact how we behave in the workplace.

Over time, our needs systems are altered by our learned responses, caregivers' developmental impact, and our ability to recreate positive emotional states experienced in infancy and childhood (Kets de Vries, 2006). Gradually, mental schemas or 'scripts' emerge, determining our interpretation of the world and influencing our actions and behaviours (Kets deVries, 2004).

Within these scripts, specific themes develop over time rooted in our deepest desires, needs, and ambitions and contribute to our unique personality styles. These repetitive patterns within our motivational need systems exert a vital influence over who we are and how we act towards others.

Metaphorically, the Clinical Paradigm is a way of exploring what Kets de Vries calls our 'inner theatre' – our own internal stage, with various actors being the people we have loved, hated, feared, and admired in our lives.

In our minds, we repeatedly re-enact the unconscious drama of our early experiences – with some being exceptionally painful and others filling us with a sense of happiness. These unconscious forces can impact our relationships at home, the people we work with (such as our bosses, colleagues and subordinates), our decision-making and management styles, and other parts of our work. Each of us brings our inner theatre with its dramas and comedies to work (Kets de Vries et al., 2016). Author Naomi Shragai has described these patterns as being hijacked by strong feelings that take us by surprise, including at work, which can have dire circumstances (Shragai, 2021).

The Clinical Paradigm helps to expose the subconscious forces underlying our human behaviour. It illuminates our human minds, a large proportion of which is unconscious. It allows us to understand the motivations behind our intergroup behaviours and dynamics, identify potential relationship conflicts, be more productive and improve our work relationships (Kets de Vries & Cheak, 2016).

Unless we can understand the motives behind our thoughts, we cannot control them. We, therefore, cannot comprehend why leaders and followers behave the way they do.

REFERENCES

Kets de Vries, M. F. R. (2004). Organizations on the Couch: A Clinical Perspective on Organizational Dynamics. *European Management Journal*, 22(2), 183–200.

Kets de Vries, M. F. R. (2006). *The Leader on the Couch: A Clinical Approach to Changing People and Organizations*. Wiley.

Kets de Vries, M. F. R., & Cheak, A. (2016). Psychodynamic Approach. In P. G. Northouse (Ed.), *Leadership: Theory and Practice* (pp. 295–328). Sage.

Kets de Vries, M. F. R., Korotov, K., Florent-Treacy, E., & Rook, C. (2016). *Coach and Couch: The Psychology of Making Better Leaders* (2nd ed.). Palgrave Macmillan.

Shragai, N. (2021). *The Man who Mistook his Job for his Life: How to Thrive at Work by Leaving Your Emotional Baggage Behind*. Penguin.

The Clinical Paradigm

Note: **Bold** page numbers refer to tables; *italic* page numbers refer to figures and page numbers followed by "n" denote endnotes.

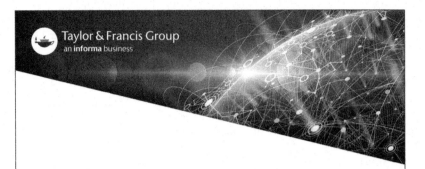

Printed in the United States
by Baker & Taylor Publisher Services